Forceful *Negotiations*

The Mexican Experience | William H. Beezley, series editor

Forceful *Negotiations*

The Origins of the
Pronunciamiento in
Nineteenth-Century
Mexico

Edited and with an introduction by
WILL FOWLER

University of Nebraska Press | Lincoln & London

Library of Congress Cataloging-in-Publication Data
Forceful negotiations: the origins of the pronunciamiento in nineteenth-century Mexico / edited and
with an introduction by Will Fowler.
p. cm. — (Mexican experience)
Includes bibliographical references.
ISBN 978-0-8032-2540-4 (pbk.: alk. paper)
1. Mexico—Politics and government—1821–1861.
2. Mexico—History—1821–1861. 3. Political
culture—Mexico—History—19th century.
4. Political violence—Mexico—History—19th
century. 5. Revolutions—Mexico—History—19th
century. 6. Government, Resistance to—Mexico—
History—19th century. 7. Legitimacy of governments—Mexico—History—19th century.
I. Fowler, Will, 1966–
F1232.F6828   2010
972 '.04—dc22
2010017777

Contents

Preface

Following the achievement of independence in 1821, Mexico entered a period of marked instability. The young nation was crippled by its eleven-year-long civil war and a hostile international context in which, apart from Britain and the United States, most European countries initially refused to recognize its independence. The following decades would be characterized by chronic turmoil. Mexico fought four international wars against Spain (1829), France (1838 and 1862–67), and the United States (1846–48). Following the Mexican-American War Mexico lost half of its national territory. Moreover, the new political order lacked authority, and its legitimacy was constantly challenged. Four different constitutions were adopted (1824, 1836, 1843, and 1857). Mexico was an empire on two occasions (1822–23 and 1864–67), a federal republic (1824–35, 1846–53, 1855–58), a central republic (1835–46), and a dictatorship (1846, 1853–55). In the wake of the War of Independence civil conflict resulted in a militarized society and a politicized army. More than fifteen hundred *pronunciamientos* erupted between the 1821 Plan of Iguala and the 1876 Plan of Tuxtepec that brought Porfirio Díaz to power. In a number of cases they degenerated into clashes of appalling violence, such as the Mexico City Parián Riot of 1828. In others they resulted in brutal civil wars (1832, 1854–55, 1858–60). In many cases, however, demands were appeased or quelled depending on how many pronunciamentos of allegiance they received. They resulted in forceful negotiations.

Often translated as "revolt," the pronunciamiento was a written protest or petition, often drafted as a list of grievances or demands and signed by a group of individuals and/or a corporate body (high-ranking officers, town council officials, villagers, etc.), that could result in an armed rebellion if the government did not attend to the demands. As early as the 1820s the pronunciamiento had already acquired in Spain and in Mexico the particular set of norms, procedures, and use of discursive strategies that set it apart from a common revolt or military uprising. The actual pronunciamiento texts or *actas* and plans became an integral part of the proceedings. These bureaucratic components were precisely what made the pronunciamiento such a distinctive revolutionary practice—one that, interestingly, would become significantly prevalent only in Spain, Mexico, and Central America. Although *pronunciamiento* is still defined in most dictionaries and encylopedias as a military uprising or coup, in reality it was not always a military action, it was generally *not* concerned with overthrowing the government, and quite frequently it was *not* a response to a development in national politics. As analyzed in the essays that make up this volume, the pronunciamiento was a nineteenth-century Hispano-Mexican extra-constitutional political practice that soldiers and civilians used to negotiate or petition forcefully for political change, both at a national and at a local level, in the absence of a clearly established constitutional order.

In this first of three planned edited volumes on the nineteenth-century Mexican pronunciamiento, we provide a collection of individual yet interrelated studies on the origins of this practice. The contributors aim to explain where this forceful way of seeking to effect change originated and how it became so widespread and popular in independent Mexico. Trendsetting pronunciamientos such as the 1821 Plan of Iguala, specific early pronunciamientos such as the 1829 Plans of Campeche and Jalapa, and the emergence of the patterns and modes of political behavior that would become a hallmark of nineteenth-century Mexico are all analyzed in individual studies that complement one another in a groundbreaking work combining essays by leading authorities in the field with the work of a new generation of scholars.

Forceful Negotiations provides an innovative and revisionist collection of essays that seek to explain the origins, nature, and dynamics of the pronunciamiento with a view to understanding the cultural-political frameworks in which an aggressive extra-constitutional practice like this could become the standard means of informing and influencing policy. We hope the volume offers readers a challenging collection of interpretations of and explanations for the ways in which Mexican political culture legitimized the threat of armed rebellion as a means of effecting political change during this turbulent period.

Acknowledgments

In June 2007 I was the recipient of a major Arts and Humanities Research Council (AHRC) research grant amounting to more than £610,000, which funded a three-year project on "The *Pronunciamiento* in Independent Mexico, 1821–1876" (2007–10). This generous award allowed me to put together a vibrant team made up of research fellows Germán Martínez Martínez and Natasha Picôt, AHRC-funded PhD students Rosie Doyle and Kerry McDonald, and database developer Sean Dooley. A further four PhD students started their doctoral programs in September 2007 on related topics under my supervision—Shara Ali, Melissa Boyd, Leticia Neria, and Ana Romero Valderrama, the last two funded by the Mexican grant-awarding body Conacyt—allowing for the emergence of a lively community of Mexicanists in the University of St. Andrews. The ultimate goals of the team were (1) to produce a major online relational database that includes transcriptions of more than fifteen hundred pronunciamientos (see http://arts.st-andrews.ac.uk/pronunciamientos/); (2) to publish three edited volumes on the origins, experience, and memory of these forceful petitions; (3) to enable the PhD students to complete their dissertations successfully; and (4) to collate the data that will eventually be analyzed in my planned monograph on the subject.

Needless to say I am extremely grateful to the Arts and Humanities Research Council. Quite simply, without the AHRC's funding, this expensive project would never have taken place. It is thanks to the AHRC that there is now a research team at St. Andrews solely concerned (not to say obsessed) with nineteenth-century Mexican politics and the practice of the pronunciamiento. It is also thanks to the AHRC that the first of three planned international conferences was held at St. Andrews, 20–22 June 2008, bringing together the St. Andrews–based research team and a formidable group of international scholars. I would like to thank El Colegio de México, the Universidad Veracruzana, the Universitat Jaume I, and the University of Manitoba for the financial contributions they made toward the travel expenses of their respective speakers.

The conference was extremely lively, generating intense discussion, and thanks are due to our conference secretary, Barbara Fleming, as well as to St. Andrews–based scholars Henriette Partzsch, Mark Harris, Ricardo Fernández, and Leticia Neria, who kindly chaired sessions and read the papers of participants who were unable to attend. Professors Paul Garner, Brian Hamnett, and Alan Knight also deserve to be acknowledged, for being such inspirational chairs and discussants, generously contributing their thoughts to the dialectics the conference unleashed. Likewise I offer my sincere thanks to those speakers who, albeit not included in this volume, offered suggestive papers on different aspects of the origins of the Mexican pronunciamiento: Francisco Eissa-Barroso, Antonio Escobar Ohmstede, Luis Medina Peña, Natasha Picôt, and Ana Romero Valderrama.

As always I thank my colleagues in the Department of Spanish and the School of Modern Languages at the University of St. Andrews for their unwavering support and collegiality. I am indebted to our former students Moira Frame, Kim Gillespie, Victoria Milton, and Rosanna Shaw for the translations they prepared of some of the papers. Andrea Boyd deserves to be thanked for translating Josefina Zoraida Vázquez's essay. Thanks are also due to Salvador Rueda Smithers and Hilda Sánchez at the Museo Nacional de Historia in Mexico City for allowing Natacha Buzalko to take the photograph of the painting entitled *Es proclamado Iturbide Primer Emperador de México, la mañana del 19 de mayo de 1822* and for ensuring that the Instituto Nacional de Antropología e Historia authorized its use on the cover of the present volume. I thank Natacha for taking the photograph and Monica Hayes for organizing the shoot. And my gratitude extends, as ever, to my wife Caroline and our children for being so incredibly patient and supportive.

Last but not least I must thank Heather Lundine and her first class editorial team at the University of Nebraska Press: in particular, Bridget Barry, Joeth Zucco, and Sally E. Antrobus. It was a real pleasure to work with them on my *Santa Anna of Mexico* (2007) and I am delighted that we have been able to continue working together. I thank Heather for believing in this project and for committing herself to publishing the books it will generate.

Introduction
The Nineteenth-Century Practice of the
Pronunciamiento and Its Origins

What was a *pronunciamiento*? It is a question that is not easy to answer given that nineteenth-century Mexicans used the term for a whole range of political interventions. To consider as a case in point the 19 May 1822 show of force in Mexico City that resulted in Agustín de Iturbide being proclaimed emperor, it was in all senses a straightforward coup d'état. It differed little from previous and subsequent coups, such as the 1808 overthrow of Viceroy José Iturrigaray or the 1846 *golpe* (coup) that brought a swift end to Mariano Paredes y Arrillaga's dictatorship, to name but two clear-cut examples.

Imitating Napoleon Bonaparte's forceful and trendsetting coup of 18 Brumaire (9 November 1799), the 19 May action consisted of a military blow in the capital, directed in this instance at the Congress, without involving the mobilization of revolutionary armies or a long drawn-out civil war. However, as may be seen in Ivana Frasquet and Manuel Chust's chapter on Iturbide's pronunciamientos of 1821 and 1822, the actors involved in 1822 called what they did a pronunciamiento.

In stark contrast, and as highlighted by Germán Martínez Martínez in his cultural analysis of this practice in chapter 11, contemporary Mexicans also used the term for what we might consider nothing other than a town council's declaration of principles. There are numerous examples of town council– and state legislature–led proclamations, initiatives, and addresses that were defined by their authors and proponents as *pronunciamientos*.

Consequently the approach adopted in this volume, almost inevitably, accepts that the pronunciamiento cannot be analyzed using too rigid a definition. After all, we cannot ignore what nineteenth-century Mexicans claimed it was if we are to attempt to understand how this practice came to permeate Mexican society at all levels during the five decades that followed independence. We have to take on board the view that a pronunciamiento could end up as a coup but that it could also be simply a statement of intent, the expression of a given political belief by a given community or group of disgruntled officers.

Yet a number of features may be seen to have been present in the great majority of conspiracies, coups, revolts, addresses, and mobilizations that were described at the time as pronunciamientos. Although there were exceptions, most pronunciamientos were in the first instance an act of insubordination or, as Miguel Alonso Baquer put it, "a gesture of rebellion."[1] They contained an expressed intention on the part of the "pronounced ones" of rebelling or disobeying, of withdrawing their support or ceasing to recognize the authority or legitimacy of a given local and/or national government. On numerous occasions the promulgators included an explicit threat of violence in the document they used to announce their act of insubordination (*acta* and plan). Typically they claimed they would have no choice but to fight if their grievances were not addressed.

The aim of these gestures of rebellion was to force the government to listen and negotiate with the pronunciados. For the original pronunciamiento to be successful it was therefore essential that following its declaration and circulation other garrisons and communities came out into the open with copycat pronunciamientos in support of it. The hope was that should the original pronunciamiento gain sufficient adherents, it would forcefully persuade or intimidate the government into backing down and attending to the original pronunciados' demands. These supporting pronunciamientos would become known as *pronunciamientos de adhesión* (of allegiance) and would constitute the "domino theory" model of this practice. Given that the pronunciamiento needed pronunciamientos de adhesión to succeed, most pronunciamiento cycles or series began in the periphery rather than in the capital. Time was needed to allow the constellations of pronunciamientos de adhesión to prosper and proliferate, something from which a pronunciamiento launched in the capital could not benefit because of its proximity to the national government. The pronunciamiento, therefore, was not a coup d'état since its dynamic was geared toward negotiation, even though as already noted, some cycles did end with the overthrow of government.

Army officers led the great majority of pronunciamientos. This was understandable given that the military had the means to make their threats of resorting to violence a reality. It was nonetheless a practice that involved active civilian participation, as may be seen in Michael T. Ducey, Kerry McDonald, and Rosie Doyle's chapters. In fact there was close collaboration between officers and civilians in most pronunciamientos either because the civilians used the soldiers to fulfill their ambitions or because the soldiers needed the civilians to legitimize and fund their actions.[2]

It was also a practice that evolved and was eventually adopted and employed by a wide range of civilian actors and subaltern groups. This can be seen, in particular, in the pronunciamientos de adhesión that did more than cut and paste or support the demands made in the original pronunciamientos. As noted by McDonald in her chapter on the origins of the pronunciamientos of San Luis Potosí it was common for regional elites to include in their *actas de adhesión* additional demands that were aimed at addressing strictly local or regional grievances.

Regardless of the pronunciamiento's evolution, it was a remarkably formulaic and ritualistic practice. In this sense it retained over time a number of characteristics that to a certain degree make possible creating a taxonomy of the phenomenon, despite the difficulties noted in defining the pronunciamiento.

Given that there would have been a grievance shared or that could be usefully exploited by a number of officers and/or villagers, the initial stage of most pronunciamientos involved a conspiracy. The potential pronunciados sought to gain adherents and establish whether they would have sufficient support from key players in the community once their forceful protest was launched. During this preparation stage the pronunciados-to-be entered into so-called *compromisos* with potential backers. This involved promising rewards to officers, merchants, priests, etc. in exchange for their support. Once the aspiring pronunciados were persuaded that they could garner a meaningful following, a meeting was convened to discuss formally the grievance or matter at hand. In the original military-led pronunciamientos, this generally took place in the leading commander's quarters. Thereafter, and once the practice of the pronunciamiento was taken up by civilians, such a meeting went on to take place in the town council rooms (i.e., the *casas consistoriales*), main square, parish church, or even in a few cases in a particular individual's house. The holding of a supposedly spontaneous meeting in which grievances were openly discussed before the premeditated resolution of launching the pronunciamiento was taken became customary. At this point, a secretary was appointed, who wrote down the minutes of the meeting—the *Acta*—which would go on to outline the plan, petition, or *grito* (cry) that was formally and almost ritualistically *pronunciado*.

Most of the pronunciamiento texts thus began with a preamble explaining how it had come to pass that those concerned had been compelled to gather and discuss the stated grievances and how, in turn, they had resolved unanimously and as a corporate body (specific garrison, *ayuntamiento*, etc.) to "pronounce." In so doing they often claimed to represent an ignored or oppressed general or popular will. They outlined their demands in the petition that ensued and noted, in the more forceful cases, that they would unwillingly resort to violence if their grievances were not addressed. The pronunciamiento invariably carried the signatures of the pronunciados, who often claimed to represent the men under their orders (e.g., a specific artillery unit or all the sergeants of a given division). The text was then circulated as widely as possible, printed and distributed as a pamphlet or inserted or reproduced in the press. It was also read out to the community where the pronunciamiento was launched, an event that could be celebrated with fireworks, tolling of church bells, music, and in some instances a fiesta. If the pronunciamiento received a significant number of pronunciamientos de adhesión, and the pronunciados could hold the government to ransom by controlling a geopolitically important town, such as Veracruz, Guadalajara, or San Luis Potosí, its chances of success were indeed great. Rosie Doyle's chapter on the 1852 Blancarte series of pronunciamientos provides a perfect case study of the dynamic outlined.[3]

In Mexico the pronunciamiento texts developed into a genre

in their own right. What is more, it is difficult to conceive of a pronunciamiento without a text. Worthy of note in this respect is Shara Ali's chapter on Santiago Imán's revolt of 1838–40 in Yucatán, where, atypically, the text was produced *after* the revolt had been launched. The importance of the text as a key element of the pronunciamiento cannot be overstated. The legalistic language employed is indicative in itself of how the pronunciamiento represented an alternative legality or bureaucracy that was on a par with the supposed constitutional order it was challenging.

It was also an appealing and addictive practice because it was ultimately a contained form of revolutionary action. The pronunciamiento was meant to be resolved without bloodshed. Its dynamic was one based on threats and counter-threats, in which rebels and government officials waited to see how much support the original pronunciamiento received before deciding whether negotiation would be necessary, or whether one side or the other would have no choice but to back down. As Josep Fontana has argued, the pronunciamiento opened up the possibility of effecting a contained or controlled revolutionary action, namely one that— although employing a threat of violence—forced change without actually unleashing a bloodbath in the manner of the French or Haitian revolutions: "It consecrated a new political formula which allowed the political and military 'liberal' minorities to carry out a controlled revolutionary process."[4] The degeneration into violence or civil war was therefore an aberration.

The pronunciamiento was certainly symptomatic of a context of institutional disarray and constitutional crisis. As was noted by Mariano Otero, whose views on the pronunciamiento Melissa Boyd discusses in chapter 8, the practice had arisen because while one political order had come to an end, that which was meant to replace it was still in the making. The effect the eleven-year-long War of Independence had had on society also influenced matters. Mexico now had a politicized military, accustomed to exerting power over civilian authorities, and a society that had grown used to settling political disputes by force. The disgruntled revolutionary officers who missed out on the post-independence round of promotions would be the first to use the pronunciamiento to further their careers and causes.

The pronunciamiento came to serve numerous purposes, moreover, as discussed in the final chapter of this volume, which in turn may help explain its appeal and popularity. Successful pronunciados used the practice to gain accelerated promotion at an individual level. However, it also allowed communities (especially the disenfranchised) to engage in politics, enabling them to make known their political views. And as evidenced in Michael T. Ducey's chapter on the pronunciamientos of the Huasteca during the First Federal Republic, it could even result in a fiesta.

Albeit intended as an extra-constitutional means of correcting perceived political injustices on behalf of the people or the nation—(in Reynaldo Sordo's chapter we find a group of congressmen pronouncing and acting extra-constitutionally in order to save the constitution)—the use of pronunciamientos became a destabilizing force. To use Otero's words, it became a *funesta manía* (baneful habit), since it became the way of conducting politics, of bringing about change, preventing a new constitutional order from setting down long-lasting roots.

Most pronunciamientos failed to achieve their aims, as Josefina Zoraida Vázquez reminds us.[5] Yet it also remains the case that most of the leading political changes of nineteenth-century Mexico were caused or provoked by pronunciamientos. The Plan of

Iguala of 24 February 1821 (reviewed here by Timothy E. Anna and Frasquet and Chust) resulted in the achievement of independence. The two 1822 Plans of Veracruz together with the 1823 Plan of Casa Mata (and all the pronunciamientos de adhesión the latter received) brought an end to Agustín de Iturbide's empire (1821–23). Manuel Gómez Pedraza's resignation and Vicente Guerrero's consequent rise to the presidency, similarly, were the result of the 1828 pronunciamientos of Perote and La Acordada. The following year, it was again a pronunciamiento, the 1829 Plan of Jalapa (analyzed by Vázquez in chapter 3) that brought down Guerrero's government and assisted Anastasio Bustamante's rise to power.

The Plan of Veracruz of 2 January 1832, after a year of daily pronunciamientos and civil war, eventually brought an end to Bustamante's term in office. The 25 May 1834 Plan of Cuernavaca was then responsible for generating such a wave of supporting pronunciamientos that Santa Anna felt justified in closing down the radical Congress of 1833–34 and repealing most of its laws. The dissolution of the 1824 Federal Constitution and the change to a centralist system were likewise provoked by the 1835 Plans of Orizaba (19 May) and Toluca (29 May) and the hundreds of pronunciamientos de adhesión they received.

Six years later, the concerted 1841 pronunciamientos of Guadalajara, La Ciudadela, and Perote—the so-called Revolución de Jalisco (touched upon in Melissa Boyd's study of Otero's writings on the practice)—ended Bustamante's second stint as president. On 11 December 1842, the pronunciamiento of Huejotzingo and its own series of plans of allegiance gave acting president Nicolás Bravo the justification to close down the Constituent Congress and abandon its proposed draft constitution. And two years later, Mariano Paredes y Arrillaga's 1844 pronunciamiento of Guadalajara, in tandem with the so-called Revolution of the Three Hours in Mexico City, ended Santa Anna's fourth presidency (discussed here by Reynaldo Sordo Cedeño). While the Guadalajara pronunciamientos of 1841 and 1844 did not bring Paredes y Arrillaga to power, his San Luis Potosí pronunciamiento of 14 December 1845 did. However, Paredes y Arrillaga was in turn deposed less than a year later (August 6) by a pronunciamiento in Mexico City, with the Mexican-American War (1846–48) having already started.

Following the defeat, it would take four years before another successful pronunciamiento series was launched on the back of the Plan of Blancarte of 26 July 1852 (discussed by Rosie Doyle in chapter 10), bringing about Santa Anna's return to Mexico from exile and his sixth term in office (1853–55). And it was a pronunciamiento in Ayutla, Guerrero, on 1 March 1854 that ended Santa Anna's dictatorship after a year of civil war and ushered in the mid-century reform period.

Notwithstanding the constitutionalist credentials of some of the men who rose to power in the mid-1850s, moderate president Ignacio Comonfort was responsible for the pronunciamiento of Tacubaya of 17 December 1857. This closed down Congress, rescinded the 1857 Constitution, and created the circumstances for General Félix Zuloaga to stage his own pronunciamiento in Mexico City on 11 January 1858, which gave the conservatives control of the capital and unleashed the particularly sanguinary Civil War of the Reforma (1858–60).

No individual pronunciamiento would prove successful at a national level between the end of the War of the Reforma in 1861 and Sebastián Lerdo de Tejada's reelection in 1876, with the country having become absorbed by the French Intervention for the greater part of the 1860s. But it would be once more a pronunciamiento, the Plan of Tuxtepec of 10 January 1876, that would bring a young Porfirio Díaz to power.

In other words, although most pronunciamientos were unsuccessful, those that triumphed were responsible for the most important political changes of nineteenth-century Mexico. To quote François-Xavier Guerra: "All the important political changes of this period, including the constitutional ones, have their origin in pronunciamientos, starting with independence itself."[6] So where did this way of conducting politics originate? And how did it become so widespread and popular?

A number of historians have argued that the origin of this phenomenon is to be found in the Masonic lodges, gatherings, and activities of the 1810s and '20s.[7] It would certainly appear to be the case that most of the conspiracies that unfolded in Spain between the return of King Ferdinand VII to the throne in 1814 and the restoration of the 1812 Constitution in 1820 were plotted, orchestrated, and led by members of secret societies, which in that period had become the main forums of enlightened or liberal opposition to absolutism, both in Spain and in many other parts of Europe.[8] In this sense Spanish historian José Luis Comellas believes that all pronunciamientos in Spain were characterized by their liberal agenda.[9] Raymond Carr endorsed this perspective, arguing that "the *pronunciamiento* was the instrument of liberal revolution in the nineteenth century," a view Frasquet and Chust espouse in chapter 2 of this volume.[10]

However, although it is possible to trace the conspiratorial stages of the pronunciamiento and its early liberal rejection of absolutism and despotism to the Masonic practices and politics of the 1810s, worthy of note was the context of contested authority in which the pronunciamiento surfaced, both in Spain and in Mexico. The constitutional crisis unleashed by the Napoleonic occupation of the Iberian Peninsula in 1808 and the usurpation of the Spanish crown, with the capture of Ferdinand VII and the imposition of Joseph Bonaparte on the throne, undoubtedly created a context of upheaval and disputed authority, raising fundamental questions about the ruling bodies' legitimacy.[11] At one level, the armed imposition of a new monarch, together with Napoleon Bonaparte's forceful activities in Europe, highlighted the extent to which authority was an incredibly fragile construct. As I have noted elsewhere, in this new and exciting revolutionary age, high-ranking officers in the mold of Napoleon could be choosers. Authority was now in the eye of the beholder. It could be questioned, challenged, overcome, and ultimately appropriated. For the generation of the Wars of Independence, in the wake of Napoleon's shake-up of most of Europe's monarchies, the mystique of authority lay no longer in the genealogy of kings or the prestige of hierarchy. Authority was there for the taking, and the strongest bidder could take all if he played his cards right in what had become a dog-eat-dog world by the teens of the century.[12]

The juntas that surfaced in Spain, and later in Spanish America, claiming to represent their country's sovereignty and the will of the people, in opposition to the usurper Bonaparte (and later the tyrant Ferdinand), similarly set a precedent whereby any group of people could claim, through the use of pseudo-legal proclamations, minutes, and eventually, constitutions, to be the true and legitimate source of authority.[13] The 1812 Constitution of Cádiz, the 1814 charter of Apatzingán, and the many short-lived *magna cartas* that were drafted throughout the Hispanic world between 1810 and 1826 empowered the written word, giving the plan, the *proclama*, and eventually the pronunciamiento their own mystique of legitimacy.

A key characteristic of the nineteenth-century pronunciamiento, evidently stemming from a context in which established governments or figures of authority were no longer perceived to be above or superior to the protesting garrison, town council, or pueblo, is that in the negotiations that tended to unfold between the holders of power and the petitioners, the pronunciados behaved as if they had the same status or rights as the supposedly official representatives of the state (presidents, military commanders, governors). In other words, for the majority of nineteenth-century Spaniards and Mexicans, the post-1808 state and its institutions had not been in place for long enough to be recognized or accepted as the legitimate incarnation of the nation or its rightful government.

Therefore it was in response to the constitutional crisis unleashed by the 1808 Napoleonic occupation of Spain that the ritualized and bureaucratic revolutionary repertoire of the pronunciamiento was developed. In Spain between 1814 and 1820 a number of conspiracies and military-led rebellions erupted following Ferdinand VII's abolition of the 1812 Cádiz Constitution, and these served as precedent and inspiration for Riego's 1 January 1820 *grito*.[14] As was the case with the proclamas and revolts that erupted in Mexico during these years, these early proto-pronunciamientos set down extremely important precedents. In a context of ongoing constitutional crisis brought about by the restored monarch's abolition of the 1812 Constitution, the Spanish *cuartelazos* (barrack revolts), *levantamientos* (uprisings), *conjuras* (plots), and *conspiraciones* (conspiracies) of 1814–19 ultimately provided Riego in Spain with a model of action which he then went on to consecrate and name in January 1820.

It was Riego who first launched a successful pronunciamiento that developed the kind of pattern of events and practices that would become widespread and common thereafter. Riego also used the term *pronunciamiento* for the first time. On 3 January 1820, two days after the grito had been given in Cabezas de San Juan, forty-eight kilometers south of Seville, he addressed his battalions in the main square of Arcos de la Frontera: "Soldiers: the glory you have acquired through your heroic *pronunciamiento* will not be erased in the Spaniards' hearts whilst the sweet name of the patria is not devoid of meaning."[15]

Riego's pronunciamiento of 1 January 1820, extra-constitutionally yet legitimately, brought back the liberal Constitution of 1812 after a slow but effective string of copycat pronunciamientos of allegiance persuaded Ferdinand VII to revive the abolished charter while remaining king of Spain. In so doing, Riego established the model that would subsequently be taken up by anybody who was somebody in Spanish and Mexican politics, in a period that Stanley Payne understandably defined as the "era of *pronunciamientos*."[16]

The prestige of this practice was soon consolidated in Mexico via the Plan of Iguala of 24 February 1821—a pronunciamiento that ultimately resulted in the independence of Mexico. Its influence as an equally trendsetting precedent cannot be overstated. The lesson was there for all to see: pronunciamientos could force a king to change his policies, even make him adopt a constitution he did not favor; now they could also bring about a country's independence. Moreover, the ritual of the pronunciamiento was given further exposure and kudos. Having gone through a *trabajos* stage whereby Iturbide finally succeeded in bringing insurgent leader Vicente Guerrero on board, and surmised that his grito would obtain significant support from key officers in the royalist army, Iturbide gathered his officers on 24 February 1821, with representatives of each military arm, and ensured that they unanimously committed themselves to backing his manifesto and plan. A secretary was appointed, who drafted the minutes of the pronunciamiento, and those present signed it. The grito of Iguala was thus launched, and copies of its pronunciamiento text or plan were dispatched to all the military and civilian authorities in the kingdom.[17] The desired domino effect did not take long to unfold. As Christon I. Archer has noted: "The suddenness of the collapse of New Spain was remarkable. The proclamation of Iturbide's Plan of Iguala and the simplicity of his message offered soldiers and civilians, royalists and insurgents, an escape from chaos and expectations of a return to prosperity."[18] Critical to the consecration of the pronunciamiento text as a legitimizing medium of change was that the eighty-five thousand men at arms who changed sides in the following months and joined Iturbide's independence movement did so by swearing their allegiance to the Plan of Iguala, the actual text, rather than to a particular individual or idea.[19]

The formulistic register and structure of the pronunciamiento text as a key legitimizing source in Mexico, with its particular characteristic features (preamble, petition, and call for action and/ or negotiation) were also piloted in the Plan of Iguala. Although Riego described his revolt as a pronunciamiento, the documents that accompanied the grito of Cabezas de San Juan were still more like *proclamas* (addresses) than the legalistic texts that became the norm in Mexico soon afterward. On 1 January 1820, Riego issued a proclama to the officers José Rabadán and Carlos Hoyos, two different proclamas "To the troops," another "To the officers and the people," a *bando* (edict or proclamation), and a *dis-*

curso (speech).[20] He did not produce a definitive single pronunciamiento text. Nor did he formulate as a petition his demand to have the 1812 Constitution restored. The Plan of Iguala, in this sense, would empower the actual pronunciamiento document in a way that was novel and would thus serve as the main model for the genre that would develop subsequently.

The pronunciamiento of Cabezas de San Juan transformed Riego into a legend; the Plan of Iguala eventually turned *criollo* officer Agustín de Iturbide into an emperor, following the self-termed pronunciamiento of 19 May 1822.[21] Pronunciamientos could thus serve liberal and libertarian causes. They could also result in vertigo-inducing promotions, such as going from being a disgruntled and demoted colonel in the royalist forces to becoming not just a *libertador* but Agustín I, emperor of the Mexican Empire. The heady mix of liberal causes such as constitutionalism, freedom, and independence, paired with the adrenaline rush of the grito and the hope of an outcome that could include personal aggrandizement as well as military and political promotion, made the experience of the pronunciamiento into an irresistible and addictive practice for most politically minded nineteenth-century Mexican soldiers. It is extremely difficult to think of an officer of the time who did not, at some stage, participate in a pronunciamiento. Here was a practice that could serve the patria, make you a hero, and even help you climb the social ladder in ways previously inconceivable. Against a background of contested authority you would be a fool not to give it a try and "pronounce." This, of course, is what happened.

The prestige of the practice was to become firmly consolidated in Mexico after the Plans of Veracruz (2 and 6 December 1822) and the Plan of Casa Mata (1 February 1823) resulted in the abdication of Agustín I. The versatility of the pronunciamiento and its ability to alter dramatically the political context of the country was there for all to emulate. Although Santa Anna and Guadalupe Victoria's 1822 *impulso* of Veracruz did not initially garner the support the pronunciados expected, it generated the context in which José Antonio Echávarri, who had been sent to crush the revolt, was able to turn against the emperor and issue his own Plan of Casa Mata in February 1823, which by creating a united front with the Veracruzan rebels the following day finally initiated the expected pronunciamiento domino effect that forced Iturbide to abdicate.[22]

Critical to the development of this practice throughout Mexico was article 9 in the Plan of Casa Mata, which temporarily empowered the provincial deputation. This article, formulated in a context in which the regional elites had greatly resented Iturbide's centralist tendencies, proved decisive in ensuring that the Plan of Casa Mata was vociferously supported by the provinces.[23] It also added a new and crucial dimension to what a pronunciamiento could do and whom it could serve. The experience of Riego's pronunciamiento had shown that this was a practice that could result in meaningful political change. The Plan of Iguala had demonstrated that it could even bring about a country's independence (and make its main instigator the emperor) and had highlighted the importance of the pronunciamiento text. The lesson to be drawn from the impact of the Plan of Casa Mata was that this was a way of ensuring that the voice of the provinces was heard and of securing devolution of power to the regions and their local governments.

Although the hundreds of pronunciamientos that erupted between 1821 and 1876 still need to be analyzed systematically, both quantitatively and qualitatively, before we can draw any firm conclusions, an initial overview of the grievances and demands that featured in a significant number of them would appear to suggest that at least in Mexico, the pronunciamiento became first and foremost a regionally led practice. Whether it was to demand the creation or reintroduction of a federalist or a centralist constitution, a tentative glance at the plans of these five decades would appear to point toward a context in which the pronunciamiento became the favorite political practice of the provincial elites when engaging with national politics.[24] If this initial impression is correct, then it can be argued that this was the result in no small measure of the manner in which the Plan of Casa Mata, and the *actas de adhesión* it received, demonstrated for the first time that through the medium of the pronunciamiento the provinces—in this instance through their provincial deputations, in tandem with their garrisons—could pressurize the national government into backing down before the demands of the regions. Iturbide abdicated, a Constituent Congress was formed, and not surprisingly, the 1824 Constitution that was subsequently drafted was a federalist one.

The pronunciamientos of Cabezas de San Juan, Iguala, and Casa Mata thus established a model of political lobbying or forceful negotiation that quickly became common and widespread throughout independent Mexico. As a political practice it was emulated, adopted, and developed in a range of major and minor towns and garrisons. To name but a sample, pronunciamientos were launched to pressurize Congress into adopting a federalist political system (Guadalajara, 23 February, and San Luis Potosí, 5 June 1823); to urge it to pass laws that would result in the expulsion of the Spanish population in Mexico (Mexico City, 23 January 1824); to demand the end of secret societies (Otumba, 23 December 1827);

to challenge the electoral results (Perote, 16 September 1828); and to end Guerrero's use of emergency powers and sack some of his ministers (Jalapa, 4 December 1829). Thereafter and following the level of political participation that was inspired and motivated by the pronunciamiento of Veracruz of 2 January 1832, it can be confidently stated that the pronunciamiento was popularized as a practice to an unprecedented degree.

The chapters in this book interpret the practice of the pronunciamiento in a broad, flexible, multifaceted, and dynamic way that allows for a wide range of lines of inquiry to be pursued. They move beyond the simplistic equation of pronunciamiento equals revolt or coup and grapple with its multiple and varied objectives, consequences, and meanings, from both regional and national perspectives, exploring the practice's origins, dynamics, and nature in the early national period. What emerges is a complex interpretation that eschews easy categorizations.

Timothy E. Anna pays attention to the evolutionary context of Mexico's transition from colony to liberal republican nation-state. Seeking to interpret the pronunciamiento's resonance as the preferred instrument for fundamental political change, he analyzes the foundational 1821 Plan of Iguala as the prototype of all subsequent pronunciamientos. Worthy of note is Anna's view that the pronunciamiento was an integral part of the Mexican "national project" and that in representing an act of political co-optation, at least in the case of Iguala, it became an effective and replicated practice in a context where there was not yet a clearly defined state, the mechanisms for transfers of power had not been in place for long enough, and the country found itself in a kind of institutional vacuum.

Anna's assessment is developed in Ivana Frasquet and Manuel

Chust's chapter on the trans-Atlantic developments that brought about Riego's grito and the Plan of Iguala, interpreting their success and resonance by stressing the way they combined military and civilian actors and defended varying brands of liberal constitutionalism. According to Frasquet and Chust the origins of the liberal pronunciamientos of the nineteenth century must be traced back to the success obtained by Riego and the Spanish liberals in 1820 and by Iturbide and his men in 1821. In the view of these authors, critical to appreciating the resonance of this practice is that it originally took place in and responded to a liberal and constitutional milieu.

Josefina Zoraida Vázquez assesses the impact the events in 1828 had both at a national and at a regional level by analyzing the contexts in which the 1829 pronunciamientos of Campeche and Jalapa erupted. Vázquez argues that the violation of the Constitution in 1828 set a precedent that would at least presage, if not legitimize, the use of extra-constitutional means in 1829 to counter what was in essence an illegitimate government. While events in Yucatán would be marked by profoundly regional concerns, the pronunciamiento of Jalapa, in contrast, would respond to national grievances. Both pronunciamientos would be temporarily successful: Yucatán was governed by the pronunciados as a quasi-independent state until November 1832, and Vicente Guerrero was forcefully replaced as president by Anastasio Bustamante, though he in turn would be overthrown.

Following on from this it is interesting to see, in Michael T. Ducey's chapter on the impact national pronunciamientos had in the Huasteca, how small town actors responded to and participated in these national movements. Ducey's research coincides with Kerry McDonald's in highlighting how local issues were ultimately the key factor in accounting for the political and violent mobilizations of given groups in rural Mexico. It is also evident that national pronunciamientos had entirely unintended consequences: municipalities and village politicos exploited them to settle old scores and promote their own factional interests in strangely superimposed contexts marred by particularly violent political rivalries and ideological polarization.

Kerry McDonald provides an overview of the grievances that were voiced in the pronunciamiento-prone state of San Luis Potosí and categorizes the *potosino* pronunciamientos' origins thematically, making a distinction between nationally and locally inspired pronunciamientos. McDonald's research highlights the importance of the pronunciamiento's metatext; that is, its unstated grievances as opposed to its visible demands. Her chapter also shows that in this region, in response to externally motivated pronunciamientos, there was a tendency to launch reactive pronunciamientos that used national issues and actors to address or rectify strictly local concerns. The pronunciamientos of San Luis Potosí may have given the impression that their defenders or aggressive proponents were using this practice simply to back or reject external pronunciamientos. In reality, more often than not, they appear to have hijacked national demands to further their own regional economic and political interests.

As can be seen in Michael Costeloe's chapter on Mariano Arista's pronunciamiento of Huejotzingo of 8 June 1833, the pronunciamiento syndrome became chronic just over a decade after independence and, from a decidedly British perspective, damaged the national government's ability to guarantee the rule of law. In this instance the pronunciados' confiscation of the British United Mexican Mining Company's cash and silver, and the authorities' inability to stop them or even to repay the money after the pronunciamiento was crushed, demonstrated that Mexican society was characterized by its lawlessness. It is no coincidence that after 1833 no new British investment went to Mexico for many years; the fallout was both symptomatic and representative of the extremely detrimental impact pronunciamientos had on the Mexican government's ability to govern the nation meaningfully or to present the republic before foreign investors as a country where the rule of law was safeguarded.

Shara Ali's chapter on Santiago Imán's revolt of 1838–40 further nuances our understanding of the origins of the pronunciamiento by analyzing what motivated Imán and his men to revolt and eventually pronounce: a concatenation of private and public concerns, micro and macro demands, concrete and general grievances. The multilayered origins of Imán's pronunciamiento, as explored in Ali's essay, provide an eloquent example of how a combination of needs could justify and legitimize a call to arms that could be both personally motivated and concerned with the general good *at the same time*, regardless of whether personal circumstances accounted for the initial urge to revolt.

Ironically—or tellingly, depending on the reader's point of view—even a constitutionalist liberal like the youthful lawyer and politician Mariano Otero from Guadalajara found ways of justifying certain pronunciamientos when these were supposedly the ones to end all others, as described in Melissa Boyd's chapter on his interpretation of the origins of the baneful Mexican national addiction to the pronunciamiento. Equally paradoxical is the manner in which Mexico's congressmen resorted to effecting political change by forceful means in December 1844, as studied in Reynaldo Sordo Cedeño's chapter on the so-called Revolution of the Three Hours. By the mid-1840s it was evidently acceptable even to ostensibly upright and law-abiding Mexican civilian legislators to employ extra-constitutional means to safeguard the Constitution.

Rosie Doyle's anatomy of the practice of the pronunciamiento, as well as providing a detailed dissection of the origins and experience of the Plan of Blancarte of 26 July 1852, explores how local concerns were hijacked by national actors to address national concerns. In contrast to the pronunciamientos of San Luis Potosí studied by McDonald, Doyle's research into what she defines as the "Blancarte series" of pronunciamientos illustrates how those originating in regional concerns could be co-opted into a national movement, which in this case resulted in the end of Mariano Arista's term in office and Santa Anna's return to power.

Germán Martínez Martínez reviews the practice of the pronunciamiento from a cultural perspective and reflects on how it contributed as a building block in the construction of Mexican national identity. Sharing Anna's view that the pronunciamiento was actually part of the national project, Martínez Martínez finds in the pronunciamiento, and particularly in its text, a site of memory where nineteenth-century actors started to express and define their incipient sense of national identity.

The final chapter uses this cultural approach, together with the interpretations offered in this volume, to explore the numerous and different purposes this practice served, above and beyond that of effecting political change. What becomes evident is that to understand the importance of the pronunciamiento in the political and cultural life of nineteenth-century Mexico, it is essential that analysis is not limited to the study of military interventions. Impacts at national and at regional levels are better interpreted by adopting a multifaceted and multidisciplinary approach that can fully encompass the complex and subtle origins, nature, and dynamics of this multidimensional and evolving phenomenon.

Such assessment of the pronunciamiento is important. As Vázquez noted in a recent article: "A careful analysis of the *pronunciamientos* will surely allow us to understand the political logic of [the time] . . . the complexity of those decades in which the republic was seeking to consolidate its state, surviving foreign threats, internal divisions, economic paralysis and bankruptcy. Given that the *pronunciamientos* were the expression of the factions and later of the parties, their analysis is a task that needs to be undertaken as a matter of urgency."[25]

The studies that follow aim to do precisely that. They analyze the many uses and forms the pronunciamiento acquired as it went on to become the favorite means to effect change in independent Mexico. They concentrate on the origins of this practice and explore what it entailed, both nationally and regionally. The conclusions drawn are just the beginning of a journey of inquiry into what was undoubtedly the most important political practice of nineteenth-century Mexico.

Notes

1. Baquer, *El modelo español de pronunciamiento*, 40.

2. For a recent article that sets out to demonstrate that the pronunciamiento was not an exclusively military practice, see Fowler, "El pronunciamiento mexicano."

3. For other accounts of the processes entailed in launching a pronunciamiento see Carr, *Spain 1808–1939*, 124; Vázquez, "Political Plans and Collaboration," 21–23; Guerra, "El pronunciamiento en México," 18; Vázquez, "El modelo de pronunciamiento mexicano," 35.

4. Josep Fontana, "Prólogo," in Castells, *La utopia insurreccional*, ix.

5. Vázquez, "Political Plans and Collaboration," 19, 21–22. Notwithstanding this, as discussed in chapter 12, the question of success/failure requires fur-

ther thought. Vázquez is right if we measure their success in terms of whether they obtained what they claimed they had set out to achieve in the pronunciamiento texts themselves. However, if, for example, the pronunciados' aim was to get noticed, to ensure that their views were aired and given coverage, as a publicity stunt of sorts, an exercise in public relations or a dramatic piece of political propaganda, then it is not so easy to determine whether they failed even if their stated demands were not satisfied.

6. Guerra, "El pronunciamiento en México," 15.

7. Vázquez, "Political Plans and Collaboration," 22. For a historiographical discussion of Vicente La Fuente and Eduardo Comín Colomer's Masonic-led interpretations see Comellas, *Los primeros pronunciamientos*, 28–29. Raymond Carr and Stanley Payne also stress the importance Masonic lodges had in organizing the civilian revolutions of 1814–20 in Spain. See Carr, *Spain 1808–1939*, 126–29, and Payne, *Politics and the Military*, 18–19.

8. See Hamnett, "Liberal Politics and Spanish Freemasonry," 222–37.

9. Comellas, *Los primeros pronunciamientos*, 24.

10. Carr, *Spain 1808–1939*, 124.

11. For a recent interpretation of these events and their consequences see Breña, *El primer liberalismo español*, especially 73–83.

12. Fowler, *Santa Anna of Mexico*, 40.

13. Jaime E. Rodríguez O.'s view that the Wars of Independence were an extension of, and part of, the constitutional crisis that arose in the Hispanic world from the dissolution of the Spanish monarchy, rather than being clear-cut anticolonial struggles, can be seen to be developed further here in the sense that the pronunciamiento was a product of this meltdown in the rules, customs, and practices that governed the Spanish orb, in Spain and in its kingdoms. See Rodríguez O., *Independence of Spanish America*.

14. For more about these early pronunciamientos in Spain see Comellas, *Los primeros pronunciamientos*; Baquer, *El modelo español de pronunciamiento*, 47–80; and Artola, *La España de Fernando VII*.

15. Gil Novales (ed.), *Rafael del Riego*, 37.

16. Payne, *Politics and the Military*, 14–30.

17. Anna, *Forging Mexico*, 79–83; Ávila, *En nombre de la nación*, 196–211; Vázquez, "El modelo de pronunciamiento mexicano," 36.

18. Archer, "Politicization of the Army of New Spain," 37.

19. For the number of men see Vázquez, "Iglesia, ejército y centralismo," 211.

20. All these documents are reproduced in Gil Novales (ed.), *Rafael de Riego*, 34–39.

21. Needless to say it was the pronunciamiento text of the Plan of Iguala that made this "legally" possible, stating "8. Si Fernando VII no se resolviere a venir a México, la Junta de la Regencia mandará a nombre de la nación mientras se resuelve la testa que debe coronarse." See chapter 2 for a translation of the 19 May 1822 text.

22. Fowler and Ortiz Escamilla, "La revuelta de 2 de diciembre de 1822."

23. For the response of the provincial deputations to the Plan of Casa Mata, see Benson, *La diputación provincial*, 122–37.

24. Having revised this chapter at the end of the second year of the three-year AHRC-funded project on "The *Pronunciamiento* in Independent Mexico, 1821–1876" (2007–10, http://arts.st-andrews.ac.uk/pronunciamientos/), it is still too early to know for certain whether this impression is correct. For an early appraisal of the nature of civil conflict in Mexico (1821–57), see Fowler, "Civil Conflict in Independent Mexico," 49–86.

25. Vázquez, "El modelo de pronunciamiento mexicano," 49.

Chronology of Main Events and Pronunciamientos, 1821–1853

1810–1821	WAR OF INDEPENDENCE
1821	
24 February	Agustín de Iturbide launches the Plan of Iguala (see introduction and chapters 1 and 2)
24 August	Iturbide and Viceroy O'Donojú sign the Treaty of Córdoba
27 September	War ends with the Army of the Three Guarantees' capture of Mexico City
1822–1823	FIRST EMPIRE
1822	
19 May	Iturbide becomes Emperor Agustín I following pronunciamiento of 19 May (see chapter 2)
26 August	Iturbide imprisons nineteen members of Congress
31 October	Iturbide closes down Congress
2 December	Santa Anna launches Pronunciamiento of Veracruz (see introduction)

1823

1 February	Plan of Casa Mata (see introduction)
2 February	Santa Anna joins the Plan of Casa Mata
19 March	Iturbide abdicates
1823–1824	THE TRIUMVIRATE
	The Federal Constitution is drafted; triumvirate is made up of generals Guadalupe Victoria, Nicolás Bravo, and Pedro Celestino Negrete

1823

5 June	Santa Anna revolts launching the Plan of San Luis Potosí (see chapter 5)
1824–1835	FIRST FEDERAL REPUBLIC
1824–1829	Guadalupe Victoria, president

1827

19 January	Arenas pro-Spanish conspiracy dismantled
10 May	First anti-Spanish Expulsion Laws
20 December	Second Expulsion Laws
23 December	Plan of Montaño, General Nicolás Bravo joins Montaño's revolt (see chapter 3)

1828

7 January	Battle of Tulancingo; *escoceses* are defeated
September	The moderate General Manuel Gómez Pedraza wins presidential elections
14 September	Santa Anna "pronounces" in Jalapa, proclaiming Vicente Guerrero president
30 November	Revolt of La Acordada (see chapter 3)
4 December	Raid of the Parián Market

27 December	Manuel Gómez Pedraza escapes and goes into exile

1829

	Vicente Guerrero, president
26 July	Isidro Barradas's expedition lands in Tampico to reconquer Mexico for Spain
11 September	Santa Anna defeats Barradas's expedition
6 November	Centralist pronunciamiento in Campeche (see chapter 3)
4 December	General Anastasio Bustamante leads the Revolt of Jalapa (see chapters 3, 4, and 5)
31 December	Bustamante takes Mexico City
1830–32	Anastasio Bustamante, president (Also known as the Alamán Administration)

1831

14 February	Vicente Guerrero is executed

1832

2 January	Santa Anna launches Plan of Veracruz (see chapters 4 and 5)
March–December	Civil war spreads across central Mexico
December	*Convenios* of Zavaleta bring an end to Bustamante's regime

1833

January	Manuel Gómez Pedraza, president (as agreed in Zavaleta, Gómez Pedraza returns to complete his interrupted term in office while elections are held)

1 April	Santa Anna, president; however, does not take up post, leaving Vice President Valentín Gómez Farías in charge
1833–34	Gómez Farías "Radical" Administration
26 May	Pronunciamiento de Escalada
1 June	Plan of Durán
8 June	Plan of Huejotzingo calling for an end to Congress's radical reforms and for Santa Anna to become dictator (see chapter 6)

1834

25 May	Plan of Cuernavaca starts a series of pronunciamientos against the reforms of the Gómez Farías Administration. Santa Anna intervenes and annuls most of the reforms (see chapter 4)

1835

January	Gómez Farías is stripped of his vice-presidential office
	Santa Anna, president; however, due to his absence the presidency is taken by Miguel Barragán
28 January	Miguel Barragán, president

1835

February	Federalists revolt in Zacatecas against the rise of the centralists
11 May	Santa Anna quells the revolt in the Battle of Guadalupe
19 May	Pronunciamiento of Orizaba calls for change to centralism

29 May	Pronunciamiento of Toluca does so as well
22 June	Revolt in Texas begins
23 October	The Federal Constitution is abolished and Mexico becomes a central republic
1835–1846	THE FIRST CENTRAL REPUBLIC

1836

27 February	José Justo Corro, president (following Barragán's death)
6 March	Battle of El Alamo
21 April	Battle of San Jacinto (Santa Anna is taken prisoner the following day)
29 December	The Siete Leyes (creating the 1836 Constitution) consolidate centralist political system and limit the suffrage
1837–1841	Anastasio Bustamante, president

1837

| April | Anastasio Bustamante, president (after winning elections) |
| February | Santa Anna returns from the United States in disgrace |

1838

March	French fleet starts blockade of port of Veracruz
May	Santiago Imán revolt in Yucatán begins (see chapter 7)
27 November	French Pastry War begins with the bombardment of Veracruz
5 December	Santa Anna forces the French to retreat and loses one leg in battle

1839

April	José Antonio Mejía and José Urrea start federalist revolt in Tamaulipas
May–June	Santa Anna acts as interim president
3 May	Battle of Acajete; Santa Anna defeats rebels; Mejía is executed

1840

15 July	Federalist pronunciamiento in the capital; Bustamante is taken prisoner in the National Palace
27 July	Revolt ends and Bustamante is restored to power

1841

August– October	Triangular Revolt (also called Revolución de Jalisco) overthrows Bustamante's regime (see chapter 8)
1841–1844	Santa Anna, president

1841

October	Bases de Tacubaya approved; Santa Anna has "almost absolute power"

1842

9 December	Pronunciamiento in San Luis Potosí demanding closure of Congress
11 December	Pronunciamiento in Huejotizingo also demanding closure of Congress
18 December	Congress is closed down

1843

8 June — Bases Orgánicas; ultimate *santanista* constitution is accepted

1844

2 November — Pronunciamiento of Guadalajara is launched by General Mariano Paredes y Arrillaga against Santa Anna

6 December — Revolution of the Three Hours overthrows Santa Anna's regime in the capital (see chapter 9)

1845

— José Joaquín Herrera, president

June — Santa Anna goes into exile to Cuba

14 December — Pronunciamiento of General Mariano Paredes y Arrillaga in San Luis Potosí leads to fall of Herrera's government (see chapter 5)

1846

— Paredes y Arrillaga's dictatorship

April — War with the United States begins

6 August — Federalist revolt overthrows Paredes y Arrillaga and replaces the centralist republic with the Second Federal Republic; Santa Anna returns, invited by the Federalists

August — José Mariano Salas, temporary president while elections are held

1846–1853 — SECOND FEDERAL REPUBLIC

1846

| December | Santa Anna, president; however, due to the war with the United States, Valentín Gómez Farías acts as president again |

1847

February	Pronunciamiento of Los Polkos against Gómez Farías and anti-clerical measures
23 February	Battle of Angostura–Buena Vista
9 March	General Winfield Scott arrives in Veracruz
21 March	Santa Anna ends Gómez Farías's administration again
18 April	Battle of Cerro Gordo
August	Caste War begins in Yucatán
11 Aug.–15 Sept.	Campaign of the Valley of Mexico
14 September	Government leaves Mexico City to become established in Querétaro
15 September	The U.S. Army takes Mexico City
September	Manuel de la Peña y Peña, president; forms new government

1848

2 February	Treaty of Guadalupe Hidalgo grants half of Mexico's national territory to the United States
1848–1851	José Joaquín de Herrera, president
1851–1853	Mariano Arista, president

1852

| 26 July | Plan of Blancarte (see chapter 10) |

13 September	Second Plan of Blancarte (see chapter 10)
20 October	Plan del Hospicio (see chapter 10)

1853

January–February	Juan Bautista Ceballos, president
February–April	Manuel María Lombardini, president
1853–1855	SANTA ANNA'S DICTATORSHIP

TIMOTHY E. ANNA

One. Iguala: *The Prototype*

The phenomenon of the *pronunciamiento* in nineteenth-century Mexico should be seen as part of the process of struggle toward political identity and the creation of the nation-state. Independence launched a history of transition, partial fragmentation, and continuity; it was the beginning of that transition, not the conclusion. As Alicia Hernández Chávez put it, when the transition from the colonial period to the liberal republican period in Mexican history is seen only in terms of a profound break that affected the central government, the result is that the first phase of Mexico's independent history incorrectly appears to be characterized by nothing but disorder and disaster. When approached from the perspective of the process of creating identity and nation, it takes on a very different look.[1] The most significant value of the achievement of independence is that it may permit a society to begin seeing social and political issues previously masked by the presence of the colonial power. We must not lose sight of evolutionary processes by which developments, once inconceivable or the object of dreams, become possible in the ongoing development of history. Independence also brought to the fore the issue of the role and power of the regions, which in three hundred years of the colonial order had never been fully factored in to political decisions at the center. The tension between centralism and regionalism is the dominant theme in Mexican history, since well before the Spanish Conquest; and during all those centuries there had not been a Mexican nationality that included the noncentral regions. Furthermore, this was a society in which, only a few years before independence, people had thought in terms of their membership in a corporate body rather than within a national identity.[2]

The pronunciamiento often appears as an assertion of regional needs, demands, identities, expressions of the *matria* against the putative *patria* (in the terms coined by Luis González y González).[3] Yet Josefina Zoraida Vázquez has written about the "true miracle" of early Mexican national history—"that New Spain resisted the fragmentation that the other viceroyalties suffered, despite the fact that its territory came from two audiencias, two autonomous governments, twelve intendancies, and one captaincy general."[4] In other words, contrary to historiography's emphasis on the early nineteenth century as a period characterized by disintegration, the true characteristic of the period was a troubled but nonetheless distinct striving for integration and union—the striving of regions and groups and interests for social, political, and economic progress in a country previously characterized by colonial centralism. It occurred in a context of profound political and ideological differences. The pronunciamiento was not merely a grab for power; it was part of the "national project."

Overall, Mexico's nineteenth-century history is a story of integration rather than disintegration. It is necessary to study the process of Mexican nationhood "through a double perspective, regional and general, particularizing and uniformizing." The choice of the federal system for the organization of the nation at large is clear evidence that the effect of the earlier Bourbon reforms was

Anna

an increase in regional strength and a weakening of the central power of Mexico City. Yet the regions, after independence, chose to pursue both differentiation and national integration.[5]

The Plan of Iguala was the culmination of the thinking of a number of individuals from Mexico's urban elites, including both liberals and conservatives as well as several clergymen and Mexican deputies to the Spanish Cortes.[6] While William Spence Robertson argued that there was no definite proof of a clerical conspiracy in 1820 to bring about a conservative form of independence, Jaime E. Rodríguez O. has said that an 1820 plan of clerical conservatives to bring about independence was actually superseded by the plan that coalesced around Agustín de Iturbide, who had been actively consulting prominent officers and clerics as well as other individuals for most of 1820.[7] Iturbide's argument in these consultations had been that the creation of an autonomous monarchy in the name of the king and the constitution was the best way to protect the interests of the Church, the army, and the nation. He consulted about the text of the Plan of Iguala with many different individuals.[8] The Plan was similar in influence to another proposal submitted to the Cortes in Spain in 1820 by a group of Mexican deputies led by José Mariano Michelena, deputy from Michoacán, which had proposed the creation of autonomous "regencies" or kingdoms in the American dominions, ruled by the king by means of Spanish princes under the constitution. The offer of a throne to the king and his brothers appears to have been aimed at overcoming the resistance of diehard supporters of Spain. After the victory of Iguala, there appears to have been very little reference to this offer. At any rate, the king refused the proposal for a separate monarchy in Mexico. The Plan was an accommodation based on a broadly shared sense among creoles that the Spanish regime in Mexico had decayed beyond repair, especially because with the reestablishment of the constitution in 1820 commanders of the regional militias were no longer able to continue levying the local war taxes upon which a military response to the insurgents depended.[9] And yet, none of the other proposals for achieving independence since 1810 had attained such a clear consensus.

Iturbide, in the memoirs he wrote in exile in Italy, took full credit for the Plan of Iguala: "I alone conceived it, extended it, published it, and executed it." In many ways Iturbide reflected the political and social interests and fears of the provincial elite from which he came. In his memoirs, for example, he explained why he and many like him had opposed the earlier rebellions: "[Miguel] Hidalgo, and those who came after him, and who followed his example, desolated the country, . . . sacrificed millions of citizens, obstructed the sources of riches, . . . destroyed all kinds of industry, rendered the conditions of the Americans still more wretched . . . and far from obtaining independence increased the obstacles that opposed it." Against this image, he contrasted the achievement of the Plan of Iguala: "Without bloodshed, without incendiaries, without murders, without robberies, in short, without tears and without lamentations, my country became free."[10] Although self-serving, this claim was held by the majority of political elites; there was a palpable sense of relief and jubilation in the first months after independence.

The speed with which the Plan of Iguala gained the support of local military commanders, provincial deputations, and city councils, extending to the far geographical extremities of Central America, Yucatán, and the far north, is its most important characteristic. So many of the royalist officers and men joined that when the remaining loyalist troops left Mexico, there were only two thousand of them.[11] The essence of the Plan's appeal was that it guaranteed no reprisals against the defeated Spaniards or royalists and it incorporated both creole and Spaniard in a proposal that protected a broad array of existing vested interests. In only five months Iturbide controlled most of the country, and only a month later the newly arrived Spanish political chief of New Spain, Juan O'Donojú, accepted the Plan of Iguala in the Treaty of Córdoba signed on 24 August 1821. Only three months later Iturbide and the Army of the Three Guarantees made their triumphal entry into Mexico City. No one had foreseen that victory would come so quickly. The regency that headed the new government declared that fewer than two hundred persons had died in the Iturbide phase, while Iturbide himself put the number at one hundred and fifty.[12] As the city council of Mexico City declared, "The will of the nation cannot be more decisive."[13] The former Spanish viceroy, Juan Ruíz de Apodaca, writing from his refuge in Cuba, declared that the means by which independence had happened "are so extraordinary that it was not possible for anyone to imagine them."[14] Many former royalists immediately became leading figures in the new independent government. No wonder one of the pamphleteers at the time referred to Iturbide as "the Surprise of History."[15]

The Plan of Iguala was the first great act of political co-optation in Mexico's independent history. Eleven years of highly destructive insurrection and guerrilla warfare were preempted by a movement created and led by urban creoles and Spanish elites and which, while not a counterrevolution, represented nonetheless a distinct modification of the goals of the revolution. Participants invariably called it a revolution. It ended the real terror that had been imposed in many areas by the royalist military in their effort to extinguish the rebellions.[16] It opened infinite, and sometimes only imaginary, vistas for future Mexican trade and development, self-government, and assertion of identity. As Servando Teresa de Mier put it, the Plan of Iguala "conciliated the interests of all parties."[17]

The rapid success of the Plan of Iguala was both the strength and the weakness of the new government. Except for the consensus of Iguala, no concordance on fundamental principles had yet developed. Immensely complex in its implications but deceptively simple in its wording, the Plan of Iguala held something for everyone. Its program brought together liberals and conservatives, rebels and royalists, creoles, Spaniards, and mestizos. The Plan consisted of twenty-three articles. Under the Three Guarantees it promised continued dominance of Roman Catholicism, establishment of a constitutional monarchy with guarantees of political and military office and rank, and even something, under the guarantee of "Union," that may be read either as national union of the myriad of provinces and regions or as the fundamental recognition of equality of the many race categories that were then recognized in Mexican society. The Plan declared that all the inhabitants of the country were citizens, which thereby elevated the majority of the population, who were Indians and persons of mixed ancestry. The preamble endorsed the "general union between Europeans and Americans, Indians and indigenous."[18] In light of the obstinate refusal of even the Spanish liberals and the government of the Cortes in 1820 and 1821 to incorporate indigenous people as fully equal members of colonial societies, this was a momentous social breakthrough, at least in theory.

There are slight variations among the several copies of the Plan that were either published or sent out to various individuals and city governments. It is not clear why the Three Guarantees are listed in the order in which they always appear by convention—Religion, Independence, Union—because in the original plan of Iguala signed by Iturbide on 24 February 1821 article 1 is religion, article 2 is independence, and article 3 is the call for a constitutional monarchy. The word *union* was not actually used in the Plan, but it and the order of the Three Guarantees appeared in the final passage of Iturbide's postscript to the original published plan, in which he declared: "Long live the holy religion which we profess! Long live Northern America, independent from all the nations of the globe! Long live the union that makes our happiness."[19] Iturbide, it should be noted, interpreted the Plan's three fundamental points as the creation of a moderate constitutional monarchy, protection of the Church, and protection of Spaniards left behind in an independent Mexico. The Plan treated separation from Spain as a fundamental fact, when it had yet to be accomplished at the time the Plan was issued. This tendency to presume that what was only a proposal was already an accomplished fact gave the Plan an air of authority and would occur in most pronunciamiento plans of nineteenth-century Mexico. The actual government created under the terms of the Plan of Iguala would not exist for another seven months.

Within two weeks after the Plan was issued, Vicente Guerrero, the major rebel leader in the south, accepted the Plan and enrolled his followers in support of it. It is sometimes mistakenly said that Iturbide and Guerrero jointly issued the Plan, but although they had previously been in correspondence, the fact is that Guerrero came out in support of it subsequently and later said he had several objections to some of its details. Nevertheless, when he became commander of the first division of the Army of the Three

Guarantees, Guerrero issued a manifesto declaring of Iturbide: "He is my chief and I am his subordinate."[20]

The Plan of Iguala was designed as an instrument to co-opt a divided elite to the side of independence and as a means for preserving the continuity of the dominant classes. It was a brilliant political compromise, even if it ultimately failed to satisfy a large enough portion of the politically active elements in the country. Each of the guarantees of the Plan of Iguala protected existing interest groups while allowing everyone to interpret the plan to include their group aspirations. The emphasis on the union of all ethnic elements and the citizenship of people of color met one major demand of such longtime rebels as Vicente Guerrero and Guadalupe Victoria. Servando Teresa de Mier, also a longtime rebel but later an opponent of Iturbide, understood that Iguala was an instrument of consensus. From his exile in the United States he wrote: "Absolute independence was the object and the base of the Plan, and the rest is a political stratagem imposed by circumstances to incorporate all parties in the network."[21]

The process by which the officers of the Spanish royalist armies went over to the Plan of Iguala was impressive, whether they were creoles or peninsulars. In about a month Antonio López de Santa Anna, commanding the coast of Veracruz, joined; then Luis de Cortázar and Anastasio Bustamante in the Bajío, followed by Vicente Filisola in Zitácuaro and the commanders in Zacatecas, San Luis Potosí, Puebla, and in Nueva Galicia General Pedro Celestino Negrete. By May Luis Quintanar, in command of Valladolid, joined independence; in June General Negrete brought Guadalajara over while Domingo E. Luaces surrendered Querétaro. In late June José Antonio Echávarri joined; in July Puebla surrendered and José Morán, its second in command, joined. Frustrated by their inability to act against the spread of the Plan, the royal army units garrisoned in Mexico City forced Viceroy Juan Ruíz de Apodaca to resign on 5 July 1821 in favor of Francisco Novella.[22] By July 1821 the Army of the Three Guarantees controlled almost all the strategic sites except Mexico City and the port of Veracruz. Then in July the new captain general and superior political chief of New Spain, Juan O'Donojú—a Spanish officer, Mason, and liberal—arrived on Mexican soil and a month later signed the Treaty of Córdoba with Iturbide, by which he recognized the political autonomy of Mexico. O'Donojú informed Spain that resistance to independence was useless, for nearly every major garrison and town had accepted the Plan of Iguala. In the four months following the treaty, almost all remaining resistance to Iguala evaporated. The garrison commander at Mexico City placed himself and his troops under the authority of O'Donojú. Only seven months after proclamation of the Plan of Iguala, independence had been achieved; Iturbide had created the largest army in the history of Mexico; and the royalist power had evaporated.

The Plan of Iguala was the basic prototype for most of the pronunciamientos of the nineteenth-century in Mexico. This came about because of its success, the speed with which it succeeded, the way in which it cut through previous impediments to independence, the daring and clarity of it, and its role as a rallying point. The balance the Plan of Iguala achieved among competing class, regional, and political forces was its cutting edge, but it was a balance that could have lasted only with the most skilled political leadership, something Iturbide himself would not provide. Among Mexican conservatives, at any rate, the feeling would linger that Iguala and Iturbide had achieved the only moment of genuine national unity for generations to come. One important effect of the Plan of Iguala was the feeling of Mexican exception-alism. No other Spanish American country achieved independence in the same way.

In the Plan of Iguala, and in the overall Iturbide phase of the struggle for independence, the army was the guarantor of the Plan and of independence itself. As a result, as Josefina Vázquez emphasizes, the military and leading civilian politicians essentially formed a "pact" in which the army was given the job of moderating political and social extremism. The civilian political leaders would finance and maintain the armed forces. This symbiotic military-civilian relationship continued for many decades. Thus the coups d'état that occurred in the First Federal Republic (in 1823, 1828, 1830, 1834, and 1835) were led by officers but always ratified by Congress.[23]

Iturbide himself represented the nascent aspirations of the creole elite of late colonial New Spain, especially the regional elite. His father was a Basque immigrant landowner and a member of the city council of Valladolid (Morelia). His father-in-law, Isidro Huarte, was the *alcalde provincial mayor* and the wealthiest man in Valladolid. In 1805, for example, the city council of Valladolid included Iturbide's father, his father-in-law, his brother-in-law, and three business partners of his father-in-law. Iturbide thus represents a whole class. His Plan, as well as the government he created, combined both the political aspirations of the elites and the consciously manipulated affection of the masses.[24] Between 1821 and 1855 he was the only leader with a truly national following, as a result of the alliance of social groups that supported him.[25] And the Plan of Iguala forged a genuine national consensus on the issue of independence. In the letter in which he dispatched a copy of the Plan of Iguala to Viceroy Apodaca in February 1821, Iturbide declared simply that "any country is free that wants to be."[26] To contemporaries, the Plan of Iguala as well as the Treaty of Córdoba were the founding documents of independence; they constituted a consensus on the great issue of whether to be independent, on whether the interests that were prominent in the Old Regime would continue, on whether the status of the Church and other institutions would remain intact. Iguala and Córdoba were a remarkably tolerant, even magnanimous break with the mother country.

The first eighteen months following September 1821 were the period of unanimity. Iturbide officiated as president of the regency, chief of state, commander of the army that he himself had created, and as liberator. Perhaps at no other time in the nineteenth century would such unanimity reign in Mexico. The second phase of the transition, from May 1822 when Iturbide was elected as emperor to March 1823 when he abdicated, was his fall from grace. It occurred because his dissolution of the first Constituent Congress on 31 October 1822 convinced provincial leaders that Iturbide opposed a provincial voice.[27] The interests of the central government and the interests of the provinces collided head on, and at the moment when provincial autonomy was rapidly gaining support as an organizing principle for the independent country. The first Constituent Congress quickly came to represent the voice of provincial power. Unfortunately for him, Iturbide believed he was the only focus of national consensus. As he wrote in his memoirs, "I was the depository of the will of the Mexicans."[28]

While we should distinguish the individual hubris of the man from the political issues of the whole, the fact is that the Plan of Iguala had failed to provide sufficient direction on two fundamental issues that would soon confront the country: the division of powers between the executive and the legislative, and indeed the possession of sovereignty itself. Iturbide believed he was the voice of sovereignty; while the Congress, in keeping with the precedent of the Cortes in Spain, declared on the day of its installation that the national sovereignty resided in itself and that it possessed not only constituent power but also ordinary legislative power in all its extent.

The question remains: is this any way to create or to run a country? The answer, in light of the prevailing circumstances of 1821, must be yes. Acceptance of the Plan of Iguala had to be founded on a consensus that incorporated the powerful European Spaniards, who numbered only fifteen thousand but who controlled much of the country's external trade, government, the Church, and textile and other manufacturing and who provided the most highly trained officers for the army. The class interests of many of the country's 1,093,000 creoles corresponded to the concerns of the European Spaniards, and they also sought the kind of guarantees provided in Iguala.[29] The Plan of Iguala and Treaty of Córdoba made this consensus possible by uniting the Europeans and the creole elite with the longtime rebels who had been repulsed in earlier attempts at a more radically based independence. The popular masses were absorbed into the alliance by their attraction to the charismatic figure of Iturbide. The political consensus O'Donojú found when he arrived in Mexico left him no choice but to acquiesce to the Treaty of Córdoba, and that consensus could not have been achieved without the Plan of Iguala. A decisive military outcome had proved impossible until the stalemate was broken by Iguala.

Nonetheless, the Plan of Iguala did have inherent weaknesses. One problem was that it was a simple political project, not a fundamental code for a nation.[30] Iturbide himself wrote: "The Plan of Iguala guaranteed the religion of our forefathers, it offered to the reigning house of Spain the only means left to keep those extensive and rich provinces; it allowed the Mexicans to give laws to themselves and to have the government residing on their own territory."[31] That, of course, is the definition of autonomy, or of responsible government and home rule, but not necessarily of independence. As Luis Villoro has argued, this was an organic transformation, or evolution, not a revolution. Iguala and Córdoba were examples of "loosening but not breaking the link with the past." Villoro argues that "the abdication of Iturbide and the reinstallation of Congress, in March 1823, may be considered the end of the Revolution of Independence because they mark the accession to power of the creole middle class which had initiated the movement."[32]

Surprisingly, when independence was achieved through the Plan of Iguala—even though it came after eleven years of protracted and destructive struggle—it was essentially a highly precipitate step. There had been no experience in institution building. Other than the fundamental choice of a monarchy with the liberal provisions of the Spanish Constitution of 1812 recently grafted on, there was no consensus on political institutions. Mexicans, after all, had been only peripheral members of a universal Spanish monarchy, outsiders looking in upon a deeply rooted set of political institutions in which they had only barely participated. The ethos of colonial dependency may have deluded some Mexicans into thinking they had a genuine political foundation upon which to build a state, but when independence transferred the burdens of political management and policy making for the future upon

Mexicans themselves, their lack of institutional preparation became immediately and tragically evident.

Another major weakness of the Plan of Iguala was the number of significant questions it left unanswered. It is not clear, for example, why Iturbide or O'Donojú believed that Ferdinand VII or members of his family would consider transferring to Mexico to become its first monarch. Although this concept had been mooted for some years, before and during the time of the Cortes in Spain, it was clear that after his troubled reign thus far, Ferdinand VII would hardly be interested in travel. Only two years later Ferdinand himself invited a French army into Spain to liberate him from the constitutional government, which he believed had his destruction as its object. At any rate, even if one of the Spanish royals had assumed the Mexican monarchy, there had been no discussion of the nature of his powers. And this, of course, became a major issue when Iturbide became the emperor in 1822.

The Plan of Iguala also failed to define the territorial extent of the Mexican Empire. In 1821 Mexico was more a concept than an actual territory. Since three hundred years of colonialism had not yet brought central control to the far north, the far south, or Yucatán, much less Central America, and in view of the separate existence of *audiencias* for Nueva Galicia and Central America, did Mexico in 1821 yet conceive of itself as a nation? This is why Iturbide called the new political entity the Mexican Empire; that is, the "empire of the Mexicans," rather than "Mexico"; he knew there was no such thing as Mexico (other than the city, valley, and province of Mexico). Indeed it was an empire precisely because it incorporated many identities, peoples, and territories. It is not clear if anyone initially foresaw that Central America would enroll itself into the Mexican Empire under terms of the Plan of Iguala. By what logic did it follow that the new Mexican Empire automatically inherited all the former territory even of the colonial dominion of New Spain? What links assured the Mexicanism of areas not part of New Spain, such as Texas, California, Chihuahua, or Yucatán? The Plan of Iguala did not take account of the urge to regional power that eleven years of internal civil war had helped strengthen. It assumed the old elite would continue in place despite the upsurge of local power brokers and military leaders in the struggle for independence. It assumed the right of Mexico to incorporate all the vast territories of the colony of New Spain and its dependencies. It assumed that the temporary alliance Iguala had forged among members of the elite would continue. It is important to note that in 1821 the Mexican Empire, at least on paper, was territorially the largest American country.

In the absence of other functioning mechanisms, the proclamation of the first successful pronunciamiento in Mexican history tells us a number of things. First, this was not yet a state; the Plan of Iguala was the attempt to create a state by fiat, but extended debate and struggle lay ahead before any possible agreement on how that state was to be defined, on how it was to know itself. Second, there was no mutually acceptable mechanism for transfer of power, either on the macro level—as from colonial subject of a European empire to independent nation—or on the micro level—as from one Mexican leader to the next. Third, the regions were conscious and demanded a voice; the process of creating a nation-state would not be complete until the regions were able to play a role in creating it and able to claim some benefit from belonging to it. Iturbide was unable to understand this, and he paid the final price when in 1824, convinced that the move toward federalism constituted the dismemberment of the country, he returned to Mexico from his European exile and was executed. And fourth, social and class structures were not developed but were still essentially colonial. Enlightenment and liberalism, and independence, had awakened demands. Popular agency was alive but embryonic and lacking means of achieving, or even sometimes of determining, its goals. Elites could not at first prevent the onset of popular action; but they soon organized to resist it. Full political polarization set in by 1826–28. Mexican elites attempted to mobilize the masses in their ongoing struggle for hegemony, but no political faction was strong enough to win a decisive victory. Hence the period was characterized by what Torcuato Di Tella called "a surprisingly non-hegemonic polity" in which neither a powerful dictatorship nor a solid civilian regime could emerge.[33] The consensus around the Plan of Iguala would be the first and last national political accord in a long time. Yet paradoxically, that was partly because the precipitate nature of the achievement of independence under the Plan of Iguala helped preclude the early possibility of developing a hegemonic polity, or at least a hegemonic authority.

Of course, the foremost problem with the Plan of Iguala—in common with all the nineteenth-century pronunciamientos—was that in addition to being only a step toward nationhood, it achieved only temporary unity. Rather than producing nationhood, we can conclude that Iguala began the process of developing one national vision, but one that would be sharply contested throughout the nineteenth century by other national visions. The civilian-military divide would dominate Mexican political life until the Porfiriato, and this was exacerbated by the fact that the Plan of Iguala was the work, at least visibly, of military leadership. Even after the 1910 Revolution, Alan Knight wrote, the objective national identity remained fragmented by region, locality, religion, ideology, age, gender and ethnicity.[34]

Perhaps the best indication of the prototypical role of the Plan of Iguala, as well as of the institutional vacuum in which politics had to play out, is the fact that Iturbide's Mexican Empire, and the rule of Iturbide himself, were brought to an end by two new plans in early 1823. Clearly, the pronunciamiento had become the preferred and almost automatic mechanism for regime change. This was partly a result of the fact that the Congress had not proceeded very far in establishing a more direct form of election of deputies or other office holders than the procedure set out in the Spanish Constitution of 1812, which had been adopted as the interim constitution for independent Mexico. Mexico, in other words, had considerably more experience in the pronunciamiento than it had in direct elections or other forms of leadership alternation. Moreover, it was Iturbide's dissolution of the first Constituent Congress on 31 October 1822 that provoked the fundamental clash of powers between the executive and Congress. In addition, the Congress was then the only direct voice at the national level for the provinces. During the Iturbide empire many provinces began to experience local self-government for the first time, and they resisted central government decision making concerning provincial affairs.[35]

The demand for the restoration of the dissolved Constituent Congress motivated both the Veracruz rebellion led by Antonio López de Santa Anna in December 1822 and the Casa Mata revolt that began in February 1823, headed by elements of the imperial army (who called for the election of a new Constituent Congress). Santa Anna's uprising was a hurried and confused affair, which he admitted in his autobiography was motivated by Iturbide's removing him from command of the port of Veracruz.[36] On 2 December 1822 Santa Anna issued two proclamations, one addressed to the citizens of the port, in which he called for the creation of a republic, and the other addressed to the troops under his command, demanding only the restoration of justice that had been denied him.[37] Four days later a longer set of "clarifications" was issued, written by Miguel Santa María, the minister of Simón Bolívar to Mexico who had been expelled by Iturbide for meddling in Mexican affairs and was then in Veracruz awaiting a ship. These items taken together were called the Plan of Veracruz. Its real appeal was that it called for creation of provincial militias, members of which would possess the *fuero militar*, and it also declared that debts incurred to finance the rebellion would be considered national debts. These were important elements encouraging both regional and military autonomy. In the first weeks, the imperial army in Veracruz province, under command of José Antonio Echávarri as captain general of Veracruz and Puebla, came close to routing Santa Anna.

Then Echávarri began to waver, under pressure from all sides to abandon his loyalty to Iturbide.[38] On 1 February 1823 Echávarri signed the Acta of Casa Mata with his fellow officers of the imperial army. The Plan of Casa Mata was intended both to ensure Iturbide's continuation on the throne and to meet the demand for the restoration of Congress. The Plan of Casa Mata declared that no attack against the emperor was intended. A clause of Casa Mata declared that the government of the province of Veracruz was to be given over to its provincial deputation until the new Congress should meet.[39] By handing the government of the province of Veracruz to a third party that both Santa Anna and Echávarri could live with, Casa Mata created the first recognized, regional self-government by a provincial deputation, something all the provinces soon aspired to have. In a very brief time the Plan of Casa Mata superseded the Plan of Veracruz and gained the adherence of almost all the provinces, in some cases specifically because it allowed provincial self-government without overthrowing Iturbide.[40] The new enterprise, which would rapidly supplant the Iturbide enterprise, was decentralization of command in the army and provincial self-government. It would soon become the drive to federalism. Iturbide, feeling betrayed by the imperial army, refused to accept an offer of the commanders of Casa Mata that he himself become leader of the movement, and abdicated instead.[41] Upon Iturbide's fall, the provinces moved immediately toward the creation of federalism. Two federalist projects emerged within a month of Iturbide's abdication.

The reason the pronunciamiento became the preferred instrument for fundamental political change is that it worked; at least the first ones did. Before the publication of Mexico's first constitution in 1824, the pronunciamiento had already brought about three fundamental changes of regime—independence itself, the fall of Iturbide's empire, and the achievement of the principle of federalism. Prior to the establishment of direct election and popular sovereignty, could there be a more effective and efficient mechanism? The pronunciamiento may have become a frequent occurrence in the years that followed, but originally it was a startling means of achieving long-sought demands in the absence of functioning vehicles to bring about such ends.

Notes

1. Hernández Chávez, *La tradición republicana del buen gobierno*, 17.
2. Hale, *Mexican Liberalism*, 113–14.
3. González y González, "Patriotismo y matriotismo," 477–95.

4. Vázquez, "De la difícil constitución de un Estado."

5. Ortega Noriega, "Hacia la regionalización de la historia de México."

6. Rodríguez O., "Transition from Colony to Nation."

7. Robertson, *Iturbide of Mexico*, 67–71.

8. Rodríguez O., "Transition from Colony to Nation," 120–22.

9. Archer, "Where Did All the Royalists Go?"

10. Agustín de Iturbide, "Memoria de Livorno," 27 September 1823, Benson Latin American Collection, University of Texas at Austin (hereafter cited as BLAC), Hernández y Dávalos Collection. This is the English translation by Michael Joseph Quin, 1823.

11. "Resumen histórico de los acontecimientos de N. Esp., dado al Exmo. Sr. Capitán General de la Ysla de Cuba y su ejército por el Ten. Coronel de Navarra Expedicionario (Vicente Bausá)," Havana, 18 December 1821, Archivo General de Indias, Seville (hereafter cited as AGI), Mexico 1680.

12. Regency to Iturbide, Mexico City, 22 February 1822, BLAC, Hernández y Dávalos Collection; Iturbide to Regency, Mexico City, 7 December 1821, Biblioteca Nacional de Antropología e Historia, Mexico City (hereafter cited as BNAH), T-3, 35, Colección Antigua.

13. "Representación del Exmo. Ayuntamiento de Méjico al comandante accidental de armas, Francisco Novella," 2 September 1821, Archivo General de la Nación, Mexico City (hereafter cited as AGN), Impresos oficiales, vol. 60, no. 103.

14. Apodaca to Minister of ultramar, Guanabacoa, Cuba, 17 November 1821, AGI, Mexico 1680.

15. Ocampo, *Las ideas de un día*, 331–32.

16. Christon I. Archer has emphasized the ways in which the loyalist response to the rebel threats constituted genuine systems of military control and terror. See his "Politicization of the Army of New Spain" and "The Militarization of Mexican Politics."

17. See especially Ocampo, *Las ideas de un día*.

18. "Plan de la independencia de México proclamada en el pueblo de Iguala en los días 1 y 2 de marzo de 1821," AGN, Impresos oficiales, vol. 60, no. 62.

19. Tena Ramírez, *Leyes fundamentales de México*, 113–16.

20. Vicente Guerrero, "Manifiesto patriótico que hizo siendo comandante General de la primera división del Ejército de las Tres Garantías," Mexico City, 1821, BLAC, García Collection.

21. Servando Teresa de Mier, "Memoria político-instructiva, enviada desde

Filadelfia en agosto de 1821 a los gefes independientes del Anahuac," Mexico City, 1822, BLAC, García Collection.

22. Anna, "Francisco Novella and the Last Stand of the Royal Army," 97–102.

23. Vázquez, "El ejército."

24. Di Tella, "Ciclos políticos."

25. Vázquez, "Un viejo tema."

26. Iturbide to Apodaca, Iguala, 24 February 1821, AGI, Mexico 1680.

27. See Anna, *The Mexican Empire of Iturbide,* and *Forging Mexico 1821–1835.*

28. Iturbide, "Memoria de Livorno."

29. Creole numbers are from "Memoria sobre la población del reino de Nueva España, escrita por D. Fernando Navarro y Noriega" (Mexico City, 1820), AGN, Impresos oficiales, vol. 60, no. 48.

30. Ortiz de Ayala, *México considerado como nación independiente y libre,* 10.

31. Iturbide, "Memoria de Livorno."

32. Villoro, "The Ideological Currents of the Epoch of Independence."

33. Di Tella, *National Popular Politics,* 247. See also Warren, *Vagrants and Citizens.*

34. Knight, "Mexican National Identity."

35. Vega, "La opción federalista en Zacatecas."

36. Santa Anna, *The Eagle,* 16.

37. "Proclamas del Brigadier Santana a los habitantes y tropa de Veracruz," Veracruz, 2 December 1822, BLAC.

38. Bocanegra, *Memorias para la historia de México independiente;* Alamán, *Historia de Méjico,* 5:488.

39. Acta de Casa Mata, Cuartel General de Casa Mata, 1 February 1823, Mexico City, BLAC, T-2, 10, Colección Antigua.

40. Provincial Deputation of Mexico to Iturbide, 1 March 1823, BLAC, Colección Bustamante, vol. 17, no. 4.

41. Bravo Ugarte, *Historia de México,* 157.

IVANA FRASQUET & MANUEL CHUST | *Translated by Kim Lauren Gillespie*

Two. Agustín de Iturbide: *From the Pronunciamiento of Iguala to the Coup of 1822*

The first decades of the nineteenth century were turbulent in most of Europe and the Americas. In Europe Napoleon challenged the absolute monarchies at the same time as their overseas territories witnessed the emergence of opposition movements in which autonomist and pro-independence aspirations were developed. For the Spanish monarchy the war against France meant more: it resulted in the questioning of the absolutist tenets of the regime and a revolutionary approach to the liberal principles that should constitute the nation-state, captured in the legislation issued by the Cádiz Cortes.[1] The definitive defeat of the Bonapartist dynasty and the reaction of the Holy Alliance provided some respite for Ferdinand VII, who from 1814 tried to restore the absolutist values of the past regime, initiating a harsh period of repression justified by belief in monarchical power that was based on the concept of divine right.

However, the restored state would not be exactly the same as it had been before 1808. The absolutist reaction of 1814 provoked a political and social divide that turned the majority of liberals against Ferdinand VII. Moreover, after 1814 the king's army found itself in the contradictory situation of having among its ranks notorious officers whose heroic actions against the French had not been duly recognized with promotion, and who thus found themselves plotting, from the barracks, military uprisings aimed at overthrowing the Ancien Régime, since it allowed no space for political negotiation. In this way a good number of liberal civilian-military *pronunciamientos* came to characterize the six-year period from 1814 to 1820.[2] The attempted uprisings of General Espoz y Mina in Pamplona (1814), of Marshal Juan Díez Porlier in La Coruña (1815), the so-called triangular conspiracy in Madrid (1816), and the planned pronunciamientos of General Luis Lacy in Barcelona (1817) and Colonel Joaquín Vidal in Valencia (1819) are all well known.[3] The 1819 El Palmar Conspiracy in Cádiz is also noteworthy.[4] In the Americas there were similar movements, such as Agustín de Iturbide's pronunciamiento in New Spain of February 1821.

One of these pronunciamientos, that of Lieutenant Colonel Rafael de Riego, was to trigger a revolutionary reaction that spread throughout the Iberian Peninsula in March 1820, forcing the king to take an oath of allegiance, for the first time, to the 1812 Constitution.

Riego's *Grito*

On 1 January 1820, Lieutenant Colonel Rafael de Riego and his men rose up in the town of Cabezas de San Juan, in the province of Seville. Riego was part of the forces stationed in Andalucia destined to set sail for the River Plate to fight against the insurgency.

Enrique O'Donnell, Count of La Bisbal, who knew of the conspiracy and whose ambiguous attitude toward the plot finally resulted in the betrayal of the conspirators in July 1819, led the expeditionary army. This denunciation led to the Count of La Bisbal being awarded the most prestigious of medals. Summoned to court to receive them, he sent in his place Félix María Calleja, Count of Calderón, governor of Cádiz, and commander-in-chief of the expeditionary army.[5]

The imprisonment of some of the plotters did not end the conspiracy, since prominent civilians such as Antonio Alcalá Galiano and Juan de Dios Álvarez Mendizábal quickly reorganized it. An outbreak of yellow fever broke communications between the conspirators located in Cádiz and the army, forcing them to postpone the date of the uprising until winter. The plot also included the participation of officers such as General Quiroga, who was detained in Alcalá de los Guazules following the conspiracy's discovery in July, Felipe de Arco Agüero, Evaristo San Miguel, Demetrio O'Daly, and Miguel López Baños.[6] As is already known, Ferdinand VII had intended to purge the army of most of its liberal officers by posting them to fight in the Americas against the insurgency.[7] Many of these officers had become hardened veterans in the Peninsular War and their promotion was due to their service in the campaign, and not as a result of their family ties, as had been the case in the Ancien Régime.

The development of the 1820 pronunciamiento and the spread of its revolutionary movement throughout the Peninsula are well known.[8] The political and social praxis of the liberal system, which had been implanted by the Cortes of Cádiz, had succeeded in establishing deep-seated roots in Spanish society. Evidence of this may be seen in the manner in which the pronunciamiento's success relied on the mobilization of the juntas that were organized in important cities like La Coruña, Pamplona, Zaragoza, Barcelona, etc.

The pronunciamiento therefore triumphed due to a combination of military and civilian factors and the resonance of liberal constitutionalism, obtaining its ultimate objective: regime change and the installation of a constitutional system. Irene Castells has analyzed the genesis of the Spanish pronunciamientos of the 1820's, explaining the way in which the conspirators operated. First came *el rompimiento* (the breaking-off); that is, the insurrection itself. Then it was essential that the different garrisons immediately supported the original pronunciamiento, with a consequent "contagious" effect among the urban civilian population. The conspirators termed this sequence of events "the general combination."[9] This strategy sought support in urban nuclei in which the liberals had their social base. Furthermore, these pronunciamientos valued public opinion as a necessary element in ensuring that the conspiracy was successful. An important point to note is that the pronunciamientos were oriented toward the periphery, seeking massive support in the cities in order to generate a wide-scale uprising. This was the case with Riego's 1820 pronunciamiento and with those that preceded it during the six-year period 1814–20.

The consequences of the pronunciamiento's success in the political context are indeed noteworthy since the revolutionary governments of the provincial juntas were reinstated and the constitutional Cortes was once more convened. During the months between the formation of the juntas and the opening of the Cortes, Spain was governed by the Junta Provisional Gubernativa (provisional junta of government) installed in Madrid on 9 March 1820 by Ferdinand VII.[10] Thereafter, following the king's oath of allegiance to the 1812 Constitution, a new period began in which the various institutions were forced to adjust to the liberal and constitutional system that came into existence, and in which the participation of the American deputies was to prove fundamental in determining the way forward for the Spanish monarchy.

Of all these deputies, the *novohispanos* (New Spaniards) were the most active and combative in the Cortes. The hope of greater autonomy, temporarily put on hold as a result of the return of absolutism in 1814, rested now on their shoulders.[11] For this reason, the events of the Peninsula and Mexico became closely intertwined and must be analyzed as an integral whole in order to obtain a complete and complex understanding of what happened.

From Iguala to Córdoba . . . Via Madrid

The news of Rafael de Riego's pronunciamiento reached the port of Veracruz on 29 April 1820 in an issue of the *Gaceta de Madrid* that also included Ferdinand VII's decree and oath of allegiance to the Constitution. Thus in not quite a month and a half the events that had taken place in the Peninsula had been heard of through the press. As we know, Viceroy Juan Ruiz de Apodaca, Count of Venadito, did not take his own oath of allegiance to the Constitution, nor did he endorse the change of system until the following 31 May, with the excuse that he had to wait to receive such news by official means.[12] Thereafter, proceedings got underway in the Peninsula to fill the vacant Spanish American seats in the Cortes with substitutes who would participate in Congress until the elected deputies arrived from the Americas. The start of sessions was set for 9 July, while 17 September was the date fixed in Mexico for the election of those deputies who would go to the Peninsula.[13]

Once the parliamentary work of the Cortes began, the Spanish American deputies set out to present a whole array of proposals aimed at consolidating their territories' autonomy and self-government. They started by demanding that the number of Spanish American representatives be increased since the decree of 22 March 1820 had designated only thirty seats for the whole continent. However, even though their call for more representatives was not heeded, the Spanish American deputies continued to participate actively and pose questions they deemed important for the autonomous development of their territories. These ranged from proposals to increase the number of provincial deputations—a fundamental institution when it came to obtaining fiscal and military control of a given territory—to developing a plan of economic decentralization for Mexico with evident federal characteristics. Moreover, they requested improvements in agricultural matters, such as the liberalization and sale of tobacco; in commercial policy, such as legalizing free trade between all the ports of the Spanish crown and cutting back on taxation; in the mining sector, abolishing the Tribunal de Minería (mining tribunal) as a restricted system with control over the ports' activities; and in education, introducing free primary schools in all towns.

The work was incessant, and the elected deputies who arrived in Madrid during the months of March, April, and May 1821 built upon the exertions of the substitute deputies.[14] The majority of the novohispano deputation had left Veracruz on 13 February 1821 in an escorted convoy of warships. Deputy Lucas Alamán, who was in Veracruz waiting to set sail for the Peninsula, recounts in his work on the period that the deputies gathered in the port were summoned at the start of January by Juan N. Gómez Navarrete—deputy for Michoacán and a close friend of Agustín de Iturbide—to acquaint them with Iturbide's plan, which consisted in proclaiming the independence of Mexico and in installing a Congress.[15] This version of the events would be reiterated with some modifications in the account deputy Manuel Gómez Pedraza gave, a short time after, in a manifesto, and would subsequently be taken up by some historians.[16] Although at this time it is likely that the novohispano deputies did not entirely support Iturbide's plan, it remains the case that they left Veracruz with some idea of the proposal that would be presented before the Cortes calling for self-government under a constitutional monarchy, with a member of the Bourbon dynasty on its throne, and with the rights of citizenship being offered to the *castas* (racially mixed people). At least, this is what Agustín de Iturbide recounted in a letter to Vicente Guerrero, to convince him that the revolution was progressing well and that it would be carried out with the support of the novohispano deputies in the Cortes of Madrid:

> Bearing in mind that the deputies who have already left for the Congress in the Peninsula, with the greatest of ideas, full of patriotism and liberalism, will manifest with as much energy as they can muster, among other things, that all the sons of the country, without distinction, should enjoy full citizenship, and that, since *señor* Don Ferdinand VII cannot be our sovereign that, perhaps, his august brother *señor* Don Carlos, or Don Francisco de Paula may come instead.[17]

It is clear that the deputies were acquainted with Iturbide's intentions. What remains uncertain is whether they shared these, given that Iturbide brought his plans forward and launched the Plan of Iguala on 24 February 1821 without waiting for the deputies to reach their destination. Nevertheless, the deputies maintained their stance in favor of self-government and hurried to request the establishment of a special committee that could deal with matters arising from the Spanish American revolutions.[18] This committee worked nonstop and involved the participation of government officials such as Juan O'Donojú, appointed field marshal and *jefe político* (political chief) of New Spain. It was in this committee that the plan agreed between Iturbide and the novohispano deputies was discussed. Although its minutes have unfortunately not been found, it can be affirmed on the basis of circumstantial comments expressed in various documents of the time that everyone approved of the plan. However, when news of the Plan of Iguala reached the Cortes at the beginning of June, events in the Peninsula sped up. The deputy for Michoacán, Mariano Michelena, ahead of his comrades, proposed the need to apply "another large measure, worthy of free men and worthy of the Spanish Congress, which has already been indicated, not only to the committee but also for the province."[19] He was clearly referring to the plan of self-government for Mexico that had been discussed in the committee. Following the same line of thought, Iturbide's friend and representative in Madrid, Juan N. Gómez Navarrete, added before parliament: "I am asking the Cortes to order the government to authorize a ship [to go to the Americas], as soon as possible, to carry the news that in the Cortes, by proposal of the deputies from overseas, a plan of government is being discussed, that may make the observance of the Constitution compatible with the vast distance which separates those provinces from the metropolis, with the request that the viceroy communicates this in straightforward terms to the dissidents."[20]

The proposal provides a glimpse of one of the arguments the Spanish Americans would use to support their plan: the vast distance that separated the overseas provinces from the Peninsula. Navarrete illustrated this point: "take for example if an uprising or a popular revolution occurred, in such a way that it became necessary to suspend a constitutional article, it would not be possible, *because the representative body does not exist there.*"[21] Moreover, he insisted, Iturbide would abandon his plans as soon as he knew the content of the Spanish American proposals, since his intentions did not entail bringing about the absolute independence of Mexico.

However, the events were rushed, and ten days later, on 14 June, the Count of Toreno told the Chamber that the committee had not been able to adopt any measure with respect to the application of the plan and that the cabinet ministers, in spite of endorsing it to begin with, had later admitted that public opinion was not ready for such a radical proposal. Therefore the committee left the solution of this matter in the hands of the government. The news must have represented a severe blow for the novohispano deputies, who were hoping for the approval of their plan in Congress. Thus they immediately set out to restructure the plan and present it on 25 June, incorporating the rest of the Spanish American territories in their federal proposal.[22]

If we analyze the plan, we see that it contained the same political bases that formed the substance of Iturbide's Plan of Iguala, namely that a constitutional monarchy should be forged with a Bourbon on the throne and that other autonomous political powers should be created, such as separate legislative and judicial branches. It was not until the following day that José Miguel Ramos Arizpe, one of the leaders of the novohispanos, presented the same plan but with the difference that it would only apply to Mexico and that the members of the Spanish royal family would not be part of the executive.

In other words, if we analyze the events it becomes evident that the steps taken by the novohispano deputies in the Cortes of Madrid in this legislature were clearly connected with the course of events in Mexico. It is for this reason that they hurried to install a committee to debate the plan that was thought up and elaborated in Veracruz. But knowing that Iturbide had brought the pro-

Frasquet and Chust

nunciamiento forward, they had to recompose their strategy and present it together with the rest of the Spanish American deputies, whose votes were fundamental if the novohispano representatives did not have the support of the government or the influential members of the committee.

Similarly, the acceptance of the Plan de Iguala by Field Marshal Juan O'Donojú and the signing of the Treaty of Córdoba on 24 August 1821 were no coincidence. Although O'Donojú left the Peninsula before the special committee recognized that he could not be authorized to deliver a report, he had attended the previous meetings where the deputies and the government ministers were in agreement over the basis of the plan of self-government. For this reason, Iturbide's proposals did not seem strange to him; rather, they conformed as a whole to the spirit of the plan he thought must have been passed in the Cortes. This is how O'Donojú expressed it in an official letter addressed to the governor of Veracruz on his arrival: "In fact our national representation, before my departure from the Peninsula, was already thinking about preparing the ground for Mexican independence. In one of their committees, with the attendance of the secretaries of state, they proposed and approved the main clauses. It was not doubted that before the Cortes closed its sessions, this important business would have been resolved for the two Spains, since the honor of both is compromised in this subject."[23]

As we know, the field marshal did not live long enough to defend himself from the accusations of treason that some peninsular deputies of the Cortes would lay on him not long afterward. But it remains clear that the events of New Spain and the Peninsula during this period must be analyzed by looking at them together, synchronically and dialectically.

The Emperor's "Constitutional Path"

Once the autonomist route was exhausted in the Spanish Cortes of Madrid, the novohispano deputies gradually abandoned the Peninsula to return to their country. More accurately, as Ramos de Arizpe hinted, it was the *Mexican* representatives (rather than the novohispano deputies) who went back home. The change of nomenclature was not unwarranted. It responded to the gradual acceptance of a new identity as Mexicans, as opposed to novohispanos, and anticipated immediate changes in Mexico as an emergent independent nation-state that was no longer New Spain.

Iturbide's military pronunciamiento of Iguala now needed to give political organization to the new state. Yet to be resolved was what this state would be like and what form its government would take. The Treaty of Córdoba and the Plan of Iguala, treated as the foundational constituent basis of the new nation-state, transformed Mexico into an empire, thus maintaining a monarchist continuity that was nonetheless constitutional, following Cádiz. For the time being the treaty reserved the throne of the empire for Ferdinand VII or another family member. The "pact" that Iturbide had signed with O'Donojú and was thus initially maintained.

The origins of the first Mexican constitutional Congress, inaugurated on 24 February 1822, were clearly revolutionary in terms of their theoretical and conceptual models. The first act of Congress was to declare itself legitimately installed and to state that "sovereignty resides essentially in the Mexican nation."[24] Then Deputy José María Fagoaga reinforced the stance of the Chamber with the following proposal: "Does national sovereignty reside in this constitutional Congress?" As was approved unanimously, the deputies, representatives of the Mexican nation, were to become the sole depositaries of the new country's sovereignty.[25] Similarly, the powers were divided equally, and in the oath that was taken subsequently, the regency was made to acknowledge the fact that the nation's sovereignty rested exclusively in Congress and was thus subjected to it. This concept of sovereignty would be one of the main sources of contention between Iturbide, who took the post of first regent after O'Donojú's death, and the Mexican Congress. As in the moderate concept of liberalism, Iturbide understood that sovereignty had to be shared between the executive and the legislative power, and not rest solely on the latter, as the deputies had proclaimed on their first day of sessions.

With the sessions commenced, the liberal Mexican deputies started to construct the state employing autonomist and revolutionary theories inherited from a political praxis acquired in Cádiz and Madrid. The first few months of Congress saw the approval of numerous decrees legislating about many aspects of the state: the tax system, education, the armed forces, commerce, national symbols, etc.

The tense relations that developed between Congress and the regent were evident from the very first sessions. On 27 February Iturbide was involved in an incident in the Chamber regarding where he had to take his seat. These formal matters, important in the initial moment of construction of the symbolic apparatus of the new state, would mark the beginning of the separation between the two powers.[26]

At the same time, the application of Cádiz legislation in Mexico provided the state with autonomous institutions that came to structure the territory politically and fiscally. The proliferation of constitutional *ayuntamientos* and provincial deputations was yet another consequence of this application.[27] Inherent in the proceedings was the problem of the treasury. The reduction or elimination of taxes and duties by Iturbide and the provisional junta, without having arranged a fiscal plan beforehand, resulted in the economic ruin of the state, so the deputies' proposals were directed toward creating direct taxes to ease the situation.[28]

The importance of these fiscal matters was apparent in the Congress's first sessions. A week in, Rafael Leandro Echenique (from Veracruz) proposed to the Chamber a wide range of articles designed to eliminate the economic debt and to address the question of outstanding loans. A few days later, on 9 March, an official letter was read in Congress from the minister of finance—Rafael Pérez Maldonado—in which an order from Iturbide was included. Iturbide complained about the lack of funds available to assist the troops and demanded that measures be taken immediately to alleviate the shortfall. The deputies interpreted this as interference on the part of the executive, which appeared to grant the government responsibility in this matter. The alleviation of the troops' needs at the time was not one of Congress's responsibilities, but establishing a public fiscal system that resolved the economic situation was. The finance committee prepared a savings plan in which the salaries of civil and military employees were to be reduced, while the army was to lose its independence by having its treasury and accounts departments abolished and control of its budget transferred to the general treasury.[29] At the same time it was demanded that the government inform Congress about the quantity of troops it required to protect strategic points and of the remissions that could be given to free the treasury from having to cover their expenses. This petition, as will be seen, triggered the crisis of May 1822 that led to Iturbide being crowned emperor.

The conflict between the regency and Congress worsened within a few days. On 23 March a new report from the finance commission was read out in the Chamber in response to the executive's request that funds be found to cover the troops' grave needs. Rafael Echenique accused the regency of slowing down Congress's activities and of altering its intended deliberations by continuously meddling with complaints about the hardships and shortages the troops were suffering. In contrast, the regency insinuated that it was neglect by Congress that was the cause of the soldiers' penury.[30]

In reply, the liberal factions protested that the regency was not publishing Congress's decrees and, furthermore, was imposing forced loans in order to get cash quickly. Congress's refusal to approve Iturbide's forced loans resulted in the deputies' having to propose raising a donation and a voluntary loan as a means of addressing the empire's more urgent needs. The loans would be returned with the sums collected in a property tax that Congress was preparing. This tax plan was presented on 24 April in the Chamber. The "direct rural pension" would force every hacienda, rancho, and farm to pay 5 percent of its gross production. In exchange for this, the sales tax would be eliminated for sale of seeds and animals prior to slaughter. As studied by José Antonio Serrano, the provincial deputations and the constitutional ayuntamientos would be in charge of establishing the fiscal census and of collecting the tax.[31] Later on, on 18 June 1822, another direct tax plan was presented, which referred to a 6 percent annual charge "on all income and capital." The fiscal theme was of great importance in these early stages due to the need to have liquid capital with which to undertake the construction of the state. Although a direct tax would not be approved until June 1823, it was already clear that the economy was one of the main issues of contention that would lead to Iturbide's clash with Congress. It was a theme that was directly related to the other problem that divided the two powers: organization of the armed forces.

The Defense of the State: Militia or Regular Army?

While the government wanted to redirect income to ease the situation of the army—the main author, in the regent's eyes, of independence-the deputies opted for measures of fiscal freedom, inspired by the spirit of revolutionary change. However, closely tied to this confrontation lay a structural problem common to the emergence of nation-states: the armed condition of the revolution. That is to say, Mexico had a revolutionary coercive force—capable of triumphing militarily over the metropolis and of subsequently guaranteeing independence against any potential aggression aimed at bringing about a reconquest—which upheld a body of liberal values aimed at defending the nation and its society.

If the fiscal question was among the fundamental factors in sustaining the new state, the army was the most fundamental and *sine qua non*. It was, in fact, of such importance that the debates about its creation would ultimately be responsible for provoking Iturbide's definitive coup of May 1822.

The problem arose early on in Congress. Only one week after the sessions had started, Deputy Francisco García from Zacatecas drew attention to the fact that the national militia bodies were not established in the capital of the empire, when they had already been established elsewhere. The deputy for Mexico, Manuel Tejada, supported the creation of the militia "as one of the pillars upon which liberty and independence and the observance of the constitution stand; and as one of the more economic means of retaining a respectable armed force, for the prosperity of the Empire."[32] Iturbide had surrounded himself in Mexico City with the army, which had helped him reach the regency and had not allowed the establishment of an armed militia corps.

The drafting of the *Reglamento* (regulations) of the militia closely followed the guidelines put forward by the Cortes of Madrid in April 1820. In Mexico, however, despite borrowing heavily from the Cádiz legislation, the name of the institution was changed so as to disassociate it from the Spanish administration. In this way the national militia became the civic militia, even if both nomenclatures were initially used indiscriminately.[33]

The debates began straight after Iturbide presented a report about the military situation and the empire's need for troops, as had been requested by Congress. The regent had prepared the report with the help of his most trusted generals, thus dispensing with the secretaries of state for this matter, as stipulated in the regency regulations. In its statement the government estimated that the regular army should be made up of 35,900 men, while the civic militia should be organized in all the provinces with much smaller numbers. In reply, Congress's war commission presented a plan in which the regular army was reduced to 20,000 men, while the number of militiamen was increased to 30,000. The arguments for these two options had been carefully thought out and the debate began on 13 May 1822.[34]

The deputies began to take sides: those who supported increasing the number of regular troops and, consequently, the regent's power, and those who prioritized the militia—made up of armed citizens, let us not forget. José María Bocanegra, deputy for Zacatecas, represented the governmental option. In his speech he spoke of the uncertainty of independence and highlighted the threat posed by the Spanish monarchy, which could attack the Mexican Empire at any time. On this basis, he defended the need to establish a permanent army. But he was also conscious of the lack of affection people felt for the army: "I know very well that the armed forces are seen with distrust and with little affection by the zealous advocates of freedom." This was no surprise, since it had been a force formed mainly by royalist veterans—such as Iturbide—who had embraced the cause of independence when it was already inevitable. What guarantees could a permanent army offer to save the liberal state? In fact, one wonders whether the deputies already feared that the military were plotting a forceful coup that would bring an end to the liberal, constitutional, and revolutionary work that had been carried out to date.

José Hipólito Odoardo defended the militia-led option, accusing the government of not obeying Congress's decrees, thus covertly accusing the regent of "absolutist inconsistencies." The construction of the Mexican state was at the center of the debate. That is to say, in a delicate context like that in which the empire found itself—in the middle of "interior and exterior dangers," as one deputy had noted—would one bet on a strong army that would consolidate the executive power, or was it preferable to create a militia force that would support the revolution and defend Congress?[35] Deputy Odoardo signaled that it was *not* safe to trust the army with guaranteeing Mexico's liberty and that its organization had to submit to the political constitution in order to make the army less dependent on the executive power. Undoubtedly, the fear that the regent could use the armed forces for his own devices was present.

On 17 May the first article of the plan was approved, granting the regular army 20,000 men. The defenders of the militia as a coercive form of defense had achieved their objective: the regular army was to be reduced to the number recommended by the

Frasquet and Chust

congressional commission, rejecting Iturbide's proposal. The next day the rest of the articles that organized the civic militia were approved.

The session closed at one o'clock in the afternoon, with the more liberal deputies believing that with the approval of the commission's report they had won the debate. However, a few hours later, early in the morning, the army of the capital would rise to proclaim Iturbide emperor of Mexico. Insisting on Congress's legitimacy, notions of national sovereignty, and constitutional and liberal ideals served little purpose, because the armed forces would dominate the sessions of the following months up until the dissolution of the legislature in October of the same year.

The End of the Regent, Long Live the Emperor!

On the mornings of 18 and 19 May 1822, the generals, chiefs, and officers of the troops garrisoned in the capital of the empire, together with their infantry and cavalry regiments, proclaimed Iturbide emperor of Mexico in a pronunciamiento that attracted significant popular support. The proclamation of the officers who staged the coup was sent to Congress:

Señor.—The infantry and cavalry regiments of the imperial army based in this capital, en masse, and with absolute uniformity, have proclaimed the most serene Señor, Admiral *Generalísimo*, President of the Supreme Regency, Don Agustín de Iturbide, Emperor of Mexican America. This *pronunciamiento* has been welcomed with the most lively demonstrations of joy and enthusiasm by the people of this capital, gathered still in the streets. The generals, chiefs and officers who subscribe [this declaration], are working toward ensuring public order and tranquility are preserved; and at the same time believe it their duty to express this idea to you; so that by taking this into consideration, you may deliberate over its importance.—May God be with you for many years.

Mexico, 19 May 1822, three in the morning.—to the Mexican Sovereign Congress.[36]

Congress was reconvened immediately the next day, in an extraordinary session to make the deputies aware of what had happened the night before. The people, overjoyed, surrounded the building shouting, "Long live the Emperor!" and fought to enter the galleries to hear the proclamation. The tense situation made the deputies demand the regency's intervention to ensure that public order was preserved and that Congress was awarded the opportunity to deliberate freely on this matter. The commission that set off to obtain these guarantees "returned without an answer that could satisfy Congress's expectations." Iturbide remained impassive. He was not going to make it easy for the legislature to discuss the approval or disapproval of his proclamation. Given that at this moment he had the opportunity to force the Chamber to accept him as emperor, he was not going to be the one to calm the excited people or hold back the army. Iturbide's connivance with the rebels has been highlighted by some historians.[37] Although the emperor himself would subsequently deny in his memoirs that he had been involved in the move to crown him emperor, his relationship with the army officers who staged the pronunciamiento would appear to demonstrate that he was involved. Perhaps it was true that Iturbide did not have anything to do with the outburst of popular support that backed the movement, but it is noteworthy that it was the former regiment of Celaya—command of which the regent had saved for himself—that led the march and the request to have him crowned emperor.

Faced with this situation, Congress decided to request the regent's presence. He appeared with an entourage of generals, applauded by the people outside the building. In this way he forced the Chamber to make the session public, relying on the crowd as an ally that would ruin any attempt to postpone the appointment. Some deputies presented a proposal to delay the nomination until the provinces had been consulted, allowing Iturbide in the meantime to be named the only regent and holder of all executive power. Others, in contrast, admitted that the powers invested in them were sufficient to appoint him emperor. The final ballot favored the acclamation of Iturbide as emperor of Mexico, and a thunderous ovation closed the session. From then on began a new stage in the construction of the Mexican state, characterized by the concentration of powers in the figure of Agustín I—which in our opinion does not mean that this entailed a return to absolutist political practices; far from it. Instead, Mexico had to wrestle with a particularly problematic contradiction, not only in having to make a prerogative of the Ancien Régime compatible with a fundamental law of the new regime but, above all, in having to make executive powers compatible with "the" Constitution of Cádiz.

Iturbide would prove himself a constitutional emperor, moderate and conservative in political state matters, but a liberal where economic affairs were concerned. His model of the state strongly supported by the army, with constitutional practices and political rights reduced to their smallest expression, would be inspired by the Napoleonic example, as some authors have already pointed out.

Conclusion

The 1820s were contextually crucial to the process of the liberal revolution, as much for Spain as for Mexico. An appreciation of the interrelationship of events on both sides of the Atlantic is necessary to understand fully the proposals and the results of the actions undertaken. The liberal pronunciamientos that characterized the century have their origins in the success obtained by Riego and the Spanish liberals in 1820 and by Iturbide and his men in 1821.

In analyzing these pronunciamientos, we should take into account some initial considerations. First, the political context in which they happened: today and in the case of Spain, few people doubt the liberal component of the pronunciamientos. We should carry on insisting that the pronunciamiento of Iguala took place in a liberal and constitutional context, and that is one of the reasons it was successful.

In our estimation, we cannot analyze the pronunciamientos that took place throughout the nineteenth century in a static and homogeneous way, since their objectives and approaches changed according to the political situation. The conspiracies designed to overthrow an absolute regime cannot be equated with those that came about after the liberal revolution—in Spain after 1843 and in Mexico after 1835. Therefore we can understand that the phenomenology is diverse and that the concept is dynamic because it is historically determined.

The same must be done with the protagonists of this particular historical moment—Riego and Iturbide, in this case—whom we must contextualize in order to comprehend their actions and their roles in the process.

Notes

1. The bibliography on the War of Independence is extensive. For a sample of general works see Aymes, *La guerra de independencia en España*; Lovett, *La guerra de la independencia y el nacimiento de la España contemporánea*; Artola, *Los orígenes de la España contemporánea* and *La guerra de independencia*; Fontana, *La crisis del Antiguo Régimen*. For recent works as points of reference

Frasquet and Chust

see De Diego, *España, el infierno de Napoleón*; Moreno Alonso, *José Bonaparte*; García Fuertes, *Dos de mayo de 1808*; Moliner, *La guerra de la independencia en España (1808–1814)*.

2. José Luis Comellas's classic work *Los primeros pronunciamientos en España, 1814–1820* has been the only study up until now that has described the pronunciamientos of the first absolutist period as exclusively military, far removed from the civilian population. Pronunciamientos recur in the second absolutist period, after 1823. For a different interpretation to Comellas's, see Castells, *La utopía insurreccional del liberalismo*.

3. Artola, *La España de Fernando VII*, 619–29.

4. Claude Morange's work on the El Palmar conspiracy shows the connection between the pronunciamientos of the six-year absolutist period and provides new data on the conspiracies. Morange, *Una conspiración fallida*.

5. The coming about of Félix María Calleja is very interesting: a general with much experience, hardened in the insurgent *novohispano* war, and furthermore viceroy and field marshal of New Spain. See Ortiz Escamilla, "Calleja, el gobierno de la Nueva España," and "Félix María Calleja: De héroe a villano."

6. Alcalá Galiano, *Recuerdos de un anciano*.

7. For more information on army matters at this time in Spain and America, see Kuethe and Marchena Fernández (eds.), *Soldados del rey*, and Marchena Fernández, *Oficiales y soldados*, "Reformas borbónicas y poder popular," and *El ejército de América antes de la Independencia*.

8. Although we are still missing detailed study of the conspiracy that led to this pronunciamiento, the following title remains useful: Gil Novales, *Rafael del Riego*.

9. Irene Castells believes that the formula used was clearly subversive and responded to the idea of staging an insurrection via the means of a pronunciamiento, conceived as a strategy to overthrow absolutism and being as a result eminently liberal. Castells, "El liberalismo insurreccional."

10. Buldain Jaca, *Régimen político y preparación de Cortes en 1820*. For the participation of the Americans and the decree convening the Cortes see Frasquet, "Ciudadanos ya tenéis Cortes."

11. Frasquet, *Las caras del águila*.

12. In Veracruz the oath took place between 26 and 28 May 1820 before the viceroy authorized it. Frasquet, "Se obedece y se cumple."

13. Rubio Mañé, "Los diputados mexicanos."

14. During the month of March, Ventura Obregón, Manuel García Sosa, Joaquín Medina, José María Gutiérrez de Terán, José Joaquín Ayestarán, Andrés Sabariego, Félix Quio Tecuanhuey, José María Jiménez de Castro, Bernardino Amati, and José Mariano Moreno appeared at the Cortes. In April Patricio López and José María Puchet arrived, and in May came Lucas Alamán, Tomás Murphy, José María Murguía, Matías Martín y Aguirre, Francisco Molinos del Campo, Manuel Gómez Pedraza, José Francisco Arroyo, José Miguel Ramírez, Tomás de Vargas, Juan N. Gómez Navarrete, Antonio María Uraga, José Francisco Guerra, Eusebio Sánchez Pareja, Andrés del Río, the Marquis of Apartado, the Count of Alcaraz, Luciano Castorena, Francisco Ramírez, Juan Bautista Valdés, and José Quirós y Millán. For more information consult the *Diario de sesiones de Cortes*, 1820; see also Rubio Mañé, "Los diputados mexicanos," 382–83.

15. Alamán, *Historia de Méjico desde los primeros movimientos*, 5:88–89.

16. Gómez Pedraza, *Manifiesto que Manuel Gómez Pedraza*; see also Rubio Mañé, "Los diputados mexicanos," 374.

17. *Carta de Agustín de Iturbide a Vicente Guerrero*, Cualotitlan, 10 January 1821, in Cuevas, *El libertador*.

18. This committee was installed on 3 May 1821 and five Americans (four of whom were *novohispanos*) participated in it: Lucas Alamán, Francisco Fagoaga, Bernardino Amati, Lorenzo de Zavala, and Felipe Fermín Paul. It was chaired by the Count of Toreno, accompanied by the peninsular deputies José María Calatrava, Juan Antonio Yandiola, and Andrés Crespo Cantilla. *Diario de sesiones de Cortes*, 4 May 1821, 1406.

19. *Diario de sesiones de Cortes*, 4 June 1821, 2046.

20. *Diario de sesiones de Cortes*, 4 June 1821, 2048.

21. *Diario de sesiones de Cortes*, 4 June 1821, 2048. The emphasis is ours.

22. For more on this plan, consult Benson, *La diputación provincial*; Rodríguez O., "La transición de colonia a nación"; Chust, *La cuestión nacional americana*.

23. *Oficio del Exmo. Sr. D. Juan O'Donojú dirigido al gobernador de la plaza de Veracruz incluyéndole el Tratado de Córdoba que trata de la independencia de México*, 26 August 1821, Benson Latin American Collection, University of Texas at Austin, Genaro García Collection, Iturbide Papers, G390, fs. 23-25vª.

24. *Actas del Congreso Constituyente Mexicano* (hereafter cited as ACCM), 1:8.

25. This revolutionary concept of sovereignty was already established in the Cortes of Cádiz by the deputies, who, assuming themselves to be the only representatives of the nation, assigned themselves all of the sovereignty that corre-

sponded to it. This is explained in Frasquet, "La senda revolucionaria del liberalismo." See also Chust and Frasquet, "Soberanía hispana, soberanía mexicana: 1810–1824."

26. The incident can be found in Rodríguez O., "Las Cortes mexicanas y el Congreso constituyente."

27. See the recent study by Ortiz Escamilla and Serrano Ortega (eds.), *Ayuntamientos y liberalismo gaditano en México.*

28. Serrano Ortega, *Igualdad, Uniformidad, Proporcionalidad.*

29. ACCM, 11 March 1822, 60.

30. ACCM, 23 March 1822, 104.

31. Serrano Ortega, *Igualdad, Uniformidad, Proporcionalidad,* 49–50.

32. ACCM, 1 March 1822, 30.

33. For studies on the national militia in Mexico, see for example Serrano Ortega, "Villas fuertes, ciudades débiles," in Broseta et al. (eds.), *Las ciudades y la guerra, 1750–1898.* In the same volume see Ortiz Escamilla, "Defensa militar, negocios e ideología," and Chust, "Milicia e independencia en México." See also Chust, "Armed Citizens."

34. A detailed analysis of the debates on this matter is found in Frasquet, "El estado armado o la nación en armas."

35. It was the deputy for Guadalajara, Santiago Alcocer, who offered this interpretation. ACCM, 15 May 1822, 260.

36. The signatories of the proclamation were Pedro Celestino Negrete, Manuel de la Sotarriva, Anastasio Bustamante, Luis Quintanar, Manuel Maria de Torres, Diego García Conde, the Marquis of Vivanco, José Antonio de Echávarri, Joaquín Parres, José Armijo, Rafael Ramiro, Ignacio del Corral, the Count of San Pedro del Alamo, José Mendivil, Manuel Barrera, José Francisco Guerra de Manzanares, Pedro Otero, Francisco de las Piedras, Francisco Manuel Hidalgo, José Antonio Matiauda, Diego Rubin de Celis, José Maria González Arebalo, Mariano Paredes y Arrillaga, Manuel de la Llata, Ramón Carrillo, José Mariano Guerra, José Maria Quintero, Tomas Illanes, Carlos de Urrutia, Antonio Ruiz de Esparza, Santiago de Menocal, Francisco de Paula Tamariz, Miguel Soto, Miguel Caballero, the Marquis of Salvatierra, Bonifacio de Hosta, Vicente Domínguez, José Camino, José Guadalupe de Palafox, the Marquis of Casa de Cadena, Bernardo Amat, the Marquis of Uluapa, Ramón Rey, Juan José Rubio, José María de Gondra, Vicente del Rivero, Narciso Sort de Sans, José María Mendiola, Felix Maria Survaran, José Maria Quintana, Mateo Qüilty Valois, Mariano Chico,

Ignacio de la Blanca (for Don Juan de Arago and in his name), the Count of San Pedro del Alamo, Francisco Olmedo, Pablo Unda, José Maria Fernández, José Ramón Malo, Juan de la Peña y del Río, Manuel de Lebrija, Manuel Francisco Casanova, Alvino Pérez, José Bernal, José Falco y Escandón, and José Portillo.

37. Di Tella, *Política nacional y popular en México*. For an interpretation that opposes this view see Anna, *El imperio de Iturbide*.

JOSEFINA ZORAIDA VÁZQUEZ | *Translated by Andrea Boyd*

Three. Two Reactions to the Illegitimate Succession of 1828: *Campeche and Jalapa*

A fter two years in which the republic enjoyed a degree of constitutional order and relative peace, political discontent surfaced as a result of the behavior of the Masonic lodges. The Scottish Lodge (or *escoceses*), introduced into Mexico by the Spanish expeditionary forces, dominated the army officer ranks and recruited a significant number of politicians. By 1825, although the lodge had lost its initial momentum and attractiveness, President Guadalupe Victoria's associates suggested that he should found another one given that Vice President Nicolás Bravo was its Grand Master in Mexico.[1] Thus the Águila Negra Lodge came into being and was registered in the Rite of York by the North American minister plenipotentiary, Joel R. Poinsett.[2] Before long its rapid expansion led to collisions with the escoceses, thereby paralyzing the running of Congress. It was in the context of this discord that Father Joaquín Arenas plotted the absurd conspiracy whereby he attempted to reestablish the old Spanish rule. As Lucas Alamán would note, "viewed impartially, it was an act of true madness," since the friar with a convoluted past, member of the Dieguino Order, assumed quite wrongly that he could expect backing from the leaders of the Mexican army.[3] So convinced was he that he invited General Ignacio Mora to take part, and Mora immediately turned him in. The affair was of little importance, except that the *yorkinos* seized on it to stoke up hatred of the Spanish and, it was rumored, so that the *iturbidistas* could satisfy their desire for revenge on the Peninsular military that had betrayed the emperor. Those involved faced a firing squad and others, who were not, were punished, and the *yorkinos* went on to draft the first expulsion law aimed at the Spanish population in Mexico.[4]

The deficit in the treasury deficit added to the heated atmosphere. This intensified with the bankruptcy of the Barclays partnership, which held more than 2.2 million pesos of the loan granted to Mexico. The result was that various bills of exchange signed by the government could not be redeemed; they bounced, forcing the government to borrow against the revenue from its customs duties.[5]

In spite of the yorkino expansion, the escoceses controlling Veracruz endeavored to resist, but Victoria weakened them by sending General Vicente Guerrero and replacing the state commander-in-chief. However, the approval of the law to expel the Spaniards, at the end of December, served to ignite a *pronunciamiento* that was already in the process of being plotted to counteract the excesses of the yorkinos. The movement was confident of producing the usual chain of affiliations. Manuel Montaño was responsible for launching the Plan of Otumba, demanding the closure of all secret lodges, a change of cabinet, the departure of Minister Joel R. Poinsett from the country, and the *literal application of the Constitution and its laws.*[6] As he had no command, Vice President Bravo, heart and soul of the enterprise, was unable to initiate it, but he immediately abandoned the capital and headed the movement. Unfortunately for him, lack of organization meant that commitments made to the plan did not materialize or were made once it had failed. Although the plan was innocuous, the participation of the vice president gave it importance. Victoria ordered Guerrero to set out for Tulancingo with a large army to subdue it. Before attacking, General Guerrero attempted to convince Bravo to withdraw the pronunciamiento, but in spite of his meager resources, he refused and was defeated in battle and captured. Many of those implicated were judged by a military tribunal, but Bravo's position as vice president meant that his case was placed before Congress. His prestige, his reputation as an honest man, and his long years of service to the cause of independence earned him his defenders. Some yorkinos tried to exaggerate his crimes, accusing him of having attacked federalism with a view to imposing a centralist system. Among the points of the plan it stressed the application of the laws, so escoceses and *novenarios* (a new lodge hostile to *yorkismo*)—as well as yorkinos such as Crecencio Rejón—were able to defend him.[7] Manuel Gómez Pedraza was another yorkino who did so.[8] As a result, Congress did not impose capital punishment, and the vice president was exiled, together with the others involved.

Guerrero's triumph over Bravo cemented his reputation, and the yorkinos capitalized on it to launch his candidacy for the September presidential elections. The Congress that was inaugurated on 1 January 1828 was thus considered to be tainted by the situation, while at the same time the yorkinos' excesses started to divide their own lodges, resulting in the departure of many of their members, who went on to favor the candidacy of Minister of War Manuel Gómez Pedraza.[9] Some well-known ex-yorkinos swelled the ranks of the new association of *imparciales*, founded by the Zacatecan Francisco García at the beginning of 1828. The press aligned itself with the positions of the yorkinos, escoceses, and imparciales until it became the dominant force behind the unrest.

Gómez Pedraza was to comment later: "In 1828, the squares and streets of the capital resounded to the cry of filthy newspapers put together by evil and dictated by rancor."[10] The yorkino press attacked ministers Francisco García and Miguel Ramos Arizpe. Their reputation as federalists led to the press accusing them of readying a secret candidate behind the country's back and urging them to disclose his name.[11] In a political setting transformed by the disappearance of the escoceses, and by yorkino resignations, rumors of centralist conspiracies started to abound. In view of the popular support for Guerrero, the yorkinos were confident he would win the presidency. Everyone respected his career, and he had the backing of the governors of the states of Mexico, Veracruz, San Luis Potosí, Durango, Coahuila and Texas, Michoacán, and Yucatán, who would be able to influence the vote in their respective legislatures. But the political elite—who did not actually represent the moneyed aristocracy or the Church, as it included such people as García, Valentín Gómez Farías, Anastasio Cañedo, and Ramos Arizpe—doubted the suitability of the former insurgent leader and were better disposed toward Gómez Pedraza. Even ardent yorkino Lorenzo de Zavala would admit that although there was merit in Guerrero's service and the purity of his intentions, "for social benefits, moral provisions, energy and mental capacity, Pedraza was undeniably preferable."[12]

In the midst of rumors of a Spanish invasion and the possible reelection of Victoria, many names were mooted as yorkino candidates. Support for Guerrero as president was unanimous, but the radicals Zavala and José Ignacio Esteva were mentioned for the vice presidency. This was counteracted by José Maria Tornel, who proposed Anastasio Bustamante, a moderate yorkino and representative of the other *independentista* wing.[13] Ramos Arizpe took over the management of the campaign in support of Pedraza in June.[14] In July the *Águila Mexicana*, the imparciales' mouthpiece, announced his candidacy.[15] It did not take long for the *Correo de la Federación* to accuse Pedraza of having been an ally of Iturbide and of being an *antifederalista*. The *Águila Mexicana* was reduced to underlining the virtues of its candidate and accused Guerrero of mobilizing troops to influence the elections in the capital. The Grand Lodge opted for organizing large gatherings in support of its candidate. Carlos María de Bustamante relates in his diary that "the primary elections of today [17 August] were decided by the yorkinos and Mexico City's riffraff, without a single honorable citizen presenting himself to vote"; from the same source we know that the elections in Oaxaca, begun on 15 August, resulted in several deaths.[16] This indicates that the yorkinos dominated the primary elections, but to no effect, since it was the state legislatures that would have the final say.

Using the pretext that the Veracruz legislature had not respected the choice of the people, and before Pedraza's triumph was made public, Antonio López de Santa Anna's pronunciamiento of Perote of September 1828 called for annulling the vote, totally expelling the Spaniards, electing Guerrero president, disregarding the legislatures that had not voted for him, and replacing them through new elections.[17] On 11 September, Santa Anna occupied the fort of Perote. The government outlawed him.[18] His pronunciamiento received scarcely any support, forcing him to march toward Oaxaca to escape the army that was sent after him. According to a letter written to Pedraza, Bustamante rejected the action of that "perverse Santa Anna."[19]

When the electoral results from the states began to arrive in September, *El Correo* rushed to confirm that its candidate had won, provoking wide unrest. This spread so widely that, on learning on 18 September that Pedraza had triumphed in the elections by the small margin of eleven votes to Guerrero's nine, yorkino fury exploded. Notable yorkinos, such as Tornel, Zavala, and even Guerrero himself, came under suspicion. Zavala attempted to demonstrate his neutrality but convinced no one. Formally accused and with his detention ordered, he chose to go into hiding. The yorkinos felt threatened and persecuted, leading Anastasio Zerecero to organize a revolt. When the government learned of this, it failed to act fast, enabling the yorkinos to occupy the Acordada building, which housed an armory. José María Lobato and Zavala soon appeared on the scene and made known their refusal to recognize Pedraza's election. From 30 November to 4 December the city was the setting of a popular uprising.[20] Up until this point, Guerrero had remained on the sidelines, but he too joined in on 2 December. The mob took advantage of the uprising to loot the Parián market, causing considerable commercial losses and arousing fears of a "caste war," in addition to marring Guerrero's administration thereafter. Victoria's weakness forced him to negotiate, leading to Pedraza's decision to resign and leave the country. He had scarcely done so before Victoria named Guerrero minister of war.

A new Congress was inaugurated on 1 January 1829 and had to solve the problem of the election of the executive. The solution should have been reached by the state legislatures, but Congress accepted the contention that they had betrayed popular opinion. After declaring Pedraza's election invalid, Congress recognized Guerrero as president and Anastasio Bustamante as vice president, on the basis of the voting, where they had come second and third. This violation of the Constitution set a precedent that would presage the 1829 pronunciamientos in Campeche and Jalapa.

The violence in the capital spread to many states, intensifying the rejection felt by the eleven legislatures that had voted for Pedraza. Tensions heightened between the state governments and the federal authorities, and many citizens became increasingly skeptical about the virtues of federalism. The governor of Zacatecas, Francisco García, would subsequently define the gravity of the situation in the following terms: "The nation marched with some regularity along the constitutional path until the end of 1828," but a faction lost their way, in spite of General Gómez Pedraza being endowed with "all the commendable qualities that are desirable in a President of the Republic."

> *From the moment* at which the revolution was perpetrated, with the statement by the Chamber of Deputies in 1829 declaring the votes cast by the legislatures in favor of General Pedraza to be invalid, *the federal pact was effectively dissolved*; but the state could neither carry into effect its separation from the general government, nor agree to *remedy one ill with the greatest of them all which is national dissolution.* It was essential and advisable, therefore, to recognize the Mexican government and the nominated president of the Republic who was governing under federal formulas, as a tie that was, in fact, preserving the union of the states [and serving as] a method of governance, the only one possible in those fateful circumstances.[21]

This consideration, and the very real news that Spain was preparing to reconquer Mexico by launching an invasion from Cuba, counteracted the states' intention of forming a coalition against the illegitimate government and led to their recognizing it, although they were preparing to uphold the federation "*with arms by means of the civil militia,*" according to García. The same justification would be proffered when recognizing the government that was imposed as a result of the Plan of Jalapa a year later. The states would have to wait until the 1832 elections before they regained their constitutional legitimacy.

When Guerrero took possession of his post on 1 April 1829, the context was an unfavorable one; the discontent that had been generated by the eruption of violence was further exacerbated by a total lack of resources, the application of the anti-Spanish expulsion laws, and the threat of a Spanish invasion. It all augured for a hapless government. Zavala, appointed minister of finance, attempted to organize the ministry, reform the federal tax system, and collect the contingency and tobacco debts from the states, so that the government could satisfy its constitutional obligations. Determined to end dependence on usurious loans, he proposed the establishment of direct taxes that took into account proportionally the taxpayers' wealth. Congress passed the law on 22 May, but resistance by the states impeded its implementation. However, once Congress invested Guerrero with extraordinary powers in response to the Spanish invasion of Isidro Barradas of July 1829, he applied a 5 percent annual contribution on income of any kind, provided that it exceeded 1,000 pesos, and 10 percent on any income in excess of 10,000 pesos, imposing on the states a forced loan that raised 3 million pesos. In order to implement its collection, he placed in each state and territory a commissioner-general with coercive powers, who could rely on the support of the state judicial system and, where necessary, that of the military authorities. This led to protests from the states, and even *guerrerista* governors considered the measure to be an attack on the federal pact.[22]

Guerrero also employed his extraordinary powers to limit the freedom of the press, a measure that was challenged by Zacatecas,

Jalisco, the state of Mexico, and Puebla and that was defied by other states following the announcement of Barradas's defeat.[23] The fiscal reform did not generate the resources necessary for the government to pay the salaries of its employees and the military. The lack of resources in many states meant that several governments sold off Church assets, to the consternation of the local populace.

The unrest was attributed to a large extent to Zavala, who resigned in October, but lacking the means, the government was not in a position to respond to requests for men and resources from coastal states afraid of further attempts at reconquest. President Guerrero had organized a Reserve Army, which he placed under the orders of Vice President Bustamante with its quarters in Huamantla. It was on receiving a communiqué from the commander-general of Veracruz that the Reserve Army moved to Jalapa.[24] When Generals Bravo and Miguel Barragán, granted amnesties by Guerrero, turned up, rumors of a conspiracy started to abound. Some claimed that Bustamante and Santa Anna were about to demand a change of cabinet and launch a pronunciamiento in favor of centralism.[25] These rumors and the Reserve Army's mobilization to Jalapa without the authorization of the minister of war raised suspicions "and the government was quick to give orders for them to disband."[26] Juan Suárez y Navarro described the atmosphere at that point: "Every day, fears mount of an approaching change, and subversive activities are attributed to the generals congregated in Jalapa. It was said that the general-in-chief, Anastasio Bustamante, and General Antonio López de Santa Anna, who *accidentally* found themselves in that town, were embroiled in a conspiracy to change the form of government."[27]

We know that the typical *trabajos* (arrangements) that preceded a pronunciamiento were under way in the Reserve Army, involving discontented officers and politicians. Nevertheless, "the tremendous cry of alarm, announced so many times, calling for [the imposition of] a central government, was to be heard [first] in a far-off corner of the Republic," raised by the garrison in Campeche and not by the Reserve Army based in Jalapa.

Yucatán, which included the current state of Campeche until the midcentury Reform period, had been at peace since 1825 under the government of José Tiburcio López Constante, a member of the federalist Liga faction. The opposing faction, the Camarilla, which was accused of being pro-Spanish, had attempted to remove him from power, but López was reelected in 1829, defeating the Camarilla candidate Segundo Carvajal, who then decided to rise to power by some other means.

The presence of commander-generals in the states was a source of tension with the federal government, and in the case of Yucatán there had also been discord over payment of excise taxes, customs duties, the cost of maintaining the army, and the costs incurred to prepare for the feared Spanish invasion. Governor López Constante had had problems with Commander-General Ignacio Mora and his demands for support, and on 11 May of that year, the legislature authorized the governor to nominate the heads and officials of the civic militia from the shortlists proposed by the *ayuntamientos* and municipal juntas, but the militia provided an inadequate defense.[28] The minister of war replaced Mora with Juan José Codallos, who started off by maintaining good relations with López. But as the rumors of a Spanish invasion increased, the scarcities forced López to restrict resources, and the commander threatened to limit himself to defending Campeche. The governor nominated the heads of the state militia and requested the resignation of Codallos, whom he accused, on the opening of the state congress on 21 August, of attempting to "supersede the powers of the state" in order to obtain resources. On 21 September 1829, the Yucatecan congress decreed not to send money in advance in "any quantity to the federal treasury without prior justification of its urgency and fair investment."[29]

The federation removed Codallos, who resigned in September 1829, but the lack of resources continued and Segundo Carvajal, who was provisionally in command, brought pressure to bear on Governor López. Such a situation favored confrontation, since unrest among the troops made them inclined to support whatever change that would promise the punctual payment of their salaries. Carvajal, complaining "of the state in which the army had been abandoned," issued a pronunciamiento on 6 November in favor of the installation of centralism.[30] In his Plan of Campeche, he pointed out that the federal system was responsible for the disorganization of the treasury and the army, and this had placed the nation in the "imminent risk in which it had been seen during the recent invasion by the Spanish troops." The federal system was complicated and ruinous for the people, so that what was needed were "less complicated institutions" and a moderate, stable, and central government. The Plan was not against the president of the republic, as long as he did not oppose it, but recognized only the general Congress as a constituent body. With regard to the Yucatecan government, Carvajal declared that its congress, senate, and governor were to be "without exercise of their functions" and that he would take over "both commands," including "all matters relating to the branches of the treasury, *of both the Federation and the state.*" Only the tribunals retained their powers "to perform their functions," although on condition of swearing allegiance to the newly established system, like all other employees. The commander-in-chief would acquire "*the authority to organize provi-sionally the internal government* of the people in a way that closely conformed to the general good."[31] As the Plan demanded that the nation adopt centralism, Yucatán was consequently separated from the federation. The pronunciamiento was immediately sup-ported by the Mérida garrison.[32] It subsequently got support from the garrisons at Bacalar, Chapotón, Sisal, and Isla del Carmen and was backed by the members of the Camarilla faction.[33]

One of Carvajal's first actions was to draft a series of regula-tions aimed at meeting the needs of "the internal government of the people" and—so that the town councils did not squander any funds—ensuring that funds were retained only in cities, towns, and villages that had *cabeceras de partido* (district heads), the re-mainder being the responsibility of a justice of the peace and a procurator. Carvajal nominated the commanders and subordinate political heads of Campeche, Carmen, Bacalar, and Sisal and the subdelegates and primary court judges in the other smaller dis-tricts. He gave the military the right to vote in their place of res-idence, and he granted retired military men and unemployed in-dividuals in the active militia the right to be elected to the town councils with entitlement to the *fuero*. The Indian republics re-tained their attributes and responsibilities, with the obligation of ensuring that "all the indigenous people of the villages sow at least fifty *mecates'* worth of maize."[34]

When the news reached Mexico City on 18 November, rumor asserted that the pronunciamiento had been orchestrated by Santa Anna, who had even sent some officials to Oaxaca to carry out a similar plan.[35] President Guerrero commissioned Zavala, originally from Yucatán, and who was planning to leave the country, "to go via the state to calm it and call it to order, using persuasion." On arrival at Sisal on 5 December, he was not allowed to proceed to Mérida, on Carvajal's orders.[36]

The expenses and difficulties entailed in any military movement against Yucatán worked in Carvajal's favor, but the fact that the government did not take any action against him led to the suspicion that he was being protected by Bustamante's Cabinet and, subsequently, even that Bustamante had been the one to orchestrate the pronunciamiento in the first place.[37] This enabled the Campeche garrison to mount an incursion into San Juan Bautista, capital of Tabasco, and put pressure on the town to toe the centralist line. However, scarcely one month later, the federal system was reestablished there.[38] Carvajal would make a further attempt in April 1830, but it would fail.[39] There was an echo of this centralist movement in Guadalajara, but it was curbed and the Senate granted an amnesty to all those involved.[40]

The Reserve Army started to plot its own pronunciamiento at this point, since it also suffered from penury; according to José Antonio Facio, it was made up of "officers with no pay [and] soldiers with no shirts, no shoes, no bread," who were convinced that Guerrero's government did not enjoy "the will and approval of the great majority of the Federation, [and] could not be sustained without employing the same system of violence and corruption that had brought it to power."[41] Bustamante had refused to acknowledge the centralist cry from Campeche. In a manifesto, he considered it "an error . . . to blame [the country's problems on] the nature of the federalist regime . . . and to attempt to cure its ills . . . with other greater ones," and he exhorted his troops to uphold the Constitution and its laws.[42] Facio and Melchor Múzquiz, instigators of the pronunciamiento of Jalapa, had to postpone its launch because Santa Anna did not want to take part and Bustamante did not want to be the one to make the first move. What finally got the ball rolling was news that the Reserve Army was to be disbanded, which circulated shortly after Zavala passed through Jalapa on his way to Yucatán and handed over to its head of cavalry the documents that, it transpired, contained the order to break up the forces. As Facio confessed in his *Memoria*, they took advantage of the army being under arms and that Bustamante was absent, to raise "the cry of 'Constitution and Laws'." On his return, "the vice president was invited to place himself at the head of the troops and, with him at our head, we marched on the capital."[43]

As justification, the Plan of Jalapa mentioned the "general disturbances [that] threaten to bring about the ruin of men and things; liberty and independence; public morale and the laws of the country, enveloping them all," making the troops victims of privation in spite of the exorbitant contributions, which were "being squandered on diverse items, and with society close to coming apart at the seams and being diverted from its principles." The army ratified "the solemn oath which it has sworn, to uphold the federal pact respecting the sovereignty of the states and conserving their indissoluble union." The Plan declared constitutional order to be reestablished and showed its authors to be committed to preserving the peace and the social guarantees. It demanded cancellation of the extraordinary powers conferred on the president and, in article 4, demanded the replacement of "those functionaries whom public opinion has shown itself to be against." This clause was to be of great utility to the new administration in ridding itself of hostile authorities in several states. Copies of the plan were sent "to the supreme governor general, the legislatures, the governors, commanders-in-chief and other political heads and to the ecclesiastical prelates," inviting generals Bustamante and Santa Anna to place themselves at the head of the army that had backed the pronunciamiento.[44] A significant number of state governments rejected the Plan but, as García was to point out, ended up by recognizing it. The Veracruz legislature did not recognize the "intrusive government installed in the capital," and Santa Anna rejected it but made no move to support Guerrero, who, after setting forth to confront the movement, drew back to Tixtla.[45]

Guerrero's departure enabled the establishment of a provisional government, which with the pronunciamiento of the commander of Mexico, Luis Quintanar, on 23 December, authorized Bustamante as vice president to take possession of the executive. The *guerreristas* controlled the Chamber of Deputies and nine state legislatures. In spite of support for the new regime being reduced to the Senate following Bustamante's ratification of federalism, Congress during its inaugural session on 1 January "recognized the Plan of Jalapa as just and national and declared it impossible for Guerrero to serve as president, thus sanctioning the revolution."[46]

The intention of the Jalapa movement was not to bring about a change to centralism but to reform the federal charter, which the majority recognized as being essential. Facio said, "The country had decided for federalism, our duty was circumscribed to upholding its will with all our might. . . . We were federalists because the entire Republic was in favor of federalism."[47] Although Alamán had defended centralism in 1824, he recognized with Luis de Cortázar that any attempt to change the system would lead to civil war.[48] Later he would reiterate that the object of the movement had been to strengthen the federal government, limit legislative predominance, and rationalize the administration so that it would be able to respond effectively to its responsibilities. Through the articles he sponsored, he promoted limiting suffrage to prevent demagogy and forming a professional army to prevent more pronunciamientos from erupting. The fact that the Constitution envisaged the possibility of reforms in 1830 favored the *pronunciados'* objectives, and in effect state proposals began to arrive that coincided in part with the aims of the Jalapa movement.[49] There are no grounds to support the accusation that the movement intended to establish a centralist system, but there is no doubt that Bustamente's government was as illegitimate as Guerrero's had been. In spite of the resolute aid of the army, this pronunciamiento cannot be considered a militaristic one like Carvajal's. Bustamante's reputation was that of a moderate federalist yorkino.

Penury forced the government to grant a broad amnesty to the Yucatán rebels. Congress approved it, but on condition that they submitted to constitutionality within a period of thirty days.[50] As they refused to do so, Congress sent Felipe Codallos and Deputy Tomás Requena with conciliatory offers. Carvajal, however, did not receive them.[51] Facio, the minister of war, then tried sending Yucatecan Martín Peraza to convince Carvajal to restore the federal system.[52] When these measures failed, remittances were suspended and it was decreed that "the goods, fruits and foreign effects proceeding from Yucatán, during the schism of that state, should pay the full customs duties established in the maritime customs general tariff, in any of the ports in the republic, Article 31 of the same being suspended."[53] Following the eruption of the War of the South in the wake of Guerrero's uprising, Yucatán became cut off, with "all communication with the individuals who exercised the authority there" being broken off, in spite of the constant calls of the yorkino congressmen José María Alpuche and Crecencio Rejón for the peninsula to be subjugated.[54]

In reality, as Eligio Ancona noted, "unfortunately for the Yucatecan pronunciados, the Jalapa uprising did not proclaim the abolition of the federal system" and left them outside the national game.[55] Carvajal insisted that the singularity of the conditions in the peninsula would require a special system and special excise duties.[56] Aware that it was difficult for the national government to launch an expedition to Yucatán, he rejected the conciliatory calls made by Guerrero and Bustamante, to the extent of calling elections on 1 December 1829 to choose forty-three representatives for an assembly to be held in Bécal. The convocation specified that only those citizens with capital of a thousand pesos in Mérida and Campeche could vote, those with five hundred in Valladolid, and those with a lesser amount in other areas. This limitation of suffrage was favored by many legislatures including Jalapa's, but unlike them, Carvajal insisted on making room for the army: the forty-three members elected from property owners were joined by thirty army officers. While the assembly was sitting, a general junta of heads and officers, meeting in Calkiní on 24 December, ratified the *Acta de Campeche* and disassociated itself from the Jalapa movement. The junta authorized Carvajal to regulate the treasury "with the greatest economy," so that he cut salaries and reduced the fiscal offices to two: one for accounting in Campeche and another for collection in Mérida. With the savings he made he assigned more resources to the army.[57]

The assembly meeting in Bécal on 4 April would do "for Yucatán what suited its true interests." Its seventy-three members drafted the representative and popular *Acta Instituyente de la República Central*, and declared the movement just and patriotic. It declared Yucatán to be *"an integral part of the Mexican Nation"* and that it upheld its independence and would recognize the government, "as soon as it becomes aware of its own true interests and decides to accept the pronunciamiento already issued." It repeated its recognition of the general Congress as a constituent body only. The provisional government maintained a watered-down imitation of the division of powers, with these being distributed between "the military commander-in-chief, the provincial council and the law tribunals." The council would consist of "seven individual property owners and an equal number of distinguished substitutes of good standing, who had capital or industry that provided them with an income of seven hundred pesos annually" and who were nominated by the assembly. Carvajal, as "commander-in-chief," would direct all the branches of the administration and would nominate civil, military, and treasury appointees. The Supreme Court of Justice would consist of three property owners nominated by the commander-in-chief. All existing laws that did not contradict the pronunciamiento were declared to be in force, and it was decided that a "Manifiesto a la Nación" should be issued explaining the aims of the pronunciamiento.[58] Bolstered by his control of the state military command and government, Carvajal secured his control of power at a local level and ensured that the town councils approved the *Acta Instituyente*.

The press in the capital commented on the events in Yucatán. *El Sol* supported the government and occupied itself with the affair for two years, including items from *La Concordia Yucateca*. *El Gladiador* and its successor, *El Gladiador o sea El Verdadero Federalista* also reproduced articles from magazines and letters from the peninsula, which criticized the situation under *the dictatorship* that had been forged there.[59] The newly created *Registro Oficial del Gobierno de los Estados Unidos Mexicanos* defended the government for attempting to promote centralism, but it focused on reforming the Constitution and included the proposals of the legislatures of Nuevo León, Puebla, Querétaro, Michoacán, and San Luis Potosí and almost ignored the events in Yucatán.[60] *El Observador de la República Mexicana* also gave preference to the reforms.

In fact, almost all the state constitutions had established centralist systems within their respective states, but they defended federalist practices vis-à-vis the federal government. What was curious about the Yucatecan stance was that they were demanding the entire nation adopt a centralist system while retaining the 1824 Constitution. Melchor Campos García is of the opinion that "the centralist coalition was the standard bearer of old unsatisfied aspirations and current demands and was presenting a new economic program aimed at industrializing agriculture," which "evoked the [ideas of] distinguished Spaniards, [Pedro] Campomanes, [J. de] Ustariz and [Gaspar de] Jovellanos in favor of agricultural development."[61] Carvajal was on close terms with the Yucatecan elite.[62] He was married to a Gutiérrez de Estrada, so it is not surprising that many of his measures benefited local merchants and property owners. Carvajal promoted free trade by annulling federal decrees, cancelling customs duties, and authorizing Xcumsuc, Angostura, and Cuyo to export lumber.[63] He expedited agricultural regulations to promote industrial agriculture, and article 18 compelled every Indian to sow fifty mecates of maize annually. Like García in Zacatecas, he promoted the formation of share capital by forming a company in 1830 for cultivation and processing henequen and promoted the extraction of lumber for export.[64]

In the general Congress, Tomás Vargas and Crecencio Rejón started to make their voices heard, demanding the restoration of constitutional order in Yucatán.[65] The government, according to the *Registro Oficial*, decided not to employ "a military force" but to exhaust "the resources of persuasion"; it insisted that the Yucatecan complaints "regarding its trade, reduced, according to them, by our prohibitive duties system," should be presented as formal "claims to Congress, with the assurance that they would be heard."[66]

Carvajal had spurned the conciliatory offers made in 1830, but when he began to encounter problems of his own he turned to opening up relations with Bustamante's administration, as his attitude was different from Guerrero's, and Bustamante appeared to have similar aims to his own. Therefore, Carvajal called a convention in order to nominate Yucatán's deputies to the general Congress. It is possible that Campos is right in believing that Carvajal was searching for a peaceful return to federalism, without great internal changes.[67] Although the deputies were elected, the general Congress refused to receive them, as they had not been elected according to the Constitution. Wealthy José María Gutiérrez de Estrada, from Campeche, who advocated the change to centralism from the capital, proposed to Congress that they should be admitted as a delegation in order to hear their "complaints and claims." Facio supported this, but all that was achieved was approval of Senator Tomás Vargas's initiative that a broad amnesty be granted as long as the national government was given its due recognition, with the proviso that the ports of Yucatán would be closed to domestic and international trade if this was refused.[68]

Cracks began to appear in the centralist movement toward the end of 1830, as confrontations between the town councils and the state government began to spread, coinciding with a heightening of generalized discontent.[69] "The coup coalition" had become fractured.[70] By Easter 1831 a conspiracy was discovered that aimed to bring about the definitive separation of Yucatán from the republic, resulting in many arrests. This tipped the balance in favor of federalism, aided by a statement from a Yucatecan functionary claiming that "Bustamante was the leading centralist in the nation," allowing him to feel confident that the republic would, in the long run, change the system.[71] A pamphlet implied that the Cabinet had sponsored the Yucatecan movement.[72]

On 8 July 1831, the Yucatecan provincial council declared that it was time to reestablish national unity, since there was no hope of the republic establishing a centralist system, but raised the need for a convention with full powers to reform the 1825 Constitution of Yucatán in order to increase the political rights of the military class.[73] In his September report Carvajal acknowledged that trade in Yucatán required the greatest possible support from the provisional government in that "it is reserved to the Supreme Powers of the nation to dispense it with all that is required by the special circumstances of this peninsula." Carvajal ensured that the convention agreed to reduce the *state Congress to twelve deputies and that a third would be army officers*. But for this reform to be approved, popular support was required. As a result Carvajal's energies were channeled into manipulating the town councils.[74] The convention met between 21 September and 11 October in Bécal and proceeded to approve a broad amnesty and name a provisional governor—by unanimous accord, Carvajal himself. Afterward the electoral procedure to reform the 1825 Constitution was set in motion.

In October 1831, inspired by these measures, Yucatán's residents in Mexico City started to issue pamphlets that commented on or contradicted them, in addition to publications that included the initiatives of the different senatorial commissions.[75] Gutiérrez de Estrada decided to support the Yucatecan cause, publishing an anonymous pamphlet that justified Yucatán's centralism, claiming, "It is desirous for Yucatán to return things to how they were in November 1829 and the people of Yucatán can then say: 'We are agreed, bring back General Guerrero to govern, bring back the legislatures and the governors that we once had in Querétaro, in San Luis Potosí, in Michoacán, in Veracruz, in Durango, in Mexico, in Jalisco, in Puebla and in other states'." In his defense of the pronunciamiento of Campeche, he pointed out that the "Plan of Jalapa, recognized by the nation, legalized, nationalized," did not correspond to any constitutional principle either. The Plan of Campeche shared "the same causes as the Plan of Jalapa, *but lacked the right choice of means*"; he considered it "an extremely dangerous political error to assume that the armed forces were responsible for everything in Yucatán and that the people were discontented with what had happened."[76] In support of his statements, he included the *Manifiesto de la Convención del Estado de Yucatán a los pueblos que lo componen* of 24 September 1831.

The new state congress met from 20 December 1831 to 1 March 1832 and elected Pablo de Lanz as vice-governor. Carvajal resigned his post, confident that one of his trusted followers would be elected, but was returned to his civil and military command. On 22 December the legislature sent a statement to the general Congress, informing it of the obstacles that stood in the way of the reestablishment of federalism and that had forced it to employ "unknown measures, as it was a unique case" in the face of the events of 1829. It was necessary "to prepare opinion for the restoration of these principles" but it was impossible to establish the authorities that had functioned in 1829, as their term had ended.[77]

However, Santa Anna's pronunciamiento of Veracruz in January 1832 complicated matters further at a national level. Santa Anna sent General José Antonio Mejía to Campeche to invite Carvajal to join the Plan of Veracruz of 2 January. Carvajal replied: "Yucatán is not about to launch any pronunciamiento, or join in with any being made, whatever their kind. The experience of the last two years has made it apparent that with regard to the rest of the republic it cannot, in any way, use extraordinary means to influence either a change or any variation or modification in the political government, whatsoever its nature." He maintained that Yucatán had decided to uphold the federal Constitution and acknowledged that the dismissal of the cabinet ministers "corresponds exclusively to the president of the republic."[78] His tone seemed to announce that the Yucatecan quandary would be resolved with the new amnesty announced on 6 March 1832, but this was not to be the case. Although the new Constitution of 3 November 1832 was returned to the state congress by Carvajal for approval, events prevented it from being promulgated.

At the same time as the 1832 Civil War ended on 11 December with the generals of the two sides signing the Treaty of Zavaleta, the Yucatecan military overthrew Segundo Carvajal and named Colonel Francisco de Paula Toro, brother-in-law of Santa Anna, as commander-in-chief. Curiously, he had delayed joining the Plan of Veracruz. He and Sebastián López de Llergo did not recognize Bustamante and recognized Gómez Pedraza as president of the republic. López Constante returned to his post of state governor on 9 November, at the same time as the dissolved Congress renewed its sessions. In this way Yucatán was reincorporated into the federal order.

Notes

1. Zavala, *Ensayo crítico* (1985), 1:258.
2. Alamán, *Historia de México* (1985), 5:824.
3. Alamán, *Historia de México*, 5:826.
4. Zavala, *Ensayo crítico*, 2:44. José María Bocanegra attempted to refute this in his *Memorias para la historia de México independiente*, 1:415–36.

5. Alamán, *Historia de México*, 5:834.

6. Jiménez Codinach (ed.), *Planes en la nación mexicana*, 1:215.

7. Echánove Trujillo, *La vida pasional*, 114.

8. Solares Robles, *Una revolución pacífica*, 71.

9. Costeloe, *La primera república federal de México*, 156.

10. Gómez Pedraza, *Manifiesto que Manuel Gómez Pedraza, ciudadano de la República de México, dedica a sus compatriotas, o sea, una reseña de su vida pública. 17 de marzo de 1831*, in Solares Robles, *La obra política de Manuel Gómez Pedraza, 1813–1851*, 172.

11. *Correo de la Federación Mexicana*, 3 February 1828.

12. Zavala, *Ensayo crítico*, 2:45.

13. Tornel y Mendívil, *Breve reseña histórica*, 312.

14. Tornel y Mendívil, *Breve reseña histórica*, 310.

15. *El Águila Mexicana*, 29 July 1828.

16. Vázquez and Hernández Silva (eds.), *Diario . . . de Bustamante*, 21 August 1828.

17. Bocanegra, *Memorias para la historia de México independiente*, 1:474.

18. Dublán and Lozano (eds.), *Legislación mexicana*, 2:79–80.

19. Bustamante to Pedraza, Matamoros, 27 October 1829, Archivo Cancelados de la Secretaría de la Defensa Nacional (hereafter cited as ACSDN), Exp. XI/III/1-235/196.

20. Di Tella, *Política nacional y popular*, 224.

21. *Memoria . . . del Estado libre de los Zacatecas.*

22. Serrano Ortega, *Igualdad, Uniformidad, Proporcionalidad*, 58–61.

23. Pakenham to Aberdeen, Mexico, 30 October 1829, Public Record Office, Foreign Office Papers, FO 50/55, fols. 287–91.

24. Facio, *Memoria que sobre los sucesos*, 109.

25. *El Sol*, 10 November 1829.

26. Facio, *Memoria que sobre los sucesos*, 109.

27. Suárez y Navarro, *Historia de México*, 169.

28. Quezada, "Formas de gobierno."

29. Flores Escalante, "Proyectos de gobierno," 31–32; Flores Escalante, "El primer experimento centralista," 50.

30. Güemez Pineda, *Liberalismo*, 157–58.

31. *Acta del Pronunciamiento de la guarnición de Campeche, por la forma de gobierno de república central;* Suárez y Navarro, *Historia de México*, 170–71; Jiménez Codinach (ed.), *Planes en la nación mexicana*, 1:225.

32. *Acta del pronunciamiento de la guarnición de Mérida por la forma de gobierno de República Central,* 9 November 1829, in Vázquez y Hernández Silva (eds.), *Diario . . . de Bustamante,* Anexes, December 1829.

33. Ancona, *Historia de Yucatán,* 3:233.

34. *Gobierno militar, político y de hacienda de Yucatán: Circular,* Campeche, 21 November 1829. Vázquez and Hernández Silva (eds.), *Diario . . . de Bustamante,* Anexes, December 1829.

35. Vázquez and Hernández Silva (eds.), *Diario . . . de Bustamante,* 19 November 1829.

36. Zavala, *Ensayo critico,* 2:157–58.

37. *El que despeja la incógnita ¿Es el Ministerio quién dirige los planes de Yucatán?* 27 August 1830.

38. *Acta celebrada en la ciudad de San Juan Bautista, capital del estado de Tabasco, en 16 de diciembre de 1829 años, por el comandante de batallón de milicia local y oficialidad que le subsigue, compañía de dragones y primera activa de la misma: Registro Oficial Extraordinario,* 23 January 1830, *El Sol,* 25 January 1830.

39. El Comisario general provisional de Tabasco al Secretario de Hacienda, Capital of Tabasco, 13 April 1830. Archivo Histórico de la Secretaría de la Defensa Nacional (hereafter cited as AHSDN), Exp. VI/481.3/744, ff. 49 and 56.

40. Ordinary Session of 22 January 1830, *El Sol,* 28 January 1830.

41. Facio, *Memoria que sobre los sucesos,* 121, 107.

42. El jefe del Ejército de Reserva, Jalapa, 17 November 1829, in Vázquez and Hernández Silva (eds.), *Diario . . . de Bustamante,* Anexes, November 1829.

43. El jefe del Ejército de Reserva, III.

44. Suárez y Navarro, *Historia de México,* 172–73.

45. Suárez y Navarro, *Historia de México,* 184–85.

46. "Noticias preliminares que sirven de introducción," in Alamán, *Examen imparcial,* 55.

47. Facio, *Memoria que sobre los sucesos,* 125.

48. Luis de Cortázar to Alamán, Guanajuato, 2 January 1830, in Alamán, *Obras De D. Lucas Alamán,* 4:189–90.

49. Catherine Andrews reviews the proposals in her article "Discusiones en torno de la reforma."

50. Decree, *Registro Oficial del Gobierno de los Estados Unidos Mexicanos,* 22 January 1830.

51. *Registro Oficial,* 19 and 28 March 1830.

52. *El Gladiador*, Supplement to no. 175, 18 September 1830.

53. *El Sol*, 10 September 1830.

54. "Defensa del ex ministro de Relaciones D. Lucas Alamán: En la causa formada contra él y contra los exministros de Guerra y Justicia del Vicepresidente D. Anastasio Bustamante," in Alamán, *Examen imparcial*, 139.

55. Ancona, *Historia de Yucatán*, 3:328.

56. *Discurso que el Esmo. Sr. D. José Segundo Carvajal gefe supremo de esta península, pronunció al instalarse la Asamblea General* (Campeche: Imprenta del Gobierno, 1830).

57. Campos García, *De provincia a estado*, 208–10.

58. *Acta Instituyente de la Augusta Asamblea General de Yucatán, reunida en el pueblo de Bécal el 28 de marzo de 1830, con inserción de todos sus incidentes, El Sol*, 28 April 1830, AHSDN, Exp. XI/481.3/744.

59. *El Gladiador y después 2a Época del Gladiador o sea El Verdadero Federalista: Diario político, crítico, literario y económico de México*, March 1831.

60. *Registro Oficial*, 26 January 1830.

61. Campos García, *De provincia a estado*, 192, 196. Güemez Pineda, in *Liberalismo*, devotes a great deal of chapter 4 to the centralist agricultural development projects.

62. Campos García, *"Que los yucatecos todos,"* 92–93.

63. Sergio Quezada, "Formas de gobierno."

64. Campos García, *De provincia a estado*, 197–200.

65. Un Yucateco, *Comentarios al proyecto de ley del señor senador Vargas para pacificar el estado de Yucatán,* Mexico City, 27 January 1831, and Un Yucateco, *Observaciones sobre el dictamen presentado a la Cámara de Senadores en la proposición del Sr. Vargas relativa a la pacificación de Yucatán*, Mexico, 31 January 1831 (Mexico City: Imprenta de Galván, a cargo de Mariano Arévalo, 1831), both in *El Gladiador o sea el Verdadero Federalista*, 31 January 1831.

66. *Registro Oficial*, 7 February and 26 January, 1830.

67. Campos García, *De provincia a estado*, 226.

68. Un Yucateco, *Observaciones sobre el dictamen presentado a la Cámara de Senadores*.

69. Flores Escalante, "Proyectos de gobierno," 100–102.

70. Campos García, *De provincia a estado*, 229; *El Gladiador*, 10 May 1831.

71. Campos García, *De provincia a estado*, 234; *El Gladiador*, 7 May 1831.

72. *El que despeja la incógnita* (see note 37).

73. Campos García, *De provincia a estado*, 236–37.

74. *Memoria que el Excmo. Sr. D. José Segundo Carvajal leyó el día 21 de setiembre de 1831 en el seno de la Soberana Convención, al hacer dimisión del cargo de Gefe Superior de Yucatán* (Mérida: Imprenta de Lorenzo Seguí, 1831), cited in Campos García, *De provincia a estado*, 237–39.

75. Varios yucatecos, *Documentos interesantes y decretos del legítimo Congreso Constitucional del Estado de Yucatán.*

76. Un Yucateco, *Observaciones sobre las iniciativas . . . relativas a los negocios de Yucatán.*

77. "Exposición de razones sobre el restablecimiento del federalismo en Yucatán," Mérida, 22 December 1831, in Congreso de Yucatán, *Exposición que el actual Congreso Ordinario de Yucatán dirigió a las Cámaras de la Unión, participando su instalación y el completo restablecimiento del régimen federativo en aquel estado* (publisher unknown), Archivo General de la Nación (hereafter cited as AGN), Gobernación, S/S, Caja 150, exp. 8, ff. 45–46.

78. Carvajal to Relaciones, Campeche, 23 January 1832, informs of the arrival of a messenger from Santa Anna in Campeche, promoting the Plan of Veracruz, but that he made him return, stating his loyalty to the general government. AGN, Gobernación, S/S, Caja 150, exp. 8, ff. 37–41.

Four. Municipalities, Prefects, and Pronunciamientos: *Power and Political Mobilizations in the Huasteca during the First Federal Republic*

One often-overlooked facet of *pronunciamientos* is their impact on society and politics in rural Mexico. This chapter explores the connections between local actors and national politics during the First Federal Republic's period of crisis, 1830 to 1834, describing how pronunciamientos unfolded in the Huasteca region and elucidating the origins and results of the political conflicts they unleashed. Pronunciamientos became an important part of Mexico's political repertoire, and this essay explores how small town actors came to participate in these national movements.

The traditional view that pronunciamientos were merely the maneuvers of barrack politicians competing for control of the national treasury has become outdated. They involved a political process that incorporated national political actors and often began with civilian leadership promoting serious political objectives.[1] It has long been noted that *pronunciados* circulated their political plans to municipal councils searching for support from "public opinion." In these communiqués, organizers cajoled *jefes políticos*, prefects, and *alcaldes* to "second" their political declarations as a means to legitimize their uprisings. This practice indicates how municipalities became political players in nineteenth-century politics: Mexicans saw them as the organs of public opinion and appealed to them as an alternative source of legitimacy outside the normal channels of elections and Congress. Within Hispanic legal traditions, town governments had a long tradition of autonomy and prestige that was only augmented under the new constitutional order.[2] As pronunciamientos became more frequent, town councils faced important decisions—national political actors urged them to endorse the use of force to change or defend the sitting government. Suddenly farmers, ranchers, and small-time merchants who occupied municipal offices were swept up into debates over the fate of the nation. Pronunciamiento leaders and governors sometimes simply ordered communities to "second" their plans in a direct top-down fashion. However, a closer look at events indicates that the reaction of local authorities was varied as they sought to challenge or accommodate national political plans to their own needs.

Although pronunciamientos in the rural areas were often bloodless, the political fallout was profound. While national leaders may have considered the "seconding" of their plans as simply consulting with the populace, these actions became critical moments in the theater of village politics. As disruptions of the constitutional order, these events became opportunities to rearrange the distribution of power and offered the possibility of dislodging the establishment in favor of upstarts. Pronunciamientos required rural office holders to take political positions on divisive national issues, creating political traditions that defined politics for years to come. As we shall see, the rhetoric of national movements, such as ultramontane Catholicism, endured long beyond any given plan.

None of the pronunciamientos considered in this book originated in the region, nor were these towns cosmopolitan political centers. In spite of this, they prove to be perfect for understanding how rural Mexicans, and the overwhelming majority of the nation's population lived in small towns, responded to the dizzying political changes of the period. Political disputes in the nation's capital became divisive national issues in part because they became connected to local interests and personalities. Only by understanding the intricate and often confusing maneuvering of village politicians can historians understand how deeply pronunciamientos changed the national order.

To understand how the plans politicized rural Mexico, the following pages briefly describe the major national pronunciamientos between 1830 and 1834. This was the crucial period when the first constitutional experiment fell into crisis, culminating in the collapse of the Federal Republic. After identifying the plans, the essay describes how they unfolded in the Huasteca, and I end with an analysis of the larger significance of the chaotic events.

New Actors and National Plans in the 1830s

The process of organizing pronunciamientos in the small towns of rural Mexico brought together national political operators and local authorities in ways that had never been contemplated by the framers of the Constitution of 1824. The federal and state constitutions created two institutions central to the 1830s events: municipalities and prefectures. The elected municipal councils administered local justice and acted as executors of state policy. Furthermore Hispanic political traditions, the process of independence, and the new constitutions infused these local institutions with considerable political legitimacy as the voice of the "people." State electoral laws granted municipalities an important de facto role in organizing the electoral process.

The region for this case study consists of the district of Huejutla, then part of the state of Mexico but today incorporated into Hidalgo. As one moves west from the lowland town of Huejutla (140 meters above sea level) to the southeast, the elevation abruptly rises to almost 2,000 meters in Zacualtipán. The district had a mostly indigenous population of 71,744 in 1833, dispersed among 175 villages that were governed by twenty-four municipalities.[3]

The second institution consisted of prefectures: midlevel administrators, appointed by the governor, who had the duty to supervise the municipalities and regulate their relations with the executive and legislative branches of state government. The district prefect located in Huejutla supervised three subprefects in Yahualica, Metztitlán and Zacualtipán.[4] Among their duties were enforcing executive orders, policing their districts, and supervising the activities of the town councils. These administrators presided over council meetings, oversaw elections, were in charge of the jails, and regulated the "internal administration of the towns."[5] Correspondence and petitions from private citizens and the councils were channeled through their offices. Likewise the state government relied on these appointees for information about the political situation in the communities. Thus these functionaries had considerable power to influence the lives of local citizens and sway the opinions of state-level officials.

Before turning to local events I must first provide a brief account of the national movements and identify their political persuasions and leadership to give the reader a national framework for understanding the Huasteca pronunciamientos.[6] In 1830 Anastasio Bustamante successfully displaced Vicente Guerrero's government via the Plan of Jalapa (see previous chapter). In 1828 Guerrero, using his strong ties to the popular classes dating back to his days as an insurgent, had come to power due to the Acordada pronunciamiento as the champion of the radical federalists. The Anastasio Bustamante government that replaced him was markedly conservative in tone and presented itself as a bulwark against the mob. In the name of the restoration of order, the new administration sought to demobilize popular politics—limiting suffrage and intervening in the administration of the states, damaging the federalist pact.

Bustamante's government was brought down as a result of the Plan of Veracruz, which began on 2 January 1832 and finally triumphed on 23 December of the same year, a long and drawn-out conflict that many now classify as a full-blown civil war. The rebellion brought together Antonio López de Santa Anna, who had originally called for the resignation of Bustamante's ministers with a group of federalist states, particularly Zacatecas, which wanted to stymie the *bustamantista* drive toward centralism. The pronunciamiento succeeded in unseating the conservative government, and in the 1833 elections Santa Anna, his vice president Valentín Gómez Farías, and a new Congress dominated by radical federalists took office.

The final series of events was extremely complicated and there is considerable debate about their supporters and the role of the then president Santa Anna. The pronunciamientos of 1833, commonly referred to as the Plans of Colonel Ignacio Escalada (Morelia), General Gabriel Duran (Tlalpan), and General Mariano Arista (Huejotzingo), occurred between 26 May and 8 June and called on Santa Anna to take dictatorial powers to defeat the projects of the radical Congress (see chapter 6). The movements, organized by army officers, eventually merged under the leadership of General Mariano Arista and found resonance in the political sectors that had supported the Bustamante government. Their slogan of "Religión y fueros" encapsulated their demand to keep the privileges of the Church and the army intact. The cause resonated with the "law and order" conservatives, who saw both institutions as critical to good government. As Michael Costeloe writes in this volume, Santa Anna vigorously rejected the path that Arista and colleagues offered him and defeated the rebels at great cost.[7] Politically, Arista's failure encouraged the Congress to pass its ambitious reform package.

The *santanistas* (politicians and officers close to General Santa Anna) soon became disenchanted with the reforms of the Church and army and organized a pronunciamiento against the Congress and the vice president on 25 May 1834, known as the Plan of Cuernavaca. From the start the movement enjoyed the support of Santa Anna and there was little doubt of its success. A week later, the garrison in the state of Mexico organized a complementary plan known as the Plan of Toluca, overthrowing the governor and state legislature dominated by zealous federalists. Via this method Santa Anna aligned himself with the more conservative elements of Mexican society and repudiated the anti-clerical and anti-military reforms.

In general, pronunciamientos became the means for thwarting one's political opponents. The Mexican state switched direction every two years between 1828 and 1834 between federalist- and populist-leaning governments to centralizing law-and-order administrations. The political whiplash that resulted eroded the constitutional order and heightened partisan tensions. Losing factions faced reprisals: the Bustamante government executed Guerrero, and the federalists exiled bustamantistas. Turning to rural Huasteca we can see how these trends reached down to the lowest level of politics.

Local Echoes of National Plans

The 1829 Plan of Jalapa unfolded so quickly—with less than a full month between the publication of the plan and Guerrero's resignation—that there was little time for political agitation to develop in the Huasteca region.[8] This may be due to the fact that, as Charles McCune noted, there had already been a kind of political divorce between the state of Mexico and the national government in the months leading up to the Plan of Jalapa. Thus although federalists controlled the state of Mexico there appears to have been little effort to mobilize state resources against the pronunciados. It was a far different situation during the subsequent events of 1832 to 1834.

We can see the growing tensions in Mexican society reflected in the way pronunciamientos played out in the Huasteca: 1832 began a cycle of increasingly bitter political competition between communities and small town powerbrokers that mirrored national conflicts. The coastal towns of northern Veracruz were the first to second the plan, and they in turn persuaded General Esteban Moctezuma to join the federalist revolt.[9] When the news of the nearby port of Tampico joining the revolt reached Huejutla on 14 March, prefect Ignacio Martínez assured the government that there "was not a single individual animated by revolutionary sentiments" in his district.[10] Ironically the rebellion quickly spread through the region and ultimately the prefect himself was not immune to the pronunciamiento fever. To attract followers in the region, the Tampico leadership resurrected the proposal to form a state of the Huasteca with all the privileges that a "free and sovereign" entity would have under a pro-federalist administration.[11] The state government later accused Cristóbal Andrade, the former alcalde and prefect of Huejutla who had organized a previous drive for statehood in 1823, as the mover behind the spread of the plan.[12] Perhaps it was the call for statehood that helped prefect Martínez abandon his earlier loyalty to Bustamante, because he began sending out invitations to other towns to second the Plan of Veracruz on 16 April. Interestingly enough, the towns quickest to join Huejutla were the largely indigenous communities of Tamazunchale, Xilitla, and Chalpulhuacan. All these communities were outside Huejutla's jurisdiction, and they joined over the opposition of their own prefects.

To propagate the movement, Martínez expanded the civil guard to more than five hundred men and began to march toward Metztitlán, where the town council and the subprefect, José M. Borromeo, had refused to join the revolt. Borromeo organized the town's defense and requested "veteran troops" from Tulancingo.[13] There was ideological jousting as well. The pronunciados denounced the government ministers as enemies of federalism, while the loyalist council of Tulancingo replied that the administration was "the best we have had since we shook off the Spanish yoke."[14]

As Martínez moved south and west the towns in his path, Tlachinol, Huazalingo, and Yahualica, joined the plan. The subprefect of Zacualtipán, Félix Arenas, tried to hedge his bets by playing both sides. According to the *alcalde primero* of Zacualtipán, José María Licona, Arenas had secret correspondence with Martínez even as he wrote to the national government pledging his allegiance: "His intention was to win regardless of the revolution's outcome."[15] Molango joined the movement supporting Santa Anna on 16 May and soon after, in the words of the state governor, the "despicable scum" led by Martínez occupied Zacualtipán.[16] After Arenas surrendered Zacualtipán without a fight, the governor replaced him with José Ruis Trejo. Martínez's success was short-lived since soon after he took the town the long-awaited "veteran troops" arrived. The battle that ensued consisted largely of the regular troops displaying their numerical superiority, whereupon 120 rebels surrendered while Martínez and the rest fled. The government commander, Colonel Fernando Franco, stated that he could not pursue the rebels because of nightfall.[17] Metztitlán officials and those from Zacualtipán who had remained loyal used their triumph to press charges against the clique that had dominated the district of Huejutla in recent years. Martínez was removed from his post, and the new officials urged that he be tried along with Rafael Melo, the treasurer (*receptor de rentas*), for participating in the revolt.

The order reestablished by government troops did not last long. Events outside the Huejutla district tipped the balance in Martínez's favor when the regular army forces withdrew to Tulancingo to face challenges elsewhere. The government counteroffensive against Martínez stalled, and it is not clear that they ever reoccupied Huejutla itself. In September the Huachinango Battalion rebelled and sent troops north into Chicontepec and Zacualtipán. The pronunciados recruited the subprefect of Chicontepec (Veracruz), Juan Meriotegui, who joined with Martínez's allies in Yahualica and captured the new loyalist prefect of Huejutla, Manuel Monteverde.[18] Towns quickly switched loyalties as Molango seconded the pronunciamiento once more, and the national government, facing uprisings on all sides, proved unable to send regular troops to the sierra as they had done earlier.

The Plan of Veracruz triumphed nationally, and that meant that Félix Arenas, Cristóbal Andrade, and Ignacio Martínez came to power and excluded their enemies from Zacualtipán and Metztitlán. However, the liberal Gómez Farías government had barely been seated when army officers organized pronunciamientos under the conservative slogan "Religión y fueros." In Zacualtipán, José Licona and José Gregorio Morales, two former municipal officials who had defended the government of Bustamante in 1832, led adherents to the conservative pronunciamientos. Morales and Licona were also captains of the *batallón activo* of Metztitlán and therefore had close ties to the town that had organized the resistance to the Plan of Veracruz.[19] The local pronunciamiento illustrates how participants in rebellions reappeared in a consistent manner as members of political factions. The conservative pronunciados reimposed the pro-Bustamante subprefect who had earlier replaced Arenas, José Ruis Trejo. Cristóbal Andrade, now serving as prefect of Huejutla, called on the people of the district not to be fooled by "those who during the last administration gave proof of their support for the oppressive system." Andrade blamed Spanish merchants and parish priests José Liberato Aldana and Lorenzo Enríquez of Zacualtipán.[20] Radical federalists had traditionally portrayed Spanish merchants as threats to the Mexican republic, while the clergy and army officers were the new enemies of the reformists of 1833–34.

The pronunciamiento collapsed when militias from Huejutla arrived, forcing the rebels to flee while officials such as Ruis Trejo and Morales abandoned the cause and requested amnesties.[21] Although short-lived, the pronunciamiento destabilized local society. Facing fiscal chaos, the loyalists raised funds to maintain a garrison in Zacualtipán by imposing a forced loan on the parish priest who had supported the uprising.[22] The pronunciados had sacked the nearby Hacienda de las Vaquerías, adding economic resentments to the existing political animosities.

While the 1833 movement failed to prosper either in the Huasteca or on the national level, the same cast of characters reappeared in May of 1834 when santanista officers issued the Plan of Cuernavaca against the reformers. While on the national level the plan was a dispute between the executive and the radical Congress, it had state and municipal dimensions. Enemies of reform sought to remove state legislatures, governors, and ultimately prefects and municipal officers viewed as committed to the radical project.

The Plan of Cuernavaca erupted at a very delicate political moment because Félix Arenas, now promoted to the prefecture of Huejutla, had tried to suppress the subprefectures of Metztitlán and Yahualica in accordance with orders from Toluca. The subprefect of Metztitlán refused to turn over his archives, and the town's militia deserted after seizing munitions from the subprefect of Zacualtipán.[23] Arenas sought to defuse the issue, ordering the subprefect of Zacualtipán to back off and sending the militia company from Molango to replace those of Metztitlán. The military emissaries of the Plan of Cuernavaca easily found followers in Metztitlán. Zacualtipán proved to be contested ground between the pronunciados in Metztitlán and the loyalists in Huejutla, but the pronunciados soon gained the upper hand by mobilizing the defeated rebels of 1833. José Gregorio Morales (the state government had pardoned him for his participation in the 1833 uprising) and the parish priest Lorenzo Enríquez came to the fore to organize a pro-Cuernavaca faction.[24] The clergy took a prominent part: the parish priest of Huazalingo, Rafael Martínez de Aragón, became one of the military leaders of the revolt. He later claimed that he, José Ordaz, the priest of Xochiatipán, and the parish priest of Yahualica worked to subvert Huazalingo in spite of the opposition from the local civic militia and prefect.[25] The Tulancingo military commander promoting the plan appointed Morales as the movement's representative and promised him army support.

The Plan of Cuernavaca sympathizers organized the election of a new town council to second the plan. Arenas described the pronunciamiento process in Zacualtipán as "an overthrow of the legitimate authorities" and a "criminal assault."[26] Under the direction of Morales, the pronunciados elected José M. Licona as *alcalde primero* and Juan Espindola as *alcalde segundo*. Arenas described a fraudulent process whereby the organizers held the election in a private home and allowed only twenty residents to vote.[27] At the same meeting Morales demanded the outgoing town council adopt the plan or "his chief, Colonel Pérez," would send troops. They also dismissed the treasurer Rafael Melo, the ally of Cristóbal Andrade in 1832, from his post. According to Arenas, the "pronunciados had the order that those [who held office] in the year 1832 should take their posts again."[28] Adhesions to Cuernavaca followed from Yahualica, Xochicoatlán, Tianguistengo, and Molango on 19 and 30 June.[29]

Santa Anna may have envisioned the Plan of Cuernavaca as a method to create a mandate for his political offensive against congressional radicals, but in the Sierra Huasteca it turned into a miniature civil war. On 31 May, the garrison of Toluca pronounced against the governor and closed the state legislature because of its sympathy for the federal Congress.[30] The new state government that resulted from the Plan of Toluca supported Cuernavaca and even sent Arenas directions to "second the said plan in all of your district."[31] Arenas delayed in responding and hampered the efforts of towns to join the plan. Arenas deposed the town council of Yahualica when it declared its support for Toluca and placed garrisons of civic militia in Yahualica and Xochicoat-lán, which prompted the Zacualtipanos to organize a military campaign against them.[32]

The Zacualtipán leadership also carried out a cultural counterrev-olution, ordering the councils of the towns they occupied to begin their meetings with a mass and that the schools teach the Catholic catechism.[33] It was armed propaganda for the conservative cause, forcing town councils to pledge their loyalty to Catholic politics. In Yahualica the pronunciados held the town meeting to adhere to the plan in the church with a ceremony that included the for-mal acceptance of a banner with the slogan "Viva la religión" and a procession led by the alcalde, Rosalino del Rosal, and the parish priest.[34] To contemporaries the banners, processions, and church services must have given the pronunciamiento the air of a patri-otic holiday. The movement leaders sought to confer the trappings of nationalism on the conservative cause. Arenas expressed much frustration over the hyper-Catholicism of the movement and ar-gued that the state of Mexico (in contrast to the federal Congress) had never attacked the Church.[35] Many Huastecan residents ig-nored the prefect's nuanced distinctions and perceived the Gómez Farías reforms as a threat to the Church. Resentment of the anti-clerical policies not only mobilized parish priests; it also seems to have generated sincere support in some of the small towns. How-ever, it is important to note that the declarations of support for the Plan of Cuernavaca sometimes specified that they were in fa-vor of annulling *only* the religious reforms and not changing the form of government.[36] Thus rumors concerning the fate of the fed-eralist pact sparked some concern in the councils that supported the plan, and the language of the declarations constituted an at-tempt to clarify how "public opinion" viewed the nature of the state. While they supported the "defense of our sacred religion," they sought to preserve federalism.

When Yahualica and Xochiatipán joined the plan over Arenas's objections, the prefect ordered the arrest of the priests and town councils. He also tried to mobilize the municipal officers ousted by the pronunciados in Yahualica and wrote to the towns subordinate to Yahualica informing them that they need not obey the new authorities in the subprefecture because in his view the Plan of Toluca violated the federal pact.[37]

In contrast to the events of 1833, the new state and national administrations supported the Plan of Cuernavaca and did not look favorably on Arenas's loyalty to the old order. The new governor wrote the Metztitlán council approving their adoption of the plan and informing them that Arenas "is not and should not be obeyed as Prefect."[38] The state governor ordered Arenas's replacement with Pedro Carrión on 24 July because of complaints from Zacualtipán about the prefect's attempt to keep the new subprefect of the town from taking office.[39]

The Plan of Toluca clearly gave the pronunciados the upper hand, yet Huejutla and its obstinate prefect refused to recognize the new order, prompting Father Martínez de Aragón and Captain Morales to march against Huejutla and occupy neighboring Huautla. Bowing to the inevitable, Arenas and the town council finally seconded the Plan of Cuernavaca on 27 July, but significantly, they included a clause that withheld recognition from the new governor of the state of Mexico.[40] The town council then wrote to President Santa Anna requesting guidance on whom they should recognize as state executive since "many of the towns have not recognized the government in Toluca as may be seen in the documents."[41] The council and Arenas accepted Santa Anna's

Plan of Cuernavaca in hope that he would maintain the local status quo against the new officials in Toluca.

Pedro Carrión reported that the town had adopted the Plan but that it remained at arms determined to resist the entrance of the pronunciamiento troops.[42] Arenas and alcalde primero Agustín Viniegra finally abandoned their posts, leaving Rafael Rocha, the alcalde segundo, to write to Carrión recognizing his authority and requesting that the soldiers retire. He stated that the expedition was unnecessary and only a result of the "resentments" of Yahualica and Xochiatipan; in addition Rocha claimed Morales and Martínez de Aragón committed abuses under the cover of the pronunciamiento.[43] The town civic militia also refused to demobilize as long as the pronunciados were in the area. Carrión called for Martínez de Aragón to retreat, and the priest later reported that he did so without entering Huejutla once he received the town's commissioners, who informed him that they had adhered to Cuernavaca.[44]

Huejutla kept their enemies out of the town but they lost control of the prefecture; in September 1834 the national government moved the district seat to Metztitlán.[45] Huejutla continued to fight a rear guard action over the events of 1834, resorting to the courts to harass Martínez de Aragón. The complaints centered on his humiliating treatment of Huautla's town council. His troops arrested the council and put them under the watch of a guard who "did not even let us speak." The pronunciados also made the town fathers carry hay for the rebels' horses on their backs.[46] In September 1834 the parish priest of Huejutla persuaded the archbishopric of Mexico to arrest Martínez de Aragón and Ordaz, to investigate the Huautla events.[47] Each town mustered followers in favor of or against the controversial curates. Matters became so heated that the state government ordered Carrión "to proceed with the utmost energy to dissolve the masses of men who have joined together abandoning their work and their families . . . [and] reestablish tranquility, putting the engines of disorder at the disposition of the proper authorities."[48] It is revealing that geography trumped the call of "Religión y fueros" since the clergy divided along geographical lines, with the Huejutla curate opposing the priests from Zacualtipán, Xochiacoatlán, and Huazalingo. Martínez de Aragón called the Huejutla priest an "enemy of order" (i.e., a supporter of the Gómez Farías government). He successfully defended himself against charges that he raided municipal coffers during the disorder, but his temporary removal allowed the region to return briefly to a semblance of normality.

Commentary: Pronunciamientos in Rural Mexico

The experiences of this corner of Mexico during the age of political crisis offer several lessons. Clearly the pronunciamientos were not only the work of politicians with epaulettes, but rather they reflected an increasing amount of polarization. The military often served as a detonator to local movements, most prominently in 1833 and 1834 when garrisons sent envoys with invitations to second the plans. In 1832 the presence of government troops hampered the spread of the pronunciamiento, but in most of these cases the military was generally absent. In this mountainous corner of the state of Mexico, district administrators and town councils held the key posts that determined whether a plan prospered. The military-civil relationship was often reversed: pronunciados needed municipalities and prefectures to mobilize the civic militias—who did most of the fighting; outside intervention by veteran troops could be decisive but was often not possible.

The organization of pronunciamientos exalted the importance of local institutions because they played a critical role in granting legitimacy to political plans. Hispanic legal tradition saw town councils as the original organs of popular sovereignty, so it was quite natural for politicians to appeal to the councils when they sought to rewrite the social contract. Town councils likewise spoke in "the name of the patria" when they propagated the plans.[49] The 1830s saw the popularization of "public opinion," and even indigenous villagers found that they too could express their desires in the context of national political movements by influencing the municipal institutions they knew intimately. Pronunciados effectively granted town councils powers similar to those of a constituent assembly: they were given the right to construct the state, not just administer its dictates.

While municipalities began as the voice of the people, they quickly deteriorated into the objective of the pronunciados. Winning the loyalty of the municipalities became paramount for the success of the movements, and the most effective way to guarantee loyalty was to manipulate elections. During the 1832 and 1834 movements pronunciados and loyalists held impromptu elections or purged town councils in the pursuit of control over these organs of public opinion. Replacing municipal officers became part of the strategy for controlling national politics, and in turn this served to erode the status of municipalities as representing local interests or the people's will. Organizers of pronunciamientos appealed to public opinion but intervened in local government to make sure it conformed to their own.

The region's power relations were inscribed in the organization of municipalities and their subordination to prefects, subprefects, and ultimately the state government. Pronunciamientos created moments of crisis during which local actors could challenge their subordination—as when Metztitlán successfully displaced Huejutla as the seat of the prefecture. Municipalities used pronunciamientos to challenge their superiors. Within the towns, individuals who had been excluded from power sought to transform the local order in their favor. Contending groups of merchants and landowners competing for power were more than willing to appeal to "outsiders" in the national government or army to further their own projects. As regional political actors formed alliances, national political divisions came to have concrete and personal meanings in the countryside. One observes a process similar to what Alan Knight described as the "logic of the revolution," in which towns often lined up on different sides of competing factions because of local rivalries.

The political competition that erupted within the local elite during these movements exacerbated tensions between municipal seats and their subordinate outlying villages, as in the attempts by Huazalingo to become independent of the district seat via a pronunciamiento led by Wenceslao Ugalde. Tensions between prefecture seats and municipalities also emerged. Chapulhuacan revolted in favor of General Santa Anna after the district capital declared its loyalty to Bustamante in 1832. The municipality of Jacala begged for assistance to put down the revolt since the Chapulhuacan Indians were "people without civilization or politics" and would destroy Jacala if they were not stopped.[50]

Towns challenged prefects with the aim of placing their own favored sons in the post. Competition for control of political posts played a role in creating geographical alliances. During the rebellions of both 1832 and 1834 administrators dismissed their opponents as ambitious office seekers. Contemporary and modern observers have often blamed nineteenth-century political instability on *empleomanía*, the drive to occupy government positions.[51] As the name implied, observers often thought that public posts held an economic and social appeal for job seekers. Implicit in this point of view was a conservative critique of the liberal state: the people seeking positions did not have incomes and social status of their own. Rather than authority being invested in the "proper" ruling class, the excesses of democracy had allowed grasping fellows to rise to power. But salary and even social status were not as important as the political power that these offices held for the residents of rural Mexico. The participants in pronunciamientos sought to control the local destinies of their districts, and to exclude their enemies, by hitching their fortunes to the different national factions promoting the plans. In other words, the salaries offered by these posts were minimal (and pay was always in arrears), but the power they held was real.

This discussion may lead the reader to conclude that pronunciamientos on the village level were all about local power arrangements and small town rivalries, but a close exploration of the history of these Huasteca pronunciamientos demonstrates heightened ideological divisions, too. The bitter disputes over the events of the Plan of Cuernavaca continued to reappear in the courts, and the positions taken by these small town officials came to define their political ties for years to come.[52] In 1838 the Huejutleños resurrected their lawsuit against Martínez de Aragón for his abusive occupation of Huautla. In the same year, the Ugalde family and a group of Huazalingo Indians rioted against Martínez de Aragón, demanding his removal as their priest. After higher authorities transferred the priest to a new town, the Ugaldes began a petition to change their district head town from Yahualica to Huejutla. Morales's efforts to become subprefect of Zacualtipán under the conservative administration in 1838 also sparked opposition.[53] An armed band led by José Bustos appeared in the area between Chicontepec and Xochiloco in 1834. Bustos took up arms after Rosalino del Rosal, the alcalde of Yahualica, singled him out for persecution because he did not support the Plan of Cuernavaca.[54]

The image of the nineteenth-century politician as a "*chaquetero*," changing political affiliations to accommodate the orders of his superiors or whoever was winning at the moment, is not supported by these events. Actors appear to have had well-defined political affiliations that they held consistently. Morales and Licona were identified with conservative movements, Andrade was affiliated with federalist projects, etc. A good counter-example indicates that fence sitting was almost impossible. Arenas, the subprefect of Zacualtipán, tried to play both sides in the early stages of the Plan of Veracruz (1832), but his failure to support Bustamante's government with enthusiasm provoked the loyalists, who later consistently opposed him. Thereafter Arenas identified with the federalist faction and became a stalwart of the anti-Cuernavaca movement long after it was a lost cause.

Actions of a town or a group of men in a pronunciamiento became part of the historical memory of the region and therefore dictated the political logic during future movements. A good example of how local officials could gain a political reputation that could later affect their careers may be seen in the petition of the Ilmatlán villagers against Juan Meriotegui, the prefect of Chicontepec, who had supported the Plan of Veracruz in 1832. In 1837 the villagers, who described themselves as "poor Indians sustaining political parasites," framed their complaints by pointing out to Bustamante's centralist government that Meriotegui associated with the *yorkino* (federalist) faction.[55] The Indians reminded the government that Meriotegui had joined with Moctezuma during the Plan of Veracruz against Bustamante's first administration, supporting the "*sanculotes*" (sic). Even the remote villagers of Il-matlán understood how the political history of local administrators could be used against them.

Ideology became intertwined with conflicts over local authority. A good example of this may be seen in 1833 and 1834: the pronunciados vociferously declared their adhesion to the ideological elements of the national movements and sought to reorganize local society to protect the Catholic faith. Much to their distress, officials such as Arenas, who claimed that Catholicism had never been questioned in his jurisdiction, found themselves cast as heretics. The adherents of Cuernavaca seem to have had a crusading zeal for their cause, but even in 1832 the correspondence between loyalists and pronunciados reveals that local actors sincerely debated the issues that the plans raised. Heightened ideological partisanship also brought harsher reprisals as contending bands mobilized militias to propagate their plans. The ideological schism became superimposed on the geographical divide as the towns in the northeast of the district became associated with federalism and those of the west and south identified as the pro-clerical centralists.

The local participants also demonstrated independence from their superiors. Local actors defied political plans, they modified them at will, and even after losing they negotiated their surrender, as in the case of Huejutla. Rural Mexico became a source of support for pronunciamientos as politicians offered to address local demands with projects such as establishing new political jurisdictions (new municipalities, prefectures, or judgeships), tax relief, and in the case of this region, the creation of a new state of the Huasteca. Thus the municipalities and prefects were not simply tools of "the superior government," or the army, or Santa Anna. Their plans reveal an understanding of the national political issues and also a savvy political calculation to achieve their own ends.

Pronunciamientos ushered in a series of political consequences that the national political actors never anticipated. The unintended political rivalry, ideological polarization, and even geographic competition had profound implications for the Mexican state. The violence and economic costs of the political plans eventually threatened the legitimacy of the new nation. Pronunciado armies threw the municipalities into disorder—seizing funds, deposing councilmen, and removing judges. Their actions undermined the basic political unit of the federal republic, revealing to even the humblest residents of rural Mexico the incapacity of the nation's ruling class. Although the Plan of Cuernavaca did not propose abandoning the federal Constitution, the fallout from the movement would lead to the eventual collapse of Mexico's First Federal Republic.

Notes

1. Tenenbaum, "'They Went Thataway,'" 194; Vázquez, "Political Plans and Collaboration"; Anna, *Forging Mexico*, 248; Annino, "Cádiz y la revolución territorial," 178. See also Guardino, *Peasants, Politics*, 159. Di Tella, *National Popular Politics*, 73–104, 116–20, 206–12, describes the role of "popular mobilizers" focusing on urban political actors. See also Fowler, *Mexico in the Age of Proposals*, 2–4; and Stevens, *Origins of Instability*, 28–29.

2. Annino, "Nuevas perspectivas," 45–91.

3. Zavala, *Memoria . . . 30 de marzo de 1833*, 18; Soto, *Noticias estadísticas de la Huasteca*, 39.

4. According to article 156 the prefect named the subprefects subject to the approval of the governor; see "Constitución política del Estado de México sancionada por su Congreso Constituyente en 14 de febrero de 1827," in Colín (ed.),

Constituciones del Estado de México, 42. See also Ley Orgánica Provisional para el arreglo del Gobierno Interior del Estado del 6 de agosto de 1824, in *Compilación de leyes y reglamentos*, 13–36.

5. The powers of the prefects and subprefects are outlined in articles 155 and 158 of the state constitution. María del Carmen Salinas Sandoval describes the role of municipalities in the state in two very useful texts: *Los municipios en la formación del Estado de México* and *Política y sociedad en los municipios*. Pages 37–59 of the second describe the municipality of the period.

6. The following brief summary draws on several texts: Anna, *Forging Mexico*, 230–31; Costeloe, *The Central Republic*; Costeloe, *La primera república federal*; Costeloe, "Santa Anna and the Gómez Farías Administration"; Fowler, *Santa Anna*.

7. Fowler, *Santa Anna*, 147–52 argues convincingly that Santa Anna was not interested in dictatorial power in 1833.

8. See McCune, *El Estado de México*, 166–68.

9. "Oficio dirigido por el Ylustre Ayuntamiento de esta Ciudad al Señor D. Esteban Moctezuma," *Gazeta de Tampico*, 17 March 1832, Biblioteca del Congreso del Estado de México (hereafter cited as BCEM), 1832/76/68, fols. 1–4; Minutes of a meeting of the town council and officers of the 4th military section in the casa consistorial of Tampico, 10 March 1832, Archivo Histórico del Estado de México (herafter cited as AHEM), 048.4/117/12, fol. 11.

10. Martínez, 17 March 1832, BCEM), 1832/76/68, fol. 1.

11. Trens, *Historia de Veracruz*, 5:130. See AHEM, 48.4/117/12, fol. 49, for reports on the advance of rebellion in Veracruz. Rangel Silva and Salazar Mendoza, "Élites," 69–92, and Escobar Ohmstede, "La conformación y las luchas," 18–19, have fine discussions of the statehood movement describing Andrade's role.

12. 23 May 1832, AHEM, 91.6/183/fol. 133. The document also accused Andrade of having stolen money from Metztitlán's town coffers when he had served as prefect; Martínez to town council of Metztitlán, 16 April 1832, AHEM, 091.6/183/3, fol. 2.

13. Gobierno del estado de México to J. M. Borromeo, 7 May and 27 May 1832, AHEM, 091.6/183/3, fols. 93–94, 126. In the 27 May note the government stated: "Neither Martínez nor his followers can withstand the stare of a veteran soldier."

14. The Plan of Veracruz originally demanded only the removal of Bustamante's ministers. Francisco Fernández, José Núñez de Caceres, 20 March 1832,

AHEM, 048.4/117/12, fols. 26–27; Ayuntamiento de Tulancingo, 24 April 1832, AHEM, 091.6/183/3, fol. 27v. On the federalist issues at stake in the appointment of ministers see Anna, *Forging Mexico*, 230.

15. Licona to Melchor Múzquiz, Zacualtipán, AHEM, 091.6/183/3, fol. 151.

16. Múzquiz, 23 May 1832, Toluca, AHEM, 091.6/183/3, fol. 150.

17. Col. Franco, Zacualtipán, 3 June 1832, AHEM, 091.6/183/3, fol. 175.

18. In Veracruz the title of the post equivalent to subprefect was *jefe de cantón*. José Cacho, comandante de México, 6 September 1832, AHEM, 091.6/177/1, fols. 38–38r. On Moctezuma's advance see Manuel Monteverde, prefect of Huejutla, Zacualtipán, 30 July 1832. In the same letter Monteverde complained that once the regular troops left his district he could not occupy the towns (such as Yahualica) under the pronunciados' control.

19. The *batallón* had also participated in Nicólas Bravo's pronunciamiento against Vicente Guerrero in 1828.

20. Andrade, Huejutla, 15 August 1833, AHEM, 091.1–.2/172/22, fol. 9, and see "Lista de los factores del pronunciamiento de este pueblo de Zacualtipán," 7 August 1833, fol. 26. He expelled a Spanish resident, Agustín Gutiérrez del Pozo, "for having joined the pronunciados de Zacualtipán," fol. 27.

21. Ruis Trejo later testified that the emissary of Arista, Alférez Ignacio Varo, intimidated him into joining; Testimony Ruis Trejo, 23 October 1833, AHEM, 91.2–.6/177/4, fol. 22.

22. The government collected the three-hundred-peso forced loan from Father José Liberto Aldana and José López Ponte; José María Saavedra to Andrade, 18 October 1833, Zacualtipán, AHEM, 91.2–.6/177/4, fol. 19v.

23. Sóstenes Vargas, Metztitlán, 15 May 1834, AHEM, 091.1–091.2/172/22, fols. 5–6; Francisco Córdova to Arenas, Zacualtipán, 20 May 1834, fol. 2.

24. Andrade described Morales as "insignificant," and "he barely knows how to write his name badly," 11 October 1833, Huejutla, AHEM, 091.1–091.2/172/22, fol. 30.

25. Martínez de Aragón to Gov. José María Esquival, August 4, 1834, AHEM, 178/4, fols. 107–8.

26. Arenas, Huejutla, 3 July 1834, AHEM, 091.2/172/4, fol. 14.

27. Arenas, Huejutla, 13 June 1834, AHEM, 091.2/178/4, fol. 11.

28. Arenas, Huejutla, 13 June 1834, fol. 11r; "Acta del Ayuntamiento," 18 June 1834, AHEM, 091.6/178/4, fol. 17. Richard Warren, *Vagrants andCitizens*, 114–15, describes how in 1833 Gómez Farías purged the town council of Mex-

ico City and summoned the 1829 council members to replace those elected under Bustamante.

29. Acta del ayuntamiento de Yahualica, 30 June 1834; Ayuntamiento de Tianguistengo, 19 June 1834; Junta Popular de San Nicolás de Xochicoatlán, 19 June 1834; Junta popular de Molango, 19 June 1834, AHEM, 091.6/178/4, fols. 35, 36, 37.

30. On the events in Toluca, see McCune, *Estado de México*, 176–77.

31. Unsigned draft of letter to prefect of Huejutla, 7 June 1834, AHEM, 091.2/178/7, fol. 172.

32. Arenas ordered the arrest of Rosalino del Rosal, alcalde segundo Fco. Rodríguez, secretario José Manuel Rodríguez, and D. Juan Del Rosal; Arenas, 14 and 15 July 1834, AHEM, 091.2/178/7, fols. 93, 95.

33. Report of Ballato, juez de paz, to subprefect of Huejutla, 22 February 1838, Huautla, BCEM, 1842/83/118, fol. 5.

34. Acta del ayuntamiento de Yahualica, sesión extraordinaria, 30 June 1834, AHEM, 091.6/178/4, fol. 31.

35. Arenas to the alcalde of Calnali, Huejutla, 15 June 1834, AHEM, 091.6/178/4, fol. 96.

36. See for example the declaration of Molango, 19 June 1834, AHEM, 091.6/178/4, fol. 37.

37. Arenas to Atlapexco, Huejutla, 23 June 1834, AHEM, 091.6/178/4, fols. 29–29r. Arenas argued that Yahualica had accepted the "revolutionary plan of the government of Toluca" under false pretenses—"it was trickery"—and urged the town council to ignore any orders from Yahualica, promising military action if Yahualica tried to enforce its will. José Rosalino de Rosal, Yahualica, 14 July 1834, fol. 52, wrote to request troops to use against Huejutla because the town "not only does not pronounce, it also encourages the towns to reject the plan."

38. Félix Aburto to alcalde primero de Metztitlán, Toluca, 29 June 1834, AHEM, 091.6/178/4, fol. 25.

39. Félix Aburto to Sixto Morales, Toluca, 24 July 1834, AHEM, 091.6/178/4, fols. 44–45.

40. Acta de Huejutla, ayuntamiento milicia y prefecto, 27 July 1834, AHEM, 091.6/178/4, fol. 76r. The council added two articles to the plan pledging support for federalism and refusing to recognize the new state government produced under the Plan of Toluca, fol. 76r.

41. Acta de Huejutla, ayuntamiento milicia y prefecto, 27 July 1834.

42. Carrión, Huejutla, 1 and 2 August 1834, AHEM, 091.6/178/4, fols. 71–72 and 74.

43. Rocha to Carrión, Huejutla, 10 August 1834, AHEM, 091.6/178/4, fols. 84–86.

44. Martínez de Aragón, Yahualica, 4 August 1834, AHEM, 091.6/178/4, fols. 107–8.

45. J. M. Coral, Toluca, 10 September 1834, BCEM, 1834/206/79, fol. 1. The order cryptically mentioned that the motive for the change was the "delicate situation" concerning "public tranquility." The town council lobbied the state government to undo the change, granting a power of attorney to Francisco González to "promote the return of the district capital to Huejutla"; Archivo Judicial de Huejutla, libro de 1835, 1 April 1835.

46. Report, Ballato to subprefect of Huejutla, Huautla, 22 February 1838, BCEM, 1842/83/118, fols. 4–5. Arenas charged that they looted the local treasury; see Arenas, Huejutla, 3 July 1834, AHEM, 091.2/178/4, fols. 14–15. The charges have some validity; the pro-Cuernavaca leadership reported that Cap. Morales seized cash inappropriately.

47. The provisorato metropolitano ordered the arrest and transfer to Mexico City of Martínez de Aragón and Ordaz on August 9; see Félix Osores, AHEM, 091.2/178/4, fol. 133. In spite of letters from the new prefect, Pedro Carrión, documenting the good behavior of José Ordaz, Carrión delayed the arrests until Toluca sent a letter supporting their detention in September; see Carrión to secretario de relaciones del estado de México, Zacualtipán, 30 August 1834, fols. 143–44, 149, 151–52. See also the arrest order Viniegra, Archivo Judicial Huejutla, libro de 1834, 14 September 1834, which mentions not only that Martínez de Aragón "captained an armed movement" but also unspecified "excesses his parishioners accuse him of."

48. Unsigned order to the prefect of Huejutla, 17 September 1834, AHEM, 091.2/178/4, fols. 149–50.

49. "Oficio dirijido por el Ylustre Ayuntamiento de esta ciudad al Sr. D. Esteban Moctezuma," BCEM, 1832/76/68, fol. 3; *Gaceta de Tampico*, 17 March 1832.

50. Mariano Reyna, Tula, 26 April 1832, AHEM, 091.6/183/3, fols. 39, 40–41.

51. See for example Bustamante, in Costeloe, *Central Republic*, 14, 58.

52. Testimony of Ballato, Huautla, 22 February 1838, BCEM, 1842/83/118, fols. 4–5.

53. BCEM, 1838/74/89, fols. 1–11.

54. Carrión to sec. de relaciones del estado de México, Huejutla, 30 August 1834, AHEM, 091.2/178/4, fols. 144–45.

55. Expediente titled "Varios indígenas de la feligresía de Santiago Ilmatlán," Archivo Judicial de Puebla (INAH), Legajos de 1837. Monteverde, the bustamantista prefect in 1832, reported that "they cannot stand him [Meriotegui] nor his troops in the many towns that have had the misfortune of accepting him into their hearts since he has demanded great quantities of cash."

Five. The Origins of the Pronunciamientos of San Luis Potosí: *An Overview*

T he purpose of this chapter is not to analyze the origins of the many *pronunciamientos* from the purely regional perspective of San Luis Potosí, which can only be accomplished through extensive archival research in the respective region, but rather to provide a thematic overview of these origins, categorizing them in terms of grievances stated in the various accompanying plans and *actas*.

It is worth noting at this point that what was said in the plans or actas was not always necessarily a reflection of what was meant. Thus categorization in terms of *stated* grievances is conducive to the study of the origins of the pronunciamiento as it highlights the need for regional contextualization, through which the existence of an underlying metatext can often be uncovered, whereby the real grievance or intention of the pronunciados (those pronouncing) is not overtly stated in the acta but may instead be cloaked by more popular political demands.[1] By addressing national political concerns in the plan, for example, the pronunciados could lend an air of legitimacy to their action; equally, by addressing more generalized grievances, they could potentially garner widespread support. The existence of a metatext is then perhaps not surprising if one further considers the importance of the text as that of a legitimizing tool, as Shara Ali's chapter in this volume suggests.

Moreover, in the case of San Luis Potosí, what this thematic overview of stated grievances (be they shared or imposed) displays is an interesting and often complex interface/tension between locally inspired and nationally inspired pronunciamientos; that is, those that reflected the needs of the *potosino* elites and those that were launched there because of the perception that San Luis Potosí offered a good vantage point.

This categorization will finally allow for a future comparative study of the origins of each pronunciamiento, in which underlying patterns in terms of their nature and dynamics, main instigators, their motivations, and support networks may be uncovered and may in turn provide a better understanding of the varying contexts from which this "anticonstitutional" form of politicking arose.

In the new independent climate characterized by its politicized military and militarized society, a plethora of actors, from military men and civilian politicians to merchants, hacienda and ranch owners, and ordinary "civilians" all played a role in the political theatricalities of the period, including the ubiquitous pronunciamiento. After failing to achieve change through the constitutional means available (political initiatives, elections, and so forth), many, upon reaching what they may have perceived to be a constitutional dead end, made use of the alternative means available to them (such as garrisons, civic militias, and state/private revenue) in order to have their grievances or proposals addressed in an attempt to bring about some kind of political change. As will become manifest, these grievances or demands (be they constitutional/political proposals, ecclesiastical issues, or local issues concerning taxes, land disputes, or personal vindications) were not always overtly stated in the actual written document that accompanied the pronunciamiento.

Having already been exposed to and participated in the changing political culture both during the Bourbon reforms and the Constitution of Cádiz from 1812 to 1814, regional elites in particular were only too eager in the early years of independence to command their region's political, and with it financial, institutions. San Luis Potosí was one of six intendancies to be granted a provincial deputation, an institution often viewed as a precursor to state federalism.[2] However, it was not always the call for federalism that would provoke so many pronunciamientos in the regions along David Brading's so-called liberal crescent.[3] Only closer analysis will uncover some of the complexities behind the regional pronunciamientos and answer questions concerning the political tendencies of the (mainly creole) elites, who, as Margaret Chowning concludes, were fundamentally conservative despite their liberal front.[4]

As Will Fowler rightly observes, "the great majority of the pronunciamientos that surfaced during this period were inspired either by the centralising or the federalising shifts of the different governments that came to power between 1821 and 1857."[5] In the political vacuum left by the collapse of a three-hundred-year colonial monarchical rule, the attempts at establishing a legitimate authority and political system were initially exposed in the federalist-centralist divide, particularly prevalent in the 1820s through to the 1840s, which served as the political platform upon which many pronunciamientos were staged. Similarly, divides along the pro-clerical vs. anti-clerical line, the monarchist-republican line, and between moderate and radical reformers also granted the *pronunciados* a political pretext in a context of widespread political debate. The main federalist-centralist divide was to be supplanted in the late 1840s with the establishment of the political parties wherein the decades from 1840s to 1880s were heavily defined by the liberal-conservative divide as well as the factions within the prevailing liberal party itself. However, this is not to say that every pronunciamiento was simply based along these lines of divide. Many pronunciados appear to have shifted seamlessly between these lines of divide depending on their interests, as subsequent studies have discovered, and to which we now look from the region of San Luis Potosí.

Located in the north-central mining belt, the region's advantageous geographic location and diversity meant that the capital of San Luis Potosí was to become of great strategic importance politically, commercially, and militarily during the first decades of independence. The opening of Tampico in 1823 also helped convert San Luis Potosí into one of the most important commercial and trading centers of independent Mexico, trading in a wide range of commercial and agricultural goods from silver and sugarcane to textiles and arms.

From the perspective of the pronunciamiento, the region of San Luis Potosí is a promising area of study; its capital experienced both local and national pronunciamientos of differing natures and outcomes, providing the strategic location and many of the actors and resources cited as necessary for a successful pronunciamiento.[6] By studying this phenomenon from the perspective of this region, we are able to explore the social and political realities behind it at the local level and how those relate to the political events at the national level.

As the basis for a thematic overview of the origins of the pronunciamientos in San Luis Potosí, the plans, *actas*, or *iniciati-*

vas are *loosely* categorized in terms of stated grievances within the framework of externally inspired and internally inspired pronunciamientos; the first primary category concerns whether the grievance or demand was national, local, or both, and the second primary category concerns whether it was political, constitutional, personal, all of the above, or other, which will highlight the interplay between national and local politics.

A set of subcategories (federalist, centralist, anti-/pro-clerical, for/against the local/general government, etc.) is also necessary for the purpose of pinpointing the multifaceted, and often ambiguous, nature of the origins as well as hinting at a possible metatext within the plans over the period of three decades (1821–1855). From such categorization one is able to draw conclusions, establish patterns of behavior, and also raise questions for further research into this phenomenon.

Externally Inspired Pronunciamientos

For externally inspired pronunciamientos, the capital of San Luis Potosí found itself on several occasions a mere launching ground, particularly in 1823 and 1845. Its geopolitically strategic location, communication links to neighboring states and to Mexico City, abundant supply network, and ready cash flow meant that it was inevitably viewed by some as an advantageous location from which to launch a pronunciamiento. Important, however, is to bear in mind that the external actors intent on using San Luis Potosí did not always represent the interests or prevailing ideology of the majority of potosino elites; depending on the size of their force and strength of national support, outside interests were able to impose on the state their own will or that of the nation. As will be displayed, these externally inspired pronunciamientos were nevertheless utilized by potosino elites, at times irrespective of their ideology, to differing ends.

One of two purely national pronunciamientos, and indeed the first original pronunciamiento to be launched from San Luis Potosí, was that of General Santa Anna and his own forces. Launched on 5 June 1823, this plan proclaimed a federal republic, putting Santa Anna and his army forth as protector of that system. Despite its stated call for a federal system, its promotion of state representation, and its stress on the importance of the provincial deputations as favored by the potosino elites (manifested in the confederate committee of Celaya), it did not receive the support of the actual majority of the then current governing class of merchant-miners and ex-royalist commanders.[7] They appeared vehemently opposed due in large part to the illegitimate threat of violence and ambivalent nature of the intentions of this external actor accompanied by his own force. It is difficult to judge whether the potosino elites were against the pronunciamiento per se, or against its potential repercussions, based on suspicion of the true intentions behind the plan. Nevertheless, Santa Anna was able to use the state as a springboard into national politics, highlighting one trend of the experience of the pronunciamiento in San Luis Potosí. Furthermore, despite being unsuccessful, he fulfilled one purpose: that of a clever public relations maneuver at the national level.

The second externally instigated national pronunciamiento of San Luis Potosí was launched from the capital on 14 December 1845 by Mariano Paredes y Arrillaga. Befitting the traditional definition of a pronunciamiento, this purely military pronunciamiento involving a network of mainly external actors succeeded in overthrowing the moderate Herrera government and establishing a short-lived military dictatorship.[8] As Michael P. Costeloe rightly

McDonald

observed, this pronunciamiento followed the conventional pattern, although in highly unconventional circumstances; Paredes found himself at the head of one of the best armies Mexico had thus far seen, receiving a significant sum of national resources. The politicization of the war over Texas, the "attack" on the army, the then current state of the country, and the apparent inertia of Herrera's administration provided Paredes with a suite of political pretexts that could appeal to a wide-ranging audience.[9] One particularly receptive audience, and presumably his target audience of choice, was the national army, hence the questioning in the pronunciamiento of the importance of the role and motivation of the army vis-à-vis that of private and state civic militia forces. Furthermore, by appealing to patriotic sentiment, the plan pledged the installation of a new administration and a Congress representative of all classes of society (article 4).

The choice of location from which to launch his pronunciamiento was in part strategic; Paredes may also have included in his calculations that the capital provided an ample source of finance, being a center for tax collection on gold and silver exported through Tampico.[10] However, national circumstances, the impending war with the United States, and San Luis Potosí's historical role as military breadbasket—rather than the political stance of the regional elites—would largely have dictated the logic for launching a pronunciamiento from San Luis Potosí.

Despite any support that Paredes, the unequivocal representative of the values of the *hombre de bien*, may or may not have received from the potosino elites, the origins of his pronunciamiento are very much of national concern.[11] Paredes was able to use the state as mere springboard. The pronunciamiento's success was attributable to Paredes's conspiratorial talent, which secured him the support of two opposing groups (the monarchists, as financiers, and the national army), and to his use of broad grievances in the plan, which garnered further support amidst building unrest.

Exceptional pronunciamientos launched by external actors, like that of Paredes, were not the rule in San Luis Potosí. If external pronunciados wished to boost their chance of success, they would add whatever provisions they could (military or verbal claims) to gain a broader support base of regional elites, incorporating issues of local concern. This is displayed in the success enjoyed by the 1829 Plan of Jalapa.

The San Luis Potosí *bustamantista* pronunciamiento of 19 December 1829, or as Manuel Muro called it, the Plan of General Luis Cortázar, was more in keeping with the sentiment of the majority of elites, at least those from the north and west of the state (hereafter referred to as highland creoles).[12] Cortázar was sent from Morelia to command the garrison at San Luis during the governorship of Vicente Romero, a radical *yorkino* governor in whom Guerrero saw a loyal supporter. The acta to which all the local authorities adhered pledged to sustain the federal system, thereby seconding Vice President Anastasio Bustamante's Plan of Jalapa (4 December 1829; see chapter 3), where the Reserve Army situated in Jalapa proclaimed, in short, the removal of general Vicente Guerrero from the presidency of the republic. The pronunciamiento heralded in a hombres de bien form of government and provided the moderate federalists the chance to eliminate the radical element from the political spectrum.

From a national perspective, this pronunciamiento (one of four of its kind) may be viewed as the imposition of *la voluntad de la nación* (the will of the nation) on the state.[13] The pronunciamiento was carried out by an external group with its own military force on the basis that San Luis had previously displayed strong federal intentions through its pact with other states to act independently of the federal government amidst rumors of a centralist system.

However, when the origins are analyzed within their regional context, there is evidence to suggest that unrest and tension among the potosino elites had been building, and so this pronunciamiento was not simply forced upon the state by national events. In terms of the local origins, many members of the potosino elite would have become increasingly vexed by Vicente Romero's first radical federalist governorship, a position he obtained in 1827 by illegitimately overthrowing the first constitutional governor, Ildefonso Díaz de León, a clearly identifiable member of the highland creole elite and a suspected *escocés*. Romero's radical federalist tendencies translated into increases in military expenditure, with the militia at his disposal as state governor, and militarization, particularly in the east and eastern lowlands of the state, from where he had gained his initial political support of the early 1820s. The culmination of his radical legislation, as Barbara Corbett has observed, convinced many highland creole elites to embrace Bustamante's Plan of Jalapa of late 1829.[14] Certain articles of the plan, particularly article 4 demanding that "functionaries against whom public opinion has been expressed be removed," must have resonated with many of the potosino elites, pointing to a metatext at the local level. That is, the potosino elites may have chosen to support the national plan to resolve a local issue: to oust the governor, Vicente Romero.

The fact that this externally inspired pronunciamiento—launched by Luis de Cortázar in response to national level events—did receive regional support exemplifies how potosino elites used national shifts to suit local needs. They chose to support the Plan of Jalapa not because they supported the plan itself but because they could use it in an attempt to resolve local grievances. At a local level this plan was initially unsuccessful as Romero, in a pragmatic shift to hold onto his governorship, adhered to the new national government. However, despite Romero's desperate federalist decree of January 1830, utilizing the civic militia to establish a pact with Guanajuato in order to protect and conserve the federal institutions, the plan of Jalapa was successfully imposed.

In the case of Lieutenant Colonel José Ramón García Ugarte's pronunciamiento of San Luis Potosí of 1837, the importance of securing a national base of support is manifest. Although he built a significant regional coalition, his inability to form a national coalition quickly and effectively would ultimately result in the failure of his pro-federalist pronunciamiento.[15] Again making use of civic militias and transcending the limits of the regional territory, Ugarte's pronunciamiento with the slogan "Federation or Death" politicized the war with Texas and vented frustration at the demands for funds made by the treasury (article 3) but channeled into the pockets of a few *agiotistas* (moneylenders; article 4). As Costeloe notes, the 1837 election campaign also provided a national opportunity for the opposition to hinder the centralist bandwagon, igniting several pronunciamientos in favor of federalism, some of which had their roots in local grievances, as in Zacatecas and Huajapam. The San Luis Potosí pronunciamiento was aided regionally by former political actors, significantly Lugardo Lechón, and by former civic militia men of 1834 as well as a new generation of "radical" federalists, such as the lawyer and civilian politician Ponciano Arriaga.[16] Also drawn in was the hacienda owner of the largest sugar-producing estates, Paulo Verástegui.[17]

The full complexities of the 1837 pronunciamiento are high-

McDonald

lighted in the network of alliances uncovered by Corbett's study "Las fibras del poder." Seemingly provoked by the national political/constitutional debate, as maintained by Ugarte, many of the merchants of *piloncillo* (cane sugar) united with the ex–civic militias under General Esteban Moctezuma's subsequent command in this federalist pronunciamiento. It received support from regional actors, such as Verástegui, and from merchants, such as Agustín Chicot (French) and Francisco Fernández (Spanish) of Tampico, and possibly received financial aid from the U.S. consul in Tampico, George Robertson, with whom it was alleged Moctezuma had a good relationship.[18] The motivation veiled in federalist discourse may for some actors, upon closer interpretation, have had less to do with liberal ideology than with economic grievances and practicalities, given the Bustamante protectionist tariffs imminent in 1837. Again the use of private and state civic militia forces, used by Ugarte, is brought into question in the pronunciamiento syndrome.

Another nationally inspired pronunciamiento was that of the three-act Plan of San Luis Potosí of 9 December 1842. From a national perspective, the origins of this pronunciamiento display the way in which national events drew powerful national actors (and their force, here the army) to utilize the state to their own ends, in this case to provide demonstrable proof of the will of the nation. It is this purported expression of *la voluntad de la nación*, as Josefina Vázquez and François-Xavier Guerra point out, that not only distinguishes the pronunciamiento from the forms of a revolt or a coup d'état but through which the pronunciamiento sought to legitimize itself.[19] Despite the role of external instigators, this pronunciamiento can be viewed as in keeping with previous local sentiment as it follows on from the initiative of 25 June 1841, in which the *ayuntamiento* (town council) of San Luis asked the departmental committee to propose the reform or renewal of the 1836 Constitution, conserving only its republican components.[20] This initiative failed, but the pronunciamiento, launched locally under the direction of national actors, served to bring about national political change with the threat of force. At the local level, Ignacio Sepúlveda was ordered to step down as governor of San Luis Potosí and was replaced by commandant José Ignacio Gutiérrez. Together with the military garrisons, not the corporate or civil authorities, Gutiérrez denounced the Constituent Congress for having contravened the will of the nation. In doing so, the pronunciamiento achieved its aim, in concert with the Plan of Huejotzingo of 11 December 1842, of ultimately securing the will of Santa Anna.

Although brief, this sketch of a range of externally inspired pronunciamientos suggests that in the majority of cases San Luis Potosí was not a mere victim when national events, actors, and their forces appeared to have hijacked their capital but rather that local actors, depending on their interests, welcomed, manipulated, or rejected the externally inspired pronunciamiento to achieve their own ends.

Locally Inspired Pronunciamientos

The political origins of locally inspired pronunciamientos became more radicalized in the federalist sense during the early 1830s, with local actors making use of local and neighboring civic militias with particular regional and associational networks at play (especially the eastern districts of the state and the "liberal nucleus" of the capital). That is not to deny, however, any apparent continuum in the traditionalist stance among the potosino elite. Locally inspired

McDonald

pronunciamientos more often than not extended their concern to the national level for a variety of reasons, perhaps to broaden their support base, gain popular support, or lend their own individual grievance or demand a more legitimate political pretext.[21]

Examples of the way in which local actors were able to hijack national issues and political events in order to address their own needs are evident in a series of pronunciamientos, as is the importance of particular individuals. The most prevalent individual actor was Vicente Romero, who allegedly made use of national political events in his attempts to retain and to return to state power. His forced resignation as governor on 11 June 1830 on grounds of embezzlement sparked what appears to have been a series of pronunciamientos shrouded in pro-federalist discourse (see appendix). To what extent were the centralizing fiscal reforms of the federal government under Bustamante a factor in the origins of these pronunciamientos? These reforms reduced state revenue of the federal customs house and the tobacco monopoly (mortgaged to the agiotistas). Or, as historians who wrote shortly thereafter claim, was this a conspiracy led by Romero in an attempt to recover his power, seeking the support of former political and military men deposed by Bustamante's administration, like José Márquez, Joaquín Gárate, and José Antonio Barragán? Romero was saved from execution, the uncharacteristically violent punishment that was meted out to Márquez and Gárate, later to claim that the rebels had risen up to take back the state government from "priests and conservative lawyers."[22]

A pattern was beginning to emerge by the 1830s of radical federalist pronunciamientos with regional origins stemming predominantly from actors of the eastern districts of San Luis Potosí. Their leading pronunciados were able to gain pledges of support and protection from some of the more powerful neighboring states, such as Zacatecas (1832 and 1837) and Guanajuato (1830), which in turn made launching a local pronunciamiento more feasible. Under such circumstances the subsequent pronunciamientos of 1832 and 1834 were claimed by observers to have originated in a conspiracy led by Romero: "In order to save himself from his conviction, the convicted resorted to conspiring against the general government, sending agents to Ríoverde, Valle del Maíz and to towns and villages throughout the Huasteca, in search of proselytes, and trying to entice General Esteban Moctezuma, with whom he had a close friendship, to promote the uprising."[23]

In an attempt to muster as much support as possible, Romero also came to an agreement with the governor of Zacatecas, Francisco García, to pronounce in favor of Manuel Gómez Pedraza as legitimate president of the republic. A pragmatic shift in Romero's stance toward Pedraza was forced; despite Romero's staunch opposition to Pedraza in the late 1820s and support of his political opponent Vicente Guerrero, Romero now threw his support behind Pedraza, who provided the "legitimate" means of ending Bustamante's centralizing administration.

The Landero/Santa Anna Plan of Veracruz of 2 January 1832 provided the opportune moment to launch their pronunciamiento. Moctezuma, military commander of Ríoverde, pronounced in Tampico on 20 March 1832 against Vice President Anastasio Bustamante and seconded the Plan of Veracruz.[24] Colonel José Antonio Barragán of Ciudad de Maíz followed Moctezuma's lead, as did the second battalion of civic militia of San Luis. Another interesting trend that can be deduced here is that of local pronunciamientos predominantly addressing local grievances, such as that of Barragán, utilizing pronunciamientos from outside the state to their own ends through their far-reaching network of alliances and support.

Subsequently Moctezuma, now "General of the second division of the liberating army" made up of militia forces from Zacatecas, turned on the capital San Luis, launching the Plan of San Luis Potosí of 5 August 1832. This plan declared Pedraza the legitimate president, denounced Bustamante, and through article 4 was able to reinstate Romero as governor (from 21 August 1832 to 18 September 1832) under the state constitution. On the one hand, the origins of the Plan may be viewed as the regional governing elite's attempt to conserve their autonomy in the face of a centralizing power, bearing in mind Barragán's pronunciamiento. On the other hand, there is also evidence to suggest the case for one man's struggle to regain regional power: it was alleged that under the circumstances, the August act was the only political measure available to protect citizens' lives and properties, and it was reversed by the 28 September manifesto upon General Bustamante's arrival in San Luis with his army.[25] Furthermore, in order to address the question of origins fully, the role of the civic militias and their political participation in this pronunciamiento must also be researched. As Fowler notes, the fact that the battle at El Gallinero (18 September 1832) between Moctezuma and Bustamante was an uncharacteristically bloody one involving forces made up of civilians may suggest that "there really was a strong and generalized sense of discontent among the population against Bustamante's government."[26] This in turn may approach answering whether this pronunciamiento was an example of cross-culture alliance, with lower classes and indigenous peoples participating in an attempt to address their own grievances, or whether it was an example of co-optation by their patron.

Despite the many pro-federalist pronunciamientos, San Luis Potosí saw a long line of pronunciamientos or actas seconding the Plan of Cuernavaca in 1834 and was also part of the stream of centralist pronunciamientos that became a national trend during May–June 1835 seconding the Plan of Orizaba.

The origins at a national level of the Plan of Cuernavaca lay in Mexico's first radical government under Vice President Valentín Gómez Farías (April 1833–April 1834). His administration was brought down by several pronunciamientos (Puebla, Orizaba, Jalapa), but the Plan of Cuernavaca was adopted as an authentic reflection of the national popular will.

From the Plan of Cuernavaca and subsequent acts seconding it, a metatext may be deduced in as far as the consensus stated in the plan appeared to stem from a condemnation of the proposed legislation that would affect the Church, instead of the far more drastic legislation directed at the army. Luis Medina Peña rightly remarks that those responsible were evidently conscious that the religious cause would drum up more support than that of the military *fuero*.[27]

The origins at the local level of San Luis Potosí may have stemmed from Romero's second state governorship/military dictatorship, which he took up thanks to the aftershocks of the 1832 pronunciamientos under the military protection of Moctezuma. Romero's failed attempts to prevent the same conservative backlash in San Luis Potosí may be viewed in reaction to events at both national and local levels; Romero demanded more forced loans, increased the size of the civilian militia, granted himself extraordinary powers, and joined together with the governors of Querétaro, Guanajuato, Jalisco, Zacatecas, and Durango in the organization of a military confederation in defense of the federal system.

McDonald

The signs of political change within the state were visible from early 1833; Ponciano Arriaga's article berates "the triumph of the aristocrats in the renewal of the state legislature," referring to the deputies elected by the districts of Catorce and Guadalcázar.[28] These deputies, together with other corporate/collective bodies such as the ayuntamientos, parish priests, etc., were in turn responsible for initiating the subsequent actas in favor of the Plan of Cuernavaca (see appendix).

François-Xavier Guerra and Josefina Vázquez have argued that such plans or actas, in this case categorized as *actas de adhesión* (plans explicitly seconding a previous pronunciamiento but that may also insert further demands or grievances), should not be considered as pronunciamientos, based on their view that the primary document of all pronunciamientos, the plan, is almost always of military origin, the army being the only corporate body that can legitimate this action through its perceived "special responsibility" toward the nation.[29] In this vein, the pronunciamiento is perceived as *the* tool of the military in its effort to establish strategic links with political actors and seek support from other actors and their civic militias. While this traditional view warrants much consideration, the restricted parameters of the present essay render lengthy fundamental debate impossible. Suffice it to say that for the purpose of this overview, I uphold the revisionist definition that the pronunciamiento was a dynamic concept (see introduction and chapter 2) popularized during the first half of the nineteenth century. Investigation has uncovered its use by civilian politicians and even the clergy, suggesting in turn that other politically minded individuals, or indeed other collective bodies, such as the ayuntamientos, were potentially in a position to utilize this form of politicking. The plans and actas of 1834 are thus considered as pronunciamientos with the marked difference of not having been initiated and composed by military players.

Although such plans were composed by nonmilitary actors, the threat of force was made explicit in several of the documents; for example, the ayuntamiento of Venado's acta refused to withdraw its forces until the other ayuntamientos of the state seconded the plan, which attests to the view that the militias were primarily the extended political arm of their respective ayuntamientos.[30] Furthermore, it is difficult to negate completely the categorization of these actas as pronunciamientos when we have yet to uncover their nineteenth-century usage among regional political actors, who may have interpreted them as a legitimate way of casting their opinion, through which they contributed to, or were themselves able to bring about, political change.

Ponciano Arriaga maintained that the Plan of Cuernavaca was not seconded in San Luis Potosí, which may hold some truth, as General Gabriel Valencia and General Luis de Cortázar did occupy the city of San Luis Potosí in order to secure its full adhesion. However, the list of eleven pronunciamientos and plans from neighboring districts (see appendix) and the nature of their grievances do provide substantial evidence to suggest at least some support, if not a fair reflection of a popular will in certain districts, particularly among the highland elites. Bearing in mind Arriaga's radical ideological stance and also this evidence of support from the highland districts of San Luis Potosí, we have indications of widespread support for a return to a stronger federalist, if not centralist system.

Growing agitation over Romero was also expressed in accusations of his enriching himself with ecclesiastical goods and in the Manifesto of San Luis Potosí, to which on 19 July a group of seventeen potosinos subscribed. Railing against the laws and decrees concerning religious reform (article 1), article 6, which was also added to the July 1834 Manifesto of San Luis Potosí, demanded that those employees unfairly dismissed by Romero be reinstated.

Furthermore, economic considerations may have had bearing upon the origins of the pronunciamientos, as the traditional elite, faced with new threats, may have felt themselves forced to accept the return to centralism in 1835.[31] Only two actas—those of the ayuntamientos of Villa de Ramos and of Ríoverde—explicitly demanded a federal system, and both were adopted under the direction of Esteban Moctezuma, raising the question of whether these districts were coerced into proclaiming the federal system. This in turn casts further questions as to how far the pronunciamiento can be considered a display of true public opinion. Notwithstanding the latter actas, it remains evident that local collective and municipal bodies were in many cases able to use national pronunciamientos as a stepping stone toward having their own demands and grievances addressed.

As way of summing up, one may conclude from this brief thematic categorization that the majority of the pronunciamientos in San Luis Potosí thus far identified were launched ostensibly in reaction to events at the national level. However, despite an overwhelming use of the national political federalist-centralist divide as the political pretext for the origin of the majority of pronunciamientos, the complexity (and near impossibility) of categorization when they are analyzed within their particular regional context suggests the possible existence within the pronunciamiento of an underlying metatext. If such a metatext can be deduced from the pronunciamiento text itself when it is viewed within the local context, it may reflect the interesting interplay between national issues and actors and those at regional level, whereby regional elites were able either to hijack certain national issues or to sway between support and rejection without losing sight of the need to address or rectify issues of a local nature that concerned them, such as retaining political power or furthering economic interests; pragmatic approaches toward politics are certainly a feature of many potosino pronunciamientos.

However, in the case of San Luis Potosí, a thorough analytical and comparative study of the body of pronunciamientos within their local context is required if we are to portray the local politics of the period. The complexity and shifting nature of alliances among the regional elites and their extensive networks of support are apparent from this brief overview, but such shifts in the motivations for launching, supporting, or rejecting pronunciamientos require further investigation to establish a closer definition of the pronunciamiento and to decipher nineteenth-century Mexico's pronunciamiento syndrome.

Appendix: Thematic Categorization
Nationally Inspired Pronunciamientos

NATIONAL→POLITICAL→FEDERALIST

5 June 1823   Plan of San Luis Potosí

NATIONAL/LOCAL→POLITICAL→MODERATE FEDERALIST
[→ Against national government and local governor]

19 December 1829   Plan of San Luis Potosí

NATIONAL/LOCAL→CONSTITUTIONAL→CENTRALIST→PRO-CLERICAL

9 December 1842   Plan of San Luis Potosí

NATIONAL→POLITICAL→CENTRALIST→MONARCHIST

5 December 1845   Plan of San Luis Potosí

14 March 1849   Sierra Gorda Plan of Ríoverde

NATIONAL/LOCAL→POLITICAL→MODERATE

[Conservative despite liberal front]

13 August 1855   Plan of San Luis Potosí

Locally Inspired Pronunciamientos

NATIONAL/LOCAL→POLITICAL→RADICAL FEDERALIST

September 1823   Pronunciamiento of Colonel José Márquez

9, 12 August 1846   Pronunciamiento of Garrison of San Luis
                     Potosí

10 August 1846   Acta of the Municipal Junta of
                     San Sebastián

LOCAL/NATIONAL→POLITICAL/PERSONAL→RADICAL FEDERALIST

[→ Local governorship]

13 January 1830   Plan of San Luis Potosí

17 November 1830   Pronunciamiento of Colonel José Márquez

8 April 1832   Pronunciamiento of Tancanhuitz

5 August 1832   Plan of San Luis Potosí

5 August 1832   Plan of Guadalcázar

LOCAL/NATIONAL→POLITICAL→CENTRALIST

[→ Pro-clerical→Economic grievances→Against local governor]

20 June 1834   Acta of the Ayuntamiento, parish priest,
                     and neighbors of la Purísima Concepción
                     de los Catorce

7 July 1834   Acta of the Ayuntamiento and subprefect
                     of Guadalcázar

8 July 1834   Acta of the Ayuntamiento of Venado

10 July 1834   Manifesto of San Luis Potosí

11 July 1834   Acta of Villa de Salinas del Peñón Blanco

13 July 1834	Acta of Villa de San Francisco de los Pozos
13 July 1834	Acta of the Ayuntamiento of Villa de Ramos
13 July 1834	Acta of the Ayuntamiento of Ríoverde
13 July 1834	Acta of Ciudad Fernández
16 July 1834	Acta of Villa de Matehuala
23 July 1834	Acta of the Ayuntamiento of Villa de Lagunillas
August 1834	Plan of San Luis Potosí

LOCAL/NATIONAL→CONSTITUTIONAL→CENTRALIST→PRO-CLERICAL

30 May 1835	Acta of Villa de San Francisco

LOCAL/NATIONAL→POLITICAL→FEDERALIST

[→Economic Grievances]

1 June 1832	Plan of Tancanhuitz
14 April 1837	Pronunciamiento of San Luis Potosí
6 May 1837	Acta of the Pronunciamiento of Ríoverde
8 May 1837	Acta of Ciudad del Maíz

LOCAL/NATIONAL→POLITICAL→FEDERALIST/MODERATE

11 December 1844	Acta of the Garrison of San Luis Potosí

LOCAL/NATIONAL→POLITICAL→FEDERALIST/MODERATE

[→Against local governor]

12 December 1852	Pronunciamiento of Ríoverde

Notes

1. See Fowler, introduction, this volume, xvii.

2. The most convincing argument is that of Nettie Lee Benson, *La diputación provincial y el federalismo Mexicano.*

3. David Brading claims that the liberal crescent around the valley of Mexico constituted a vast area of territory stretching from Guerrero through to Michoacán, Jalisco, part of Guanajuato, Zacatecas, and San Luis Potosí to Veracruz. Brading, *Origins of Mexican Nationalism*, 96.

4. Chowning, *Wealth and Power*, 41.

5. Fowler, "Civil Conflict in Independent Mexico," 60.

6. Vázquez, "El modelo de pronunciamiento" and "Political Plans and Collaboration," and Guerra, "El pronunciamiento en México."

7. The state of San Luis Potosí was one of several provinces that, through a perceived political inequality vis-à-vis Mexico City, took steps in the form of a league of states to seek redress and promote the need for state representation at the national level. The political league of deputations consisted of Valladolid, Guanajuato, Querétaro, and San Luis Potosí. Calvillo Unna and Monroy Castillo, "Las apuestas de una región," 331.

8. Costeloe, *The Central Republic in Mexico*, 280–81; Vázquez, "Political Plans and Collaboration," 32–35; Vázquez, "El ejercito."

9. Further information regarding the historical context of this period, including the political debates surrounding the Herrera administration being confronted with the annexation of Texas to the United States and a potential war with the United States, see Soto, "Mariano Paredes y Arrillaga."

10. Hamnett, "Partidos políticos mexicanos," 583.

11. Manuel Muro claims that the local political class opposed Paredes's plan, thus proving the presence of a significant group of federalist politicians. Muro, *Historia de San Luis Potosí*, 2:348. However, recent research by Barbara M. Corbett has proved that local support for Paredes existed; the creole elite coalition emerging from the 1841–42 historical conjuncture cheered Paredes's promise to "return to the productive classes their lost influence and to grant to wealth, industry, and work their corresponding roles within the Government of this society." Mariano Paredes y Arrillaga, "A La Nación Mexicana," reprinted in *Boletín Oficial*, 20 December 1845, quoted in Corbett, "Republican Hacienda," 232.

12. Muro, *Historia de San Luis Potosí*, 1:527–28.

13. The other three known bustamantista plans of 1829 are the Plan of Tehuantepec, 17 December; the Plan of Mexico City, 19 December; and the Plan of Jalisco, 24 December.

14. Corbett, "Republican Hacienda," 145.

15. Arnold, "José Ramón García Ugarte."

16. Several regional historians have maintained that Ponciano Arriaga was the so-called intellectual leader of the movement. However, according to recent findings based on the testimonies of those involved, it is claimed that Ponciano

Arriaga was later invited by Moctezuma to join the movement. See Arnold, "José Ramón García Ugarte."

17. Márquez (ed.), *San Luis Potosí*, 148–51.

18. Corbett, "Las fibras del poder," 383.

19. Francisco Manuel Sánchez de Tagle, one of the authors of the 1836 Constitution, confesses that public opinion and national will are always the pretext for all the convulsions. Noriega, *El pensamiento conservador*, 217.

20. Velázquez, *San Luis Potosí*, 204.

21. Thomas David argues that for plans "to be considered worthy of the name they were supposed to be serious in purpose and national in scope." David and Ricon Virulegio (eds.), *Political Plans of Mexico*, xv.

22. 1833 RAG Collection, cited in Corbett, "Republican Hacienda," 158.

23. Translation is my own. Velázquez, *San Luis Potosí*, 168. Muro also firmly agrees that Romero was the instigator, as political change would be his only salvation from the judicial process against him in 1831. Muro, *Historia de San Luis Potosí*, 2:10.

24. Antonio Escobar Ohmstede notes that Moctezuma also pronounced for the creation of a Huastecan state in order to gain the support of important sectors of the Huastecas, and that this support was inspired by economic interests. Escobar Ohmstede, "La confirmación y las luchas," 19–20.

25. For the allegation see Velázquez, *San Luis Potosí*, 171.

26. Fowler, *Mexico in the Age of Proposals*, 230.

27. Medina Peña, *Invención del sistema político*, 250.

28. The quote is the title of an article in *El Yunque de la Libertad*, San Luis Potosí, no. 14 (27 January 1833): 4, cited in Márquez and Abella (eds.), *Ponciano Arriaga*, 1:38–40.

29. Guerra, "El pronunciamiento en México," 17.

30. Medina Peña, *Invención del sistema político*, 265.

31. Corbett, "Republican Hacienda," 178.

Six. The British and an Early Pronunciamiento, 1833–1834

Confirmation of the occupation of Mexico City on 27 September 1821 by Agustín de Iturbide and his victorious insurgent army reached Britain early in December of that year. The first newspaper to report the event, as far as I have been able to ascertain, was the *Caledonian Mercury*, published in Edinburgh. It carried a very brief report on Thursday, 6 December, with information it had found in American newspapers that had just arrived in Scotland. Within days the London papers published the news, and in just a couple of weeks the independence of Mexico was known throughout the United Kingdom, with details published in many provincial papers all over the country. There is no doubt that the British welcomed the news of Mexico's emancipation, and in the following three or four years, from 1822 to 1826, thousands of people from every corner of the United Kingdom invested what in our terms amounted to hundreds of millions of pounds of their savings in the new nation. These investments, it must be emphasized, did not come from wealthy banks or financial institutions but directly from the pockets of private individuals who were persuaded that Mexico was a better place to invest their money than any of the alternatives open to them, such as British or European government stocks or companies. To cite just a handful of examples, among the investors were the four Cazenove brothers, founders of the well-known merchant bank; the three Twining brothers of the tea trade; Dr. Peter Roget, author of the *Thesaurus* that most of us sooner or later still use to this day; Henry Fox Talbot, the photography pioneer; George Sandeman, of the port company fame; and Benjamin Disraeli, then young, ambitious, and anxious to make his fortune. In addition to these famous names, many others could be cited: members of Parliament, fellows of Oxford and Cambridge colleges, brewers, bankers, lawyers, farmers, ironmasters, not to mention an array of local clergy, solicitors, doctors, retired military, widows, and pensioners from towns throughout Britain.

There were two principal ways in which the British were able to invest in Mexico without actually traveling to the country. The first was to buy Mexican government bonds, which were first offered for sale in the London market in 1824 and 1825. Thousands of British investors chose to put millions of pounds into those bonds on the expectation of receiving a secure and reasonable level of return on their money. I have looked into the whole issue of the bonds and the bondholders already in a book published in 2003 and so I am not concerned with them in this study.[1] What I am concerned with here are the alternative investments on offer in Mexico and across the whole Latin American continent. Very briefly, in 1824 and 1825 there was a stock market bubble in London, the like of which had not been seen in Britain for a hundred years and was not to be seen again until the dot.com bubble of 1999. Over a period of a few months, around seven hundred new companies were announced and shares in them were offered for sale with a total value of over £372 million. There were insurance, canal, mining, construction, transport, and a wide range of other companies. Many were what were described at the time as "ephemeral follies," designed as fraudulent schemes to swindle people out of their money; but investors, swept up in the irrational enthusiasm of the time, ignored press warnings. As one contemporary observer recalled, "I could not have conceived that madness could be so universal."[2] The bubble reached its peak in January–February 1825, by which time some share prices had reached huge premiums, but by March–April prices began to fall, and market panic followed. By December 1825 banks up and down the country began to fail, and of the seven hundred companies that had been announced, only 127 survived.

About 10 percent, or seventy, of the seven hundred new companies involved projects to invest in the new nations of Latin America, and among these there were about twenty-five schemes for Mexico. These included companies formed to develop whale fishing off California; others were to raise Spanish galleons in the Gulf of Mexico with their holds believed to be full of doubloons; some were to work pearl fisheries in Mexican waters, which by exploiting the recent invention of a diving bell were expected to make investors rich. There were projects for land development and colonization that promised to find thousands of Scottish and Irish families to colonize Mexico's northern provinces, and there were all manner of other schemes involving shipping lines and trading links.

Most of these proposed companies did not get beyond the planning stage and shares were not offered for sale. The biggest group of companies, however, did get off the ground, and these were the mining companies. Mexico's silver mines had yielded rich profits to their owners and substantial tax revenues to Spain during the colonial period, but the whole industry had been devastated during the ten years of the War of Independence. Mines across the country had been abandoned by their owners, and by 1821 many were flooded and seemingly impossible to restore to production. Then, with independence, both the new Mexican government and the mine owners decided to rescue the mining industry. They knew that what they needed was capital in large amounts, and they came to London to look for it. In their view there was no doubt that experienced European miners, supported by British capital, mining skills, and above all the application of technological developments such as steam power would easily be able to rescue the abandoned mines.

Several mining companies, therefore, were formed in London and hundreds of mines were leased to them by their Mexican owners. For the purposes of this chapter only one of the mining companies is of interest. This was the United Mexican Mining Association or Company. Its origins were in Paris, where Lucas Alamán, the mining engineer and, of course, very important conservative politician in Mexico, had tried to form a company and raise capital. His efforts in Paris were not successful and he came to London in July–August 1822 in search of backers. He quickly found support from the merchant bankers, Hullett Brothers, and with their help the United Mexican Mining Association was formed and announced to the public in January 1824. The company was initially to have £240,000 in capital divided into 6,000 shares of £40 each. Alamán, who by then was back in Mexico and a minister in the government, was named as the head of the Board of Management in Mexico. During the next few months of 1824 and 1825 he contracted dozens of mines on behalf of the company. He personally inspected some, especially in his home state of Guanajuato, and agents were employed to check on and contract others in the states of Mexico, Michoacán, Zacatecas, and Oaxaca. Mining equipment was acquired and shipped to Mexico, especially steam engines, and dozens of miners, many from Cornwall, were recruited and sent out to work the mines.

It was soon clear that some of the mines would never yield a profit and they were abandoned, but the company representatives, including Alamán, sent back optimistic reports about the potential of many others. Over the next few years substantial amounts of additional capital were raised in London by selling shares, and more and more money, equipment, and men were sent to Mexico in the belief that with just one extra effort, a silver bonanza would be found and everybody would get rich. The company's main hopes rested in several mines in Guanajuato. Contracts to work these had been entered into with the owner, the Marquis de Rayas. At first there were no difficulties, but by the early 1830s, there were serious contractual problems between the marquis and the company, mostly concerning the accounts. The events were neatly summarized in a legal opinion formulated in London in 1834: "The Mine of Rayas did not become productive until about the middle of June 1832 when it appeared likely to yield a large return. As soon as this event occurred, the Marquis de Rayas (who is not only a man of rank but of personal influence in those parts) in direct violation of his contract resumed dominion over the mine for the purpose of assuming to himself the profits of his shares in it."[3]

What this meant was that on 11 March 1833, the marquis had persuaded the local *alcalde* (mayor) to issue a decree of sequestration whereby the proceeds of the mining operations were required to be paid into the state treasury rather than to the United Mexican Company. In other words, while the mines continued to be worked, the British company was denied access to any profits or cash until such time as the dispute with the marquis had been settled. In London the news of this event caused "a strong sensation" among the company's shareholders, as the *Morning Chronicle* put it (21 May 1833), and the share price fell by about 10 percent in one day. At this time the £40 paid-up shares were selling at around £10–12. In other words, investors had already lost three-quarters of the money they had invested.

Why did so many British people invest their money in Mexico? There are all manner of answers to that question—belief in the future prosperity of the country; the almost mystical attraction of the Mexican silver mines and the fabulous tales of bonanzas during the Spanish dominion; blind faith in the skills of British miners and their expertise; the statistics of Alexander von Humboldt; and so on. All these factors certainly played a part, but there was also another major consideration for the potential shareholder in a Mexican mining company. Although it sounds perhaps trivial or even patronizing to say it, British investors believed in what we might describe as the rule of law. Like any investors then or now, they wanted to be sure that the place where they were putting their money was politically stable. It was important that the rule of law prevailed and that in the case of disputes fair treatment and justice were assured. Investing in a recently emancipated nation like Mexico could and would only be justified if guarantees of the rule of law, the rights of property, an established judicial system, and protection of individual rights were properly established.

There were two ways in which the British investors were reassured that these conditions were met in Mexico. The first was through the British press, from which they derived most of their information about the country. Mexico's early experience of independence was disappointing—the Iturbide empire and its rapid collapse were not encouraging, and it is noticeable that no British companies were formed to invest in Mexico before the end of

Costeloe

1823. By that time the image of Mexico in the British press changed radically. Now there was frequent reference to the establishment of the federal republic, the creation of an executive branch of government, a congress, a supreme court, and above all, in 1824, the publication of the Federal Constitution. These words—*constitution, congress, supreme court, presidential elections, states, legislation,* and *legislators*—all served to give the impression that now that the initial problems of the Iturbide episode had been resolved, the future of Mexico was that of a politically stable and economically prosperous nation where the rule of law would prevail. As the *Hampshire Telegraph and Sussex Chronicle* told its readers on 3 January 1825, "the Constitution of Mexico has been settled upon a footing which seems to promise durability."

Of course, British investors were not naïve, or at least some were not, and while these reassuring terms were coming out of Mexico, they wanted more tangible guarantees that their money would be safe. For these guarantees they relied on their government and the negotiations that were undertaken by British diplomats, notably Henry Ward, in arranging treaties of commerce and friendship between the two countries. Looking at the treaty that was negotiated, the terms seem to be quite unequivocal, and persons and property were given full guarantees. Article 8, for example, says: "The citizens and subjects of the contracting parties in the Territories of each other shall receive and enjoy full and perfect protection for their persons and property; and shall have free and open access to the Courts of Justice in the said countries respectively for the prosecution and defence of their just rights." Article 10 states emphatically that "no forced loans shall be levied upon them," and article 12 confirms that as long as they do not contravene the laws, "their goods and effects of whatever description shall not be liable to seizure or sequestration." Article 13 confirms that British subjects residing in Mexico "shall enjoy in their houses, persons and properties the protection of the Government."[4] Finally, as a petition by British merchants resident in Mexico City put it in 1836, "it was on the faith of that Treaty that British merchants were induced to adventure their lives and property."[5]

This treaty was concluded in December 1826, which was after the first phase of the major investment of private capital that took place. The terms of protection of persons and property that I have cited, therefore, cannot be said to have dictated the investment decisions taken by the British investors, but there is no doubt that they influenced the subsequent decisions of the various companies to proceed with more and more expenditure. The directors and managers of the companies, all based in London, repeatedly expressed their confidence that Mexico was a safe place to invest because it had created all the right institutions of government and because investors could rely on the protection of both the British and Mexican governments, as stipulated in the Treaty of Commerce and Friendship. The internal or domestic political problems that Mexico experienced after about 1825—events like the rebellion against the 1828 election result; the rise to power of Vicente Guerrero; the successful *pronunciamiento* against him by Anastasio Bustamante; the Santa Anna–led pronunciamiento of 1832, and so on—were matters of regret but of no great concern to the British companies because they were not directly affected.

Now I want to turn briefly to the situation in Mexico in 1833. Santa Anna had defeated the incumbent government by the end of 1832. Manuel Gómez Pedraza had acted as president for a couple of months until elections could take place, and they in turn had brought about the election of Santa Anna as president and

Valentín Gómez Farías as his vice president. Santa Anna chose not to take up the post in April 1833, and Gómez Farías exercised the executive power. A radical majority in Congress began to enact a series of measures of clerical and military reform. Those measures promptly provoked a reaction neatly summarized in the slogan of the time, "Religión y fueros." Both sides—the conservative, pro-clerical, pro-military versus the progressive radicals—prepared to fight for their cause. Pronunciamientos were announced in various places in May–June 1833. The one that concerns me took place on 8 June at Huejotzingo, a village or pueblo just north of the city of Puebla. The leading rebel, or senior army officer, was Mariano Arista. His demands, stated in the written or published plan of the pronunciamiento, were the protection of clerical and military privileges and that Santa Anna should be given dictatorial powers. This Arista plan echoed earlier ones, and he was almost certainly in collusion with General Gabriel Durán, who had pronounced a few days before with much the same demands. As the bizarre events of the next week or so are explained in Will Fowler's recent book on Santa Anna, only a brief summary is needed here.[6] Santa Anna left Mexico City heading south to suppress these rebellions. Having entered into talks with rebel representatives, he was allegedly arrested by them. He managed to escape and returned to Mexico City, where he issued a manifesto condemning the rebels, denying that he had any dictatorial ambitions, and promising to defeat them.[7]

Santa Anna's escape and his refusal to back the pronunciamientos left the rebels in a difficult position, especially Arista and Durán, who were still camped near Puebla. At first they led their military units in a futile attack on Puebla, but knowing that Santa Anna was coming after them, they decided to move on. At this point geography and the logistics of rebellion become significant. In the first place, we do not know how many rebels there were. Contemporaries, including Mariano Arista himself, cite various figures, at times referring to large numbers, even thousands; but it seems unlikely that there were more than a few hundred, consisting of some cavalry but mostly foot soldiers.[8] Numbers also fluctuated for various reasons, including desertion and disease. In particular, the rapid spread of a cholera epidemic decimated the rebel forces and Santa Anna's units. It may have been because of the cholera that Arista decided not to lead his men eastward to the Gulf Coast and the relative safety of Veracruz, the usual port of escape for unsuccessful rebels, or westward to the Pacific Coast. Instead, he first headed south toward Oaxaca but then, deceived by what turned out to be false reports of rebel successes in Toluca, he decided to march northward. In his account of the events Arista gives a day-by-day narrative of his movements, explaining where he led his men, where they stopped for the night, and the route they took.[9] Following a circuitous route, they went round Mexico City and headed northeast for Pachuca and the mining town of Real del Monte. Then they passed near to or through San Juan del Río and Querétaro. After that they continued north, tried and failed to enter San Luis Potosí, Arista's birthplace, and veered toward Guanajuato, which they reached at the end of July 1833.

The distance from Huejotzingo to Guanajuato is roughly 300–400 miles, but because of the twists and turns of the march, it is impossible to calculate exactly how much ground the rebels covered. What is clear from Arista's account, however, is that they experienced major difficulties. Arista and other officers had horses but most of the foot soldiers did not, and the march for them was slow and painful, especially with cholera reducing their numbers day by day. The weather was bad and there were days of "constant rain" followed by suffocating heat. They survived by living off the land, confiscating, stealing, taking whatever they needed as they progressed, but even so the men lacked uniforms, shoes, and basic equipment. Citing what he describes as "the imperious law of necessity," Arista explains that he ordered forced loans in various places as well as confiscating money wherever he found it.[10] Also, it seems that as soon as they arrived in a town or village, the first thing he did was confiscate and sell to the highest bidder the contents of local tithe barns where agricultural produce was stored. Perhaps curiously, and with an eye on the possibility of failure, detailed financial records were kept by the commissary of each military unit.[11] They noted the forced loans, the costs of pasture and fodder taken from haciendas for the horses, the produce taken from the *colecturías*—for example, twenty *cargas de frijol* (boxes of beans) that fetched sixty pesos—and there are even entries in their accounts for office costs, wages of servants, printing costs, and always "secret expenses." All the infantry received a pair of shoes, two reals a day, and four reals a month for "common expenses." The cavalry were also paid, as were the officers. In total, 229,277 pesos were raised and spent by the Arista rebels. All this apparently careful bookkeeping appears incongruous given that this was a disparate group of poorly equipped, disease-ridden soldiers fleeing to escape the rapidly approaching forces of Santa Anna. Their final destination was Guanajuato, but why Guanajuato?

This narrative brings me back to Guanajuato at the end of July 1833. Outside the city and fast approaching were Arista and his rebels. In the city were the United Mexican Mining Company and its British managers, in dispute with the Marquis de Rayas. About 81,000 pesos of the revenues of the mining operations had been placed in the state treasury. Then, on 1 August, the alcalde who had ordered the sequestration of the company's assets back in March suddenly lifted the order and instructed that the 81,000 pesos must be returned to the company offices. That was done immediately. The reason for this sudden change of mind soon became clear. The Guanajuato authorities knew of Arista's impending arrival and they also knew that the first place rebels went when they entered a town or city was the treasury. Hence they wanted no cash on deposit. Arista and his force arrived a day or so later and, finding that there was no money in the treasury, soon learned that there were at least 81,879 pesos in the mining company office. Officers and soldiers went to that office and demanded the cash. The British managers refused to hand it over, but the soldiers seized it anyway. Other rebels were stationed outside the office to make sure that if further funds were brought from the mines, they would know about it.

The seizure of the cash was not the only thing Arista did. He sent soldiers to the reduction plant or *hacienda de beneficio* where the ore removed from the mines was processed. They seized or took control of the ore and sold it in a public auction at which Arista himself was present. According to the British reports, the ore was worth 14,000 pesos but sold for just 6,000 pesos. The rebels also found 27,000 pesos' worth of silver at the company works, and they took that as well.[12]

These confiscations or seizures of cash and silver were not the only problems suffered by the United Mexican Company. There were several British managers working for the company in Guanajuato. Arista and his officers decided that their houses were the best places to live while they were in the city and they simply moved in, forcing the British owners to feed and accommodate them.

Costeloe

Military guards were stationed outside the front door of each house or, as company employee Simon McGillivray, expressed it, "I have had the additional honour of a sentry parading at my door."[13] The rebels also had a large number of horses, and these were taken to company stables, where they were fed and watered with company supplies set aside for the animals used at the mines. The British protested against all these actions but to no avail, the only response being, as one put it, "gross personal insult and occasional arrest." Finally Arista imposed forced loans on the residents, and the British had to pay. To cite again one of those affected, Captain Vetch reported that "the troops now occupying this city are plundering the Company in every possible way and to the most shameful extent."

In sum, the rebels ransacked the British, and there was nothing the British could do about it. The United Mexican Company was the main target, but there were other British companies operating in Guanajuato. One was the mining company called the Anglo-Mexican Mining Association, and it claimed to have lost between two and three thousand pesos. Among the various other British residents, a Mr. Dudley suffered losses amounting to fifteen hundred pesos.[14] They all appealed for help from the local authorities, including the Mining Tribunal, but were ignored. There were several reasons for this. According to the British managers, the local authorities, anxious to protect their own money and properties, more or less openly directed Arista and his men toward the foreigners. It was far better, they said, to take the cash from them than from their own compatriots. Second, Arista wanted to attract the support of the local population, and he realized that taking British rather than Mexican goods was a popular move. Third, when the British appealed to the courts and other authorities, they found that key figures—judges and others—had prudently left the city in anticipation of the rebels' arrival. The Mining Tribunal refused to meet on the pretext that one of its members was related to an employee of the Marquis de Rayas, with whom the company was still in dispute.

Eventually the rebellion was suppressed when Santa Anna arrived with his military units at the beginning of October. There was some military action in the first week of October and that brought about the surrender of the rebels. Arista was exiled and went to Cincinnati, funding his travels, it was said, with the cash he had seized from the United Mexican Company, although it must be added that he denied taking as much as a centavo. The British welcomed Santa Anna because they assumed that as the nation's president, he would want to ensure the rule of law. They met him on the day he entered the city, but they were rebuffed. He told them he could and would do nothing because his government could not be held responsible for the actions of rebels.

Over the next few months, from October 1833 onward, the several British managers affected by all this sent back reports to their head office in London. These make interesting reading, revealing the almost total contempt the managers had for the Mexican way of doing things. The Mexican workers were thieves, inefficient and lazy; judges and the courts were corrupt; laws and legal processes were totally ignored; influence peddling was commonplace; Mexicans were hostile to foreigners even though it was their money that was bringing employment to the mining areas. All this is well summed up in one of the managers' reports, sent from Guanajuato on 16 October 1833 as "the thievery of the operatives up to the dishonesty and in many cases the villany of the Mine Owners, countenanced and supported by the partiality of judges, the inefficiency of the laws, and in effect the total negation of justice to a foreign company, against Mexican citizens or interests."

Back in London, the United Mexican Company directors appealed to the British government for support. They demanded that diplomatic pressure be put on the government in Mexico City and that the federal government be held responsible for the actions of Arista and his rebels. They wanted the state authorities of Guanajuato to repay the money that had been taken from the British, and if they would not or could not oblige, the debt must be recognized as a federal or national debt. If the Mexicans would not cooperate, then force must be used. Force, it was said, was "the only manner in which interference with a half-civilized nation can be effective." If the Mexican government refused to respond, "then the Directors conceive that war will be inevitable, at no very distant period, or that all beneficial mercantile intercourse between this country and Mexico must cease."[15]

Although it is always difficult to draw conclusions about pronunciamientos or place them in categories, it seems we can say that this one had little or no political or ideological character unless we accept that Arista and Durán were in collusion with Santa Anna, who betrayed them. The declared aims of defending ecclesiastical and military privileges were dismissed as a pretext at the time, but Arista insists strongly in his own account that he acted precisely to defend the Church and the army. More likely, perhaps, is the traditional explanation that this was an example of ambitious military officers seeking promotion and personal profit and that they were able to attract some support from military units because they promised booty and cash to the lower and usually unpaid ranks. As always, however, we have the problem of finding evidence. Arista certainly was in contact with many people about the revolt, but he tells us himself that "I ordered that all the correspondence that could compromise the individuals we had dealings with be burned." Certainly Carlos Bustamante—not the most reliable source—was convinced that Arista's aim was personal profit.

Even if we accept this interpretation of the Arista rebellion as of little or no significance in the ideological struggles that were developing in Mexico at the time, it was nevertheless an important event for other reasons. First, in terms of Mexico's internal domestic politics, Arista justified his actions with these words: "When a society's corruption becomes extreme, in the words of one wise politician, the preservation of good laws is not enough—it is essential to employ force as the only means of reestablishing order; and this was the situation in which we found ourselves."[16] Army intervention in the civil sphere on the grounds that incumbent governments were acting unconstitutionally or that "social disintegration," to use the contemporary phrase, was threatened by a breakdown of public order, was to become common in later years. Arista himself was involved in some of these later pronunciamientos, and the most notorious general of the time, Antonio López de Santa Anna, regularly justified his rebellions as being intended "to restore public order."

Second, as noted earlier, it seems that this was the first pronunciamiento to have a direct impact on the British mining community. Previous political and military disturbances had left the miners alone, but Arista had gone to Guanajuato, presumably because he knew that there was money or booty to be had. The whole episode proved a major blow to Mexico's reputation among the British in the country and also back in the United Kingdom.[17] The British press reported the events and the diplomatic efforts to get justice for the United Mexican Company. The dispute with the Marquis de Rayas was eventually settled amicably. In a separate accord promoted by Richard Pakenham, the British minister in Mexico, the Mexican government agreed to repay the United Mexican Company 89,003 pesos compensation for the money taken by Arista and also the sums claimed by the Anglo-Mexican Company and Mr. Dudley. This final agreement for what was known as the "Guanajuato indemnity" was reached in April 1836, when Pakenham and the companies' representative, George O'Gorman, met with a representative of the Mexican government.[18] The compensation was supposed to be paid in five annual installments, and while orders were certainly given to the Mexican treasury to pay up, I have not been able to confirm that money was in fact paid. While it is always imprudent to make too many deductions from events, it may be significant that apart from the companies that were already there and committed, almost no new British investment went to Mexico for many years after 1833. Perhaps we can presume that the Arista pronunciamiento had a much greater impact on Mexico than we have hitherto appreciated.

Notes

1. Costeloe, *Bonds and Bondholders*.

2. Cockburn, *Memorials of His Time*, 432.

3. Public Record Office, Foreign Office Papers (hereafter cited as FO), FO 50/89, fols. 73–74.

4. A convenient source for the text of the treaty is Johnston, *Missions to Mexico*, 257–64.

5. FO 50/99, fol. 191.

6. Fowler, *Santa Anna of Mexico*. For another useful summary, see Samponaro, "Santa Anna and the Abortive Anti-Federalist Revolt."

7. There were strong suspicions that Santa Anna was in league with the rebels but changed his mind when he realized that there was insufficient support

for his dictatorial ambitions. See Bustamante, *Continuación del cuadro histórico*, iv, 227; González Pedrero, *País de un solo hombre*, ii, 366–92.

8. Arista's own account of the course of events during the rebellion includes various statistics of troop numbers: see Arista, *Reseña histórica*.

9. Arista, *Reseña histórica*.

10. Arista, *Reseña histórica*, 137.

11. The financial statements are included as appendices to the *Reseña histórica*.

12. Arista includes various sums that he took from the British mining companies in his financial records of the rebellion at the end of his *Reseña histórica*. The amounts do not always correspond to those given by the British managers.

13. The details of what happened in Guanajuato during the Arista occupation are all taken from a series of reports the British managers sent back to London in the weeks after the end of the occupation. These and other relevant documents are in FO 89, fols. 38–95.

14. Details from a report sent by R. Pakenham to Lord Palmerston, 21 April 1836, FO 50/99, fols. 67–69.

15. J. Easthope, Chairman of United Mexican Company, to Duke of Wellington, 14 March 1835, FO 50/96, fols. 100–104.

16. Arista, *Reseña histórica*, 68.

17. A similar incident took place in 1833 in Zacatecas, where the United Mexican Company also had its properties sequestered on the orders of a local judge, acting for the Mexican mine owners. It took years to settle the dispute: FO 50/96, fols. 114–23.

18. George O'Gorman was the brother of Charles O'Gorman, British consul in Mexico City. Later generations of the O'Gorman family in Mexico include well-known architects and historians.

Seven. The Origins of the Santiago Imán Revolt, 1838–1840: *A Reassessment*

The pro-federalist-turned-secessionist Santiago Imán *pronunciamiento* of 1838–40, which was claimed to have erupted in direct opposition to the Mexican centralist Anastasio Bustamante administration of 1837, was probably the epitome of the unstable relations that existed between Yucatán and Mexico during the early nineteenth century. While Yucatán was itself home to dozens of pronunciamientos during this period, and it also seceded from Mexico several times (1840–43, 1846, 1847–48), the Imán revolt was in fact the only popularly motivated pronunciamiento that resulted in Yucatán's complete secession from Mexico.[1] It was also the most widespread revolt in the peninsula, with the three major cities of Mérida, Campeche, and Valladolid and numerous towns across the region supporting its call for a federalist system (and if federalism was not possible, then independence). It was thus one of the most significant pronunciamientos of nineteenth-century Yucatán, and it is consequently useful to determine the motivations that inspired its support and its consequent success. In this context, I attempt to establish in this study the true origins of and the initial actors in the Imán revolt. Was there a genuine desire on General Imán's and his supporters' part to achieve federalism for Yucatán, as is believed? Or was the revolt originally sparked by more localized military concerns, and was its call for federalism thus a means of guaranteeing essential political and civilian support? In this aspect, I hope the chapter contributes in more general terms to explaining the relationship between the genuine factors (micro origins) and the larger-scale factors (macro origins) *believed* to be behind pronunciamientos in nineteenth-century Mexico.

The historiography on the origins of the Imán pronunciamiento has generally concluded that the Imán revolt arose from the Yucatecan powers' opposition to harsh administrative, political, and economic decrees emanating from the Bustamante administration.[2] In this aspect, it can be argued that the Imán revolt has been categorized as one of the many regional pronunciamientos that arose as a reaction to the oppressive Bustamante centralist government, pronunciamientos such as the 1836 revolts of Texas and Sonora; the 1837 revolts of San Luis Potosí, Michoacán, and Zacatecas; and the 1838 revolts of Tampico and Aguascalientes, to name but a few. While this is indeed true to an extent, I propose that the Imán pronunciamiento initially arose because of much more intimate (and even personal) concerns within the Yucatecan military. Eric Van Young has proposed the theory that regional (and even national in some cases) conflict in nineteenth-century Mexico was originally sparked by and rooted in more *local* than large-scale concerns.[3] Van Young thus believes that in order to comprehend the genuine origins of some of the major revolts of nineteenth-century Mexico, one must take into account the role of the deeply intimate factors in starting these revolts; that is, the "hyper-localist" atmosphere (involving local conflict, attitudes, and actors).[4] This chapter first synthesizes the general factors interpreted by historians to be the origins of the Imán revolt. The apparently more genuine and concrete origins of the pronunciamiento (which become apparent when one analyzes the local historical context and the actual text of the pronunciamiento), are then discussed. In conclusion, using this pronunciamiento as an example, an attempt is made to analyze the typology of motivating factors behind pronunciamientos in nineteenth-century Mexico.

First it is necessary to understand the dynamic of relations between Mexico and Yucatán during the early nineteenth century in order to grasp the macro factors behind the Imán revolt. The Mexican-Yucatecan relationship was weak throughout the colonial era and would continue to fluctuate during post-independence years, and this situation was due to generally opposing stances. Yucatán's elites, its two main political parties (the Campeche-based Liga and the Mérida-based Camarilla parties), and its business class all possessed a *generally* defensive and pro-autonomous attitude, which clashed with Mexico's covetous tendency toward the peninsula (see chapter 3). This overarching situation was due to the peninsula's status as a peripheral state. A substantially "marginal" state, to use Justo Sierra's phraseology, the region was situated 1,150 kilometers from Mexico City, separated from it by geography and practically nonexistent communication.[5] This meant not only that it was far removed from significant movements experienced by "mainland" Mexico (such as the War of Independence) but also that distance from Mexico's authority gave Yucatán's leaders a chance to "pioneer."[6] Situated on the southern tip of Mexico with access to the sea, Yucatán also had practically independent trade relations with Cuba, Belize, and Jamaica.[7] Thus at the time of independence Yucatán's holders of power had long been accustomed to an autonomous form of government policy and economic activity and had no interest in letting a strange capital situated more than 1,000 kilometers away dictate its internal policies and destroy its self-proclaimed "love of freedom."[8] Indeed, as early as 1822 Yucatán announced that the centralist Agustín de Iturbide empire would be recognized only "if it guaranteed respect to the civil liberties established in the Spanish Constitution."[9] Subsequently the most principal condition (as ordered by Yucatán's governing *junta* on 7 June 1823) under which Yucatecan deputies were allowed join the nascent Mexican Republic was: "First, that the union of Yucatán will take place in a federal republic, and not in any other form: and therefore, Yucatán will possess the right to form its own Constitution and establish laws which it believes are conducive to its happiness."[10] Thus Yucatán's congress officially recognized Mexico's 1824 federalist Constitution on 23 April 1825.[11]

A decade of republicanism under a federalist Constitution had not been a positive experience in Mexico. With the exception of Guadalupe Victoria's, no presidency had lasted its full term. The economy was weak, with severe recession and prominent poverty. The Mexican political class and the *hombres de bien* (men of the higher classes, especially those who owned property or had an income exceeding a thousand pesos per annum) began to believe that certain states were now enjoying an excessive amount of "regionalism."[12] In 1834 Texas, Zacatecas, and Yucatán—without the permission of the government—reinstated the legislatures that had been abolished in 1832 under the Anastasio Bustamante administration.[13] The blame was now placed on the 1824 Federal Constitution for causing poverty, instability, liberalism, and excessive regionalism. The Constitution was seen as overly empowering the legislature, weakening the center with its federalist structure, and thus encouraging regional political instability.[14] A centralist constitution seemed to be the solution to order.

The centralist constitution known as the Siete Leyes (Seven

Laws) was thus implemented on 29 December 1836 under the presidency of Anastasio Bustamante (who held office from 1837). Political power was now restricted to the higher social classes, in terms of both suffrage and access to office.[15] More important, the centralist administration was determined to reign in any states that may have been enjoying an excessive measure of autonomy, with Yucatán being one of those. The measures taken by the centralist government in 1836–37 would not only be heavily denounced in the Imán pronunciamiento but would also most significantly be used by the Yucatecan congress and its governor throughout 1840–42 to justify the Imán revolt after its success. It is thus understandable that historians would believe these macro factors to be the sole and genuine motivations behind this pronunciamiento of 1838.

There are several reasons to believe that the Imán pronunciamiento was a simple manifestation of regional opposition to centralism. First, the pronunciamiento text contains heavy criticism of the Bustamante government and its actions as well as a call for the reestablishment of a federalist system. It is important to recall that the centralist system of 1836 was completely in contradiction to the conditions under which those in power in Yucatán had agreed to join Mexico in the first place; thus the importance of a federalist constitution in their eyes cannot be underestimated. The pronunciamiento therefore condemned "the countless evils that have been afflicted upon the peoples of this state, whose misery and poverty have reached the extreme, due to the continuous and multiple demands which the present administration has afflicted on the landowners and all the other classes."[16]

Furthermore, in its very first article, the pronunciamiento declared "the reestablishment of the Constitution of the Free State of

Yucatán, sanctioned and adopted in 1824."[17] This reason was most significantly reinforced in October 1841 by the Yucatecan congress, which stated that the Imán revolt occurred because "the 1824 Constitution . . . was scandalously destroyed by the 1836 Congress."[18] The pronunciamiento's articles 2 and 3 further declared the temporary institution of Yucatán's own congress, governor, and senators until new elections had occurred. This indeed heavily implies that the pronunciamiento's primary aim was to check the centralist zeal of the Bustamante administration and allow Yucatecans to regain the level of autonomy they had enjoyed under the federalist system. As Will Fowler has highlighted, the success of the 1823 Plan of Casa Mata (a pronunciamiento that arose in opposition to the centralist Iturbide empire and subsequently forced the emperor's abdication) demonstrated just how effective a method the pronunciamiento was with regard to serving the demands of the regions. Indeed, Fowler suggests that an analysis of the general origins of pronunciamientos in independent Mexico implies that the pronunciamiento "became first and foremost a regionally led practice" (see introduction).

The Imán pronunciamiento can also be interpreted as a regional reaction as its supporters believed themselves to be representing, above all, the general will of a people who were clearly in opposition to the centralist Bustamante administration. Josefina Vázquez and François-Xavier Guerra have rightly stated that one of the key elements distinguishing the pronunciamiento from a standard coup d'état was the idea that it looked to "legitimize" its existence because it justly represented public opinion.[19] The Imán pronunciamiento text stressed that "many citizens from different classes proposed their opinions" with regard to the demands outlined.[20] In this respect the pronunciamiento can be seen as arising from the dissatisfaction of all classes of Yucatecan society and thus representing the view that Yucatecans believed they had every right to get rid of a system not beneficial to them. Interestingly, the pronunciamiento claimed to be serving the federal interests not only of Yucatán but of other dissenting departments. It declared that its supporters were "protecting the opinion of their compatriots and this, in keeping with what has been explained in several ways in the different states in the Republic, is in favor of the reestablishment of the Federal system."[21] As Fowler, Guerra, and Alfonso Noriega have correctly pointed out, by the mid-nineteenth century no post-independent Mexican government had ever been established long enough for Mexican citizens to respect the institution of the state as the rightful and legitimate representation of the nation.[22] Once it was proven that the will of the people could successfully overpower a political institution or constitution (as in 1821), this was to remain the pattern for most of the nineteenth century. The Imán pronunciamiento can thus be interpreted as a regional force challenging the centralist government.

This pronunciamiento can be interpreted as a large-scale regional reaction, as its stated purpose was to negotiate "legitimately" with the center for the reestablishment of the federalist system (note that the pronunciamiento, which was seconded in Mérida on 18 February 1840, included the condition of separation from Mexico *unless* a federalist constitution was restored).[23] Indeed, the Imán pronunciamiento text would declare that one of the principal purposes of its existence was to ensure the prevention of an "illegitimate" revolt; that is, "to avoid the scandalous disorder that was threatening to erupt in all branches of society . . . [and] to put the people at ease and silence the general clamor."[24]

It is noteworthy that this element of outside forces "legitimately" negotiating with the established central authority to effect political change was one of the distinguishing features of the pronunciamiento. From the very first successful pronunciamiento in Spain (that of Rafael de Riego in 1820, challenging the royal decree that Spanish troops be sent to Latin America to combat the Wars of Independence), this practice of negotiation was established. The process was repeated in Mexico's first pronunciamientos—Agustín de Iturbide's 1821 Plan of Iguala (which declared Mexico's independence; see chapters 1 and 2), and the 1823 Plan of Casa Mata—and was then recognized as an official practice by hundreds of subsequent *pronunciados.* Guerra, Fowler, and Vázquez thus all agree that the pronunciamiento gradually became the norm in seeking local and national political change through negotiation.

However, it is significant to note, then, that in 1838 the Imán pronunciamiento was seen as the primary method of negotiation not only because of its established commonality but also because in 1836 (as in 1821), suffrage was restricted to the higher political class, and thus it was believed that the most effective way to make one's voice heard legitimately—without resorting to an outright revolt—was through a pronunciamiento. This applied especially to the military, who, because of their moderate salaries, were not recognized as "citizens" and thus were not eligible to vote in elections. For them the pronunciamiento was therefore a way of extra-constitutionally, yet legitimately, negotiating political change.

Nevertheless, a more intimate examination of the demands outlined in the Imán pronunciamiento text and a clearer picture of the concrete context in which the event arose reveal that the actual origins of the pronunciamiento were initially more distinct and localized than historians have claimed. Indeed, the picture that emerges from the following examination is clearly different from what has previously been depicted concerning the origins of the Imán pronunciamiento, with much more specific aims and actors than was formerly believed.

The most significant and powerful factor provoking the Imán revolt was undoubtedly Yucatecan military opposition to the central decree that they go to far-away Texas to battle the secessionist war there (approximately twenty-five hundred Yucatecan troops were sent to Texas in 1836). It should be noted that Yucatecan troops were not formally trained or armed like other Mexican battalions. The centrally installed General Commander Joaquín Rivas Zayas admitted that the Yucatecan troops were mainly made up of aged and inexperienced men, and a decision to send them to Texas was nonsensical: "The battalions of this class are made up of craftsmen and farm workers, generally married and established in their respective villages, and are only called upon in extraordinary circumstances."[25] These men were now violently separated from their families, society, and even language (many of them spoke Maya), to go to war.

Furthermore, it is of extreme significance that the military *sorteo* (lottery-style recruitment) for Texas-bound troops would most heavily affect the areas where the Imán revolt would eventually arise—the regions of Espita, Izamal, and Tizimín, where the districts of the First and Third Active Battalions were situated. The plans for revolt in 1838 would thus actually begin with these resentful battalions destined for Texas. Santiago Imán, who was then captain of the Third Active Battalion of Tizimín, would be the instigator. Imán was a fairly wealthy landowner and merchant from Tizimín and was heavily preoccupied about the loss of his workforce, as his employees were among those targeted for enlistment for Texas. Of equal significance was the fact that he was now captain of a regiment destined for Texas. His previously respected military position (pre-1836) now became unpopular, as he had the problematic responsibility of gathering unwilling troops for battle against the northern state. These factors, undoubtedly combined with a *personal* lack of desire to go to Texas, spurred Imán's decision to revolt against the Bustamante government.

The most striking element of the Imán pronunciamiento text is therefore the denouncing of the recruitment of troops bound for Texas (and its opposition to the war itself), condemning "the dreadful decree of *sorteo* with which the government has dared to insult the dignity of the men in a free *pueblo*" and claiming that "the deportation of the sons of this Peninsula to support . . . a ruinous war for the Republic must come to an end."[26] Furthermore, article 9 of the pronunciamiento specifically declared the dissolution of the Third Active Battalion, "whose organization and existence have been until now been so destructive, undiplomatic and ruinous to the districts of Izamal, Valladolid and Tizimín."[27]

In this context, therefore, it is imperative to emphasize that the pronunciamiento, not only in Yucatán but in all of nineteenth-century Mexico, was seen above all as a military exercise. According to Vázquez, almost every single pronunciamiento was carried out by military figures claiming to seek political change.[28] In Guerra's view this applied to them all.[29] A leading figure of the military would usually gain support from other members of his forces through promises of pay rises or promotions.[30] Imán had more than a decade of military experience; he was practiced in the art of recruitment.[31] This experience of bribery would be essential when he decided to obtain troops for his pronunciamiento (indeed, Imán's principal pronunciamiento officers, Antonio Trujeque, José Cosgaya, José Dolores Cetina, Pastor Gamboa, and Vito Pacheco, would all be permitted to file sizable land claims in 1840).[32] The Imán pronunciamiento is therefore seen as arising *initially* from purely military dissent. This brings us back to the original question: *whose* crisis or conflict exactly was it? It was the military's, and on an even more personal level, Santiago Imán's. In this regard, it is interesting to note the striking parallel between Imán's pronunciamiento and the very first successful pronunciamiento as we know it: that of General Rafael de Riego in Spain in 1820. Riego's pronunciamiento initially arose because he and other members of the Spanish military did not want to go to Latin America to fight in the Wars of Independence. The pronunciamiento, however, ended up proclaiming the reestablishment of the Constitution of Cádiz. Like Riego's pronunciamiento, dissent in Yucatán began with troops unwilling to migrate to distant lands to fight battles but would end up with an attempt to negotiate for federalism. We now need to examine how this development took place in order to realize what other motivations and actors were *subsequently* incorporated into this pronunciamiento.

The supposition that the origins of this pronunciamiento resided within the military underscores that it had a dual purpose, gradually encompassing broader and more general political concerns into the revolt. Although there was some desire on the part of Imán and his supporters to achieve the "greater good" of federalism for the region, the inclusion of civilian demands in the pronunciamiento was undoubtedly more important as a means of broadening the necessary core and gaining essential political and financial support. It is hardly likely that powerful political and financial players would have assisted in a pronunciamiento strictly geared toward ending military enlistment to go to Texas. Thus, as was the case in the standard initial conspiratorial process of a pronunciamiento, military officers formed alliances with key civilian actors, including landowners, businessmen, and powerful political figures, whose backing would be useful to the officers in terms of sponsorship, protection, and support.[33] These actors in turn would receive rewards or incentives for their support; rewards that at the very least undoubtedly entailed inclusion of civilian demands in the pronunciamiento text. It is thus worth examining in more detail which sectors of society supported Imán in order to understand more fully the civilian demands included in his pronunciamiento.

In Yucatán the *criollo* (creole) civilian support would be drawn from two main sectors of society: the political class and the business/landowning class. The federalist party stationed in the capital of Mérida would play a crucial role during the initial months of planning for Imán's revolt. Indeed, in the late months of 1836 Imán's early conspiratorial pronunciamiento plans were discovered by the centralist authorities, and he was imprisoned in Izamal; nevertheless, he was out nine months later in the custody of an herb doctor, pleading hemorrhoids.[34] Throughout 1837 Imán broadened his range of allies and followers, liaising extensively with prominent members of the federal party in order to gain support, resources, and protection (he is referred to in the history chronicles of Yucatán as "the *caudillo* of the federalists").[35] There was reason for discontent among these members of the civilian population. The power of the centrally appointed governor (Pedro Marcial Guerra) and officials occupying roles in Congress, the tax collection offices, and the treasury threatened the traditional strongholds of Yucatecan power.[36] In exchange for support from the political class, the pronunciamiento would thus include specific political demands in its text, the most prominent being the all-important call for federalism. Indeed, the pronunciamiento ordered the removal of all centrally appointed officials, the reestablishment of "all authorities that were in power as of January 1834," and the institution of a temporary governing junta composed of the same men who had lent their support and aid to Imán: "five individuals; Lic. D. Pablo Castellanos, D. Agustín Acereto, D. Miguel Cámara Curas, D. Buenaventura Pérez and D. José Antonio García."[37] These very individuals signed the pronunciamiento text. Thus, in the words of Van Young, "from this point of view, at least some political crises begin to look invented, almost conspiratorial," as it is possible that the "crisis" of federalism was added to the pronunciamiento cause in order to broaden its appeal to encompass political causes as well.[38]

The business and landowning sector would also have an important role in supporting the pronunciamiento. The centralist government had imposed a series of harmful economic decrees on Yucatán; on 11 March 1837 the Mexican administration abolished Yucatan's privilege of paying only three-fifths of the standard Mexican import duties.[39] Tariff rates were raised on many imported products, such as fruits, clothing materials, medicine, furniture, and jewelry (which encouraged flourishing contraband trade practices with Belize, Cuba, and Jamaica).[40] The government also decreed the removal of the one-fifth reduction on import duties in the Campechean port.[41] Moreover, it was ordered that 50 percent of departmental income go toward national spending and making the situation worse was that the increased contributions were meant to raise funds for the war against Texas).[42] Finally, there was the administration's demand that 62 percent of profits from Yucatán's ports be given to maintain state finances.[43] The Yucatecan business and landowning sectors' voices were thus also heard in the pronunciamiento, as the text stated that their "poverty was to the extreme, due to the continuous and multiple demands which the present administration has afflicted upon the landowners and all other classes."[44]

It is imperative to examine the largely ignored (and ironically perhaps the most significant) sector of civilian aid in the Imán revolt: the Maya. This is important not only because their participation was a key factor in the pronunciamiento's success but because their support would also influence the demands in the pronunciamiento text. In the initial attempts of Imán's revolt, from 5 May 1839 to 12 December 1839, the centralist forces commanded by General Rivas Zayas defeated Imán's considerably weaker forces in Espita, Chancenote, San Fernando Aké, and finally Tizimín.[45] While Imán gained extra troops when the members of a Yucatecan battalion destined for Texas forced the captain of their ship to return them to Yucatán, this was still insufficient—it was time to turn to the Maya for extra support. The decision made sense. The Maya, formerly forbidden to own arms, now had in their possession shotguns and machetes, as they had recently been forced to enlist in units destined for Texas; and they numbered in the thousands.[46] In Chemax, Imán began to mobilize Maya troops through bribery: if he won his revolt with their support, he would eliminate their most dreaded tax—the obvention. The response was astounding. Thousands of Maya took up arms with Imán. Only after gaining this Mayan support did Imán manage to defeat the centralist forces and finally claim victory in Valladolid on 11 February 1840, issuing his pronunciamiento the very next day. Article 10 declared "the termination of the obvention contributed to the parish priests under the hateful classifications which up to now [the Maya] have been designated."[47]

Finally, there is the distinct probability that the Imán pronunciamiento arose from a personal desire for aggrandizement by Santiago Imán. As Fowler points out in the introduction to this volume, Agustín Iturbide had demonstrated in his 1821 Plan of Iguala that not only could a pronunciamiento serve the interests of a state—it could also change a "disgruntled and demoted colonel" to ruler of the Mexican Empire. Thus, combined with the pride of heading a movement that could serve your interests, benefit your homeland, and make you popular and respected for your success, there was also the possibility that the pronunciamiento could result in improvement in political as well as military stature. This, according to Fowler, made the pronunciamiento "an irresistible and addictive practice" for military officers who had grand ideas of advancement.[48] In support of this theory, the Imán pronunciamiento would declare in article 7 that Santiago Imán would be entrusted with the title of General Commander of the Liberating Army, with article 11 stating that the president of the junta would pledge obedience to the Constitution and laws that would be controlled by Imán.

One striking element that deserves mention is the time frame in which Imán issued his pronunciamiento text. Certain pronunciamiento critics such as Guerra and Vázquez maintain that in the established process of a pronunciamiento, the text is issued *before* the mobilization of the participants in the revolt. This initial circulation and official publication of dissent is in their view one of the key defining elements of a pronunciamiento. According to Guerra, the first step in a pronunciamiento is "a programmatic declaration of principles and proposals," which is then followed by an appeal to supporters, a propaganda campaign, and finally the revolt itself.[49] However, the Imán pronunciamiento followed an almost opposite route—Imán and his supporters had been in a state of revolt since 5 May 1839 without any sign of a text. It was not until he defeated the centralist troops on 12 February 1840 that a text was issued, the excuse being "that the distressing circumstances . . . have not allowed it until now," those distressing circumstances meaning Imán's failure to win a single engagement until then.[50] The fact that Imán issued his text *after* such a long period of revolt implies that his was indeed initially a simple revolt, only later involving the issuing of a text to legitimize its existence and convert it into a pronunciamiento.

However, looking back at the very first successful pronunciamiento known in history, this argument may not seem as valid. General Rafael de Riego was the first person ever to refer to his 1821 revolt as a pronunciamiento, as he believed it was more a method of representing the will of a people attempting to negotiate forcefully with the authorities in power than a simple coup d'état. But as Fowler points out, although Riego issued two *proclamas* (official announcements), "he did not produce a definitive single *pronunciamiento* text."[51] Therefore, if this is considered the first pronunciamiento, it seems questionable to argue that lack of a pronunciamiento text prevents the Imán revolt being called a pronunciamiento. What seems to be more significant is the effort at representing the desires of the people and at negotiation with the established authorities. This would imply that the Imán revolt was indeed a pronunciamiento all along.

It is thus evident that while sweeping reforms made by the Bustamante administration did engender significant resentment in the Yucatán Peninsula, the fact remains that the initial origins of the Santiago Imán pronunciamiento resided in a relatively small faction for a very specific reason: Imán and his troops were extremely

Ali

reluctant to go to Texas, and they decided to do something about it. The recruitment of civilian support—while possibly an attempt to incorporate the federalist element into the pronunciamiento— was more likely a mechanism to guarantee protection, resources, and support. This would explain the many standpoints that come together in the pronunciamiento text. The text is pervaded with the declarations of an indignant military but includes elements representing dissenting federalists, businessmen, and Maya. The micro factor of the military, however, is essential if one wants to understand either this pronunciamiento or the majority of others in nineteenth-century Mexico. An intimate examination of the origins of the major pronunciamientos can not only determine the real local factors that sparked these revolts but can also aid one in understanding how and why broader sectors of society were incorporated in this practice. This prevents one from generalizing the pronunciamiento phenomenon as simply a regional reaction to a federalist/centralist government and instead places the pronunciamiento into a more realistic context: with real people, having real (even personal) problems, and choosing this means as the avenue for addressing their problems.

Notes

1. Zuleta Miranda, "El federalismo en Yucatán," 44.

2. The Yucatecan Creole historians' account of this topic (Serapio Baqueiro, Joaquín Baranda, and Eligio Ancona) are significantly biased against the centralist government and tend to denounce heavily the Bustamante administration's political and economic actions, tallying these as the reasons behind the pronunciamiento of 1838. Terry Rugeley has concentrated briefly on the origins of this revolt with more emphasis on the consequences of this pronunciamiento concerning the bringing about of the 1847 Caste War. Nelson Reed mentions the revolt in his work and also concentrates on the role it played in eventually provoking the Caste War.

3. Van Young, "Of Tempests and Teapots," 31.

4. Van Young, "Of Tempests and Teapots," 27.

5. Costeloe, *The Central Republic*, 243; Fowler, *Mexico in the Age of Proposals*, 29.

6. Cline, "Regionalism and Society in Yucatan," 1.

7. Rugeley, *Yucatán's Maya Peasantry*, xii.

8. Méndez, *Representación que el gobernador de Yucatán*, 3.

9. Anna, *El imperio de Iturbide*, 57.

10. Mena Brito, *Reestructuración histórica de Yucatán*, 1:23.

11. Rugeley, *Yucatán's Maya Peasantry*, 62; Fowler, *Santa Anna of Mexico*, 86; Williams, "Secessionist Diplomacy," 132.

12. Costeloe, *The Central Republic*, 17–18.

13. Fowler, *Mexico in the Age of Proposals*, 55; Costeloe, *The Central Republic*, 37.

14. Costeloe, *The Central Republic*, 22.

15. Costeloe, *The Central Republic*, 73.

16. Baqueiro, *Ensayo histórico*, 1:487.

17. Baqueiro, *Ensayo histórico*, 1:488.

18. Augusta cámara de diputados, *Dictamen de la comisión especial . . . de 1 de octubre 1841*.

19. Vázquez, "El modelo de pronunciamiento mexicano," 31; Guerra, "El pronunciamiento en México," 21.

20. Baqueiro, *Ensayo histórico*, 1:488.

21. Baqueiro, *Ensayo histórico*, 1:487.

22. Fowler, introduction, this volume, xxiv–xxv; Guerra, "El pronunciamiento en México," 21; Noriega, *El pensamiento conservador*, 1:153.

23. Baqueiro, *Ensayo histórico*, 1:493.

24. Baqueiro, *Ensayo histórico*, 1:487.

25. Acereto, *Evolución histórica*, 70.

26. Baqueiro, *Ensayo histórico*, 1:490.

27. Baqueiro, *Ensayo histórico*, 1:489.

28. Vázquez, "Political Plans and Collaboration," 20. It should be noted that Will Fowler debates this idea in his works on pronunciamientos.

29. Guerra, "El pronunciamiento en México," 17.

30. See introduction.

31. Reed, *The Caste War of Yucatán*, 30; Rugeley, *Yucatán's Maya Peasantry*, 118.

32. Rugeley, *Yucatán's Maya Peasantry*, 125.

33. See introduction.

34. Rugeley, *Yucatán's Maya Peasantry*, 118.

35. Baranda, *Recordaciones históricas*, 331.

36. Campos García, *De provincia a estado*, 314.

37. Baqueiro, *Ensayo histórico*, 1:488.

38. Van Young "Of Tempests and Teapots," 49.

39. http://www.campeche.gob.mx/Campeche/Estado/Historia/cap5siglo19e.php; Suárez Molina, *La evolución económica de Yucatán*, 1:90.

40. Suárez Molina, *La evolución económica de Yucatán*, 1:96; http://lyncis.dgsca.unam.mx/harvest/cgi-bin/DUBLANYLOZANO/muestraXML.cgi?var1=3-1835.xml&var2=3; Acereto, *Evolución histórica*, 61.

41. Acereto, *Evolución histórica*, 70.

42. Campos García, *De provincia a estado*, 114; http://lyncis.dgsca.unam.mx/harvest/cgi-bin/DUBLANYLOZANO/muestraXML.cgi?var1=3-1678.xml&var2=3; Acereto, *Evolución histórica*, 60.

43. Baranda, *Recordaciones históricas*, 328.

44. Baqueiro, *Ensayo histórico*, 1:487.

45. Arrangoíz y Berzabal, *México desde 1808 hasta 1867*, 376–77; Rugeley, *Yucatán's Maya Peasantry*, 119.

46. Reed, *The Caste War of Yucatán*, 30.

47. Baqueiro, *Ensayo histórico*, 1:489.

48. See introduction.

49. Guerra, "El pronunciamiento en México," 15; Vázquez, "Political Plans and Collaboration," 20.

50. Baqueiro, *Ensayo histórico*, 1:487.

51. See introduction.

Eight. A Reluctant Advocate: *Mariano Otero and the Revolución de Jalisco*

As the ideological standard bearer of the *moderado* or moderate movement, Mariano Otero was firmly opposed to the practice of *pronunciamientos*. He was vehemently opposed to military interference and any dominant role by the army in politics, although he did make one important exception. Originally from Jalisco, he had graduated as a lawyer in 1835. He became known to the politicians of Mexico City only after giving the 16 September 1841 Independence Day speech in Guadalajara, news of which traveled as far as the capital, where it was published in *El Siglo XIX* newspaper in October of that year. The speech is significant because it outlines Otero's thoughts on many of the issues that he would later go on to explore in his works and which were to define his ideology and political position. After his arrival in the city he was fully absorbed into its political life and took his seat in the 1842 Constituent Congress, which was debating the new constitution. His *Ensayo sobre el verdadero estado de la cuestión social y política que se agita en la República Mexicana,* published in the same year, laid out the theoretical parameters of the political beliefs of the moderate faction, most particularly that revolution only ever bred counterrevolution and therefore *pronunciamientos* could never lead to long-term productive change. From this stemmed the moderado belief that all reform needed to be gradual in order to achieve and maintain its goals.

Yet his *Ensayo* was published in defense of what he himself described as the "Revolución de Jalisco," a term he used to encompass Mariano Paredes y Arrillaga's Plan of Jalisco (8 August), Gabriel Valencia's Plan of La Ciudadela (4 September), and Antonio López de Santa Anna's Plan of Perote (9 September), all issued in 1841 and redefined by Michael P. Costeloe as the Triangular Revolt.[1] It is this nexus of pronunciamientos, *actas*, and *planes* that Otero referred to as the Revolución de Jalisco in his 1842 *Ensayo*. In Otero's own words, the *Ensayo* was written as a defense of the Jalisco movement. However, it is much more than that. The *Ensayo* sought to explain the causes of the 1841 revolt and, in doing so, to present the reader with an overview of the state of the Mexican nation from independence up to the date of its publication.

The origins of the revolution that Otero was writing about can be traced back to the unrest that had been widespread since the beginning of 1841, with minor disturbances being recorded in the first few months in Chiapas, Orizaba, Durango, and San Luis Potosí, among others.[2] This unrest led to rumors circulating of a potential revolution being plotted in Jalisco and Veracruz.[3] Santa Anna emphasized these in writing to the government in July 1841 to draw its attention to the demands of the merchants of Veracruz. They were unhappy with the *derecho de consumo*, a 15 percent import tax introduced in 1839, which had raised the overall taxation on imported goods to 49.5 percent, and announced their intention to stop levying it.[4]

Shortly after Santa Anna's contact with the central government, news began to arrive from Jalisco, where the state government was hinting at rising unrest that it too attributed to the high level of taxation, further suggesting that it was a result of the central government's reluctance to address it.[5]

By 8 August rumors had become fact. Mariano Paredes y Arrillaga staged a *pronunciamiento* in Guadalajara and issued his Manifiesto y Plan de Jalisco, known as *el plan mercantil*, on the basis of its origin being the call by both overseas and Mexican merchants and traders for the repeal of the taxation on foreign goods. The demands of the Plan moved beyond insistence on changes in the rates of taxation; it sought the removal of General Anastasio Bustamante from power, his substitution by an interim president to be named by the Supremo Poder Conservador, and called for the election of a new Constituent Congress.[6] The Supremo Poder Conservador had been created by the Siete Leyes of 1836, which came to be known as the centralist constitution and was designed to maintain those laws.[7] The Plan itself moved away from a mere representation of the interests of one group, the merchants, and proclaimed itself as representative of the will of the nation. "The entire nation," "men from all parties," and "save the country" are all expressions used in the Plan to ensure that it was seen not as a move to benefit a specific group but as a generalized cry for help stemming from all sectors, unhappy with Bustamante's government.[8]

Bustamante's government had been under attack for some time prior to the Plan of Jalisco, and a number of these issues are listed in the text of the Plan. Texas was no closer to being reconquered than it had been in 1836, when Bustamante came to power in 1837 with the promise of an immediate focus on this issue; few of the reforms promised by the ministers when they took power had ever materialized, and those that did had no visible effects; and revolts in 1840 in Yucatán and in Tabasco further sullied the government's reputation. Moreover, the floundering state of the national economy forced the government to take further loans from national sources and from their allies, and its inability to repay any of these led to strains in foreign relations with Britain and France. Increased taxation was the only other source of revenue for the government, the implementation of which alienated many of its supporters, especially since even these taxes were insufficient to cover the necessities of the government.[9] Taxation, more specifically a call for the repeal of the derecho de consumo, was the main rallying cry in garnering support for the Plan of Jalisco.

On 4 September Valencia pronounced in the Ciudadela garrison in Mexico City, calling for an interim president and the convocation of a new Constituent Congress, and as such, he was seen to be publicly backing Paredes's Plan of Jalisco. Once the pronunciamiento had been established as a real force strong enough to succeed further, more *planes* emerged seconding the revolution that had begun in Jalisco. Zacatecas followed suit on 5 September and Jerez on 7 September. Two days later, on 9 September, Santa Anna published his Manifiesto y Plan de Perote, dropping all pretence of neutrality and mediation and demanding that Bustamante step down.[10] The pronunciamiento had succeeded. The three generals, Santa Anna, Valencia, and Paredes, reached an agreement that produced the Bases de Tacubaya, a thirteen-point plan that included calling for a new congress and an interim president. With the signing of these Bases by the three generals, Bustamante was ousted from power and Santa Anna was sworn in as the interim president.

Otero shied away from any kind of chronological narration of events. Nor was he writing, like so many of his contemporaries did, a history of what had occurred in some specific period during the twenty years following independence. He was analyzing what could perhaps be described as a social history of these decades. Otero used the *Ensayo* to draw the reader's attention to the origins of the 1841 pronunciamientos and divided them into two categories: persistent and immediate.

He gave little detail on the immediate, short-term factors that led to the revolt, mentioning almost in passing the unrest and combination of factors that led to Bustamante's fall from power and providing only a brief outline of the events. He was concerned with the persistent causes, and he moves beyond the immediate causes in order to ascertain and present the importance of "la cuestión social."[11]

This "social question" was far more than just the current state of affairs in Mexico in 1842 and far more than the buildup to the 1841 pronunciamientos. It was the underlying social conditions, Otero argued, that had caused all instability in Mexico since independence; this was the real origin of all pronunciamientos, revolts, and constitutional shortcomings. This is why Otero argued that the Revolución de Jalisco was more than a reaction to the discontent felt at that particular time, 1841; or against that particular government, headed by Bustamante; or addressing one particular grievance, the repeal of the derecho de consumo. It was a general discontent that ran more deeply and had its roots firmly planted in the nation's history.

Therefore from Otero's point of view the revolution combined two objectives or goals: to remove the current ineffective government from power, and to allow the nation to decide. The latter involved examining the persistent causes and the need to establish institutions, laws, and individuals so as to remove the underlying causes of the revolution.[12] Otero argued that the first of these objectives was achieved by the Bases de Tacubaya. At the time of publication the second objective had not been met, and therefore the Revolución de Jalisco was not yet over. If it had merely ended with the signing of the Bases, it would have been like any other pronunciamiento, ceasing when only the immediate causes of unrest had been removed. Otero believed that the Revolución was still under way and that the Congress and the nation were facing the momentous task of deciding on the best course for the future. Consequently Otero used his *Ensayo* to explore the options available to the nation readying itself to decide on a new constitution and the best forms of government and legislation to lead it into the next phase and finally conclude the Revolución de Jalisco. The persistent causes of unrest would have been addressed, and that "fatal mania for revolutions" would be ended once and for all.

Otero identified these persistent causes as being embodied in certain specific problems relating to public wealth, the deplorable state of the country's bureaucracy, and the appalling conditions in agriculture, industry, transport, communications, mining, and commerce. In addition he drew attention to the lamentable state of the distribution of property in Mexico.

These were some of the problems underlying the main causes of the discontent that reigned in Mexico at the time of Otero's analysis in his *Ensayo* and that he felt were the real origins of the 1841 revolts and, indeed, of all pronunciamientos. By analyzing the *cuestión social*, therefore, one would be better able to understand the causes of the 1841 movement and thus to expose the needs and their potential solutions so that the revolution would be successful.

His analysis of the causes of the pronunciamientos and of the general instability Mexico had been experiencing during the twenty years since independence was followed by a presentation of the needs of the country, and it is here that his moderate beliefs become evident. Otero strongly believed that the first and foremost necessity of any country was a strong constitution, which would become unchallengeable. From this would emerge a firm government whose main task was to protect the individual's rights while remaining non-interventionist to the highest possible degree. This would be supported by legislation and an independent judiciary.

The rights of the individual, as described by Otero in the *Ensayo*, were the right to ownership of property, the right to security, freedom of expression, and equality before the law. Otero shared many radical views on reform, although he disagreed with the means of achieving this; he called for moderation and criticized previous administrations for their abrupt radical reforms that led to an instant backlash from opposing parties. He was totally against Church intervention in matters of government and repeatedly called for a separation of Church and state, while at the same time emphasizing its positive role as a social institution.

However, it is Otero's views on the army that are illuminating when contrasted with his defense of the 1841 Revolución de Jalisco. Although the Revolución was seen as a plan that set out to protect the interests of the merchants, it is essential to note that it would have been impossible without the support and initial impetus of the army. Furthermore, it was military support from all points of the nation—Mariano Arista in the north, Juan Álvarez and Nicolás Bravo in the south, Paredes in the west, Santa Anna in the east, and Valencia in Mexico City—that gave the illusion of an entire nation's support for the Plan.[13] As with a number of the pronunciamientos in nineteenth-century Mexico, those in the summer of

1841 were reflections of a practice that sought to attack the constitutional order while at the same time maintaining that they were merely fulfilling the will of the nation and enhancing their image as the "ultimate arbiter of the national will."[14]

The movement in Jalisco was portrayed as a reaction to the failures and shortcomings of the Bustamante government and to the state of affairs in Mexico in 1842. It was not considered as a move initiated by Paredes and the garrison in Guadalajara. The army was intent, therefore, on portraying itself as merely the tool of the national will, thus avoiding the common accusation that it was looking only for self-benefit and internal promotions. In addition, to achieve success it was necessary for the army to ensure that the Plan was seen as being launched as a last resort, a call for the addressing of grievances that had received no consideration when put forward by "legal" means.[15]

As such, the preamble to the points in the Plan of Jalisco underlined the specific failures of the Bustamante government despite the nation's constant reminders. These were taxation, Texas, and the state of public revenue, thereby supporting the need for the pronunciamiento.[16] This would suggest that these pronunciamientos could be seen as a legitimate political step when all other avenues had been unsuccessfully explored. In Jalisco, Paredes was not only the head of the garrison and main author of the pronunciamiento; he became provisional governor and as such played an important political role. This shows that it was often impossible to distinguish between politics and the military, to such an extent that military politics often became national politics.

The *Ensayo* appears to support the Revolución de Jalisco but, at the same time, presents Otero's views on the position of the military within Mexico as an embryonic nation. Otero was born in

1817 and was thus a toddler at independence, and when the *Ensayo* was published he was merely twenty-five years old and had recently started to participate actively in the political scene. Unlike many of his contemporaries, Otero had only ever been a civilian, his education leading to his career as a lawyer and, until 1842, his political contribution to the events of the time occurring in minor political roles. He had attended the Junta de Notables, which had been called as a result of the events in Guadalajara in August 1841, and from there had moved on to Mexico City as the delegate for Jalisco to the Junta de los Representantes de los Departamentos on 24 December 1841—hardly starring roles, either of them, particularly when compared to the careers of some of the individuals he would go on to join in Congress in 1842.[17] Thus, in contrast to Lucas Alamán, Carlos Maria de Bustamante, or any of his contemporaries publishing around the same time, he was never involved in any of the fighting or the military and political machinations that followed the initial break from Spain.

His views of the military, therefore, were those of a generation slightly removed from the events of Independence, whence the military drew its image as savior and protector of the will of the nation. He never poured scorn on the role of the army during independence and, indeed, believed that it was essential to the well-being of the nation; he supported the need for an armed force at all times. The army, he argued, could only be involved in politics when war was the first necessity and the main way of life of a nation. Where this was not the case, as with Mexico, where the War of Independence had ended in freedom for Mexico, the army should take on a secondary role.[18] In times of peace, therefore, the army's position should be that of a purely military force, and as such, Otero was of the opinion that it should cease all political involvement except as a tool of the legally elected government.

He was vehemently against the practice of the pronunciamiento, which he saw as interference by the army in the proper constitutional running of the country, and referred constantly to the country's need to "make the fatal mania for revolutions disappear once and for all." The army's key role in orchestrating the pronunciamientos in 1841 was therefore not in keeping with Otero's views on its role, as presented in the *Ensayo*. He had always insisted he was opposed to any interference by the army in politics or governance. So why did he present the *Ensayo* in support of the Revolución de Jalisco? The contradiction is startling. He stood for the complete separation of army and state, and yet he published a defense of three pronunciamientos led by senior army officers in the late summer of 1841.

In an endeavor to shed some light on this apparent inconsistency, it is important to explore Otero's views on this specific set of pronunciamientos and compare them with the generic views he expressed on revolution as a political tool, leading us to a better understanding of the reasons behind his wholehearted support of the Revolución de Jalisco.

The "state of society," as Otero presented it in his *Ensayo*, created a view of Mexico as an unstable country, with weak governments, constant battles for supremacy between the *partido del progreso* (seeking reform) and the *partido del retroceso* (preserving the status quo), and no properly viable constitution. As such, revolutions and pronunciamientos were the expected outcome of the state of the nation at the outbreak of the rash of 1841 pronunciamientos. Otero went so far as to argue that there are times "when political agitations are . . . the constitution" and in doing so provided a better understanding of why he defended the 1841 revolts.[19] He understood that as things stood in 1841, political unrest was a manifestation of the general will of the nation, but at the same time he believed that this would no longer be the case when the persistent causes of the unrest were addressed.

The weakness of the nation was due to a variety of factors. There was a distinct lack of a proper middle class, again something that Otero felt was due to the dismal state of the nation, where commerce was floundering and education was guided by the Church. What little middle class did exist was unable to challenge the rule of the military with any temperance, due to the fact that the country was governed by passion and not by reason, force being called upon to resolve questions and grievances that should be addressed by the constitution, legislation, and the government. The army could well have argued that in pronouncing, they were merely coming to the aid of the nation, but Otero did not agree with this; he was fervently against military dominance or intervention of any kind. He believed that the great challenges and questions faced by Mexico should be addressed by peaceful means and not by military force.

Otero asked rhetorically where it was written that the way the nation's grievances were resolved should be decided by the minority, simply because they had the military strength to back their positions. He argued that the devastation of war had replaced free debate; all that was left was war and the army. As a result, everything would be lost, no constitutional equilibrium would be achieved since the military power would always dominate, unsettling events to fit its needs and aspirations.[20]

Yet at the same time Otero was writing in strong defense of the specific stages and outcomes of the Revolución de Jalisco. This contradiction can be explained because Otero divided events into two sections: first, those that had already happened, such as the lack of national development since independence, the failure to establish a strong constitution, and the 1841 pronunciamientos, which were all things that could not be changed; and second, the future of the Mexican nation, with growth in all sectors of society and in commerce, the need to forge a new constitution able to withstand attack from any quarter, and an end to all pronunciamientos.

When he was writing in 1842, the state of the nation was deplorable, and it had been in a fragile condition since independence. The only viable way that Otero saw to address the *cuestión social* in 1841 was by means of a pronunciamiento. He did not agree with the practice and insisted that one of the first goals of the country must be to put a stop to it, but in view of the state of the country under Bustamante's second term in power, he realized that there was no other option. Pronunciamientos had become an established, acceptable way of getting one's point across, especially since the "slow work" of building a nation and of setting up a constitution and all the appropriate governmental bodies had been overtaken by the "fatal apprenticeship of the revolutions."[21] But these revolutions, Otero argued, could only ever address the immediate causes of discontent and dissatisfaction; they were unable to provide a solution to the persistent causes underlying the nation's unrest.

Otero argued that the pronunciamiento, and eventually the full-scale war that brought independence, were perfectly acceptable. They were necessary in a society where the military were the only hope against Spanish dominance. However, he also believed that it was in the years directly following independence that the Mexican mania for revolutions began. All change was expected to happen immediately, as the country went from colony to independent nation almost overnight.

However, the slow, lengthy process that was needed to build a nation was overlooked, so that the absence of coherent political bodies, the deficiencies of the 1824 Constitution, and therefore the lack of powerful constitutional and judiciary frameworks meant that no alternative to pronunciamientos had been provided to assist the nation in redressing its grievances, leaving the Mexican nation with what Otero called a predisposition for civil war. Furthermore he compared different potential states of a nation in order to demonstrate the lack of possibilities facing Mexico: "In properly constituted societies, there is a dominant principle that decides the political or administrative questions that always arise: the will of a tyrant in despotism: the interests of the nobles in an aristocracy and the vote of the majority in democratic states, solve all these questions when the institutions are in all their vigor: but, when these annihilate each other . . . this authority does not have true force, civil war is established."[22]

Such was the case in Mexico, where following independence, the lack of a proper constitution and the weakness of the governing bodies stood out in sharp contrast against the strength and the position gained by the military. It was because of this decline in the political structures, Otero felt, that "civil war," or in the case of Mexico the pronunciamiento, became the commonplace way of getting one's views heard, of making any necessary or simply desirable changes, and of running the country.

By 1841 a centralist and a federalist constitution had failed. The *partido del progreso* and the *partido del retroceso* had met with little success in government, and pronunciamientos had produced some outstanding results, including the Plan of Iguala. This eventually led to Mexican independence from Spain. What few government institutions there were failed to fulfill even the basic constitutional needs. However, Otero believed the Revolución de Jalisco to be the watershed between the tumultuous past of the nation, when revolutions were the commonplace way of airing grievances, and the future of the Mexican nation, when political power would be played out within the constitutional and legitimate framework.

Otero was able to support the Revolución de Jalisco because he truly seemed to believe that it was different from those that came before it. It sought to address a broader set of issues and had a wider support base than most. It was "a revolution that could not be taken as a rebellion, and which profoundly moved the foundations of society, producing a general movement that excited the interest and action of all men and all parties."[23] We know that this was not exactly true. Further pronunciamientos came out in support of the Plan of Jalisco, whereas others disagreed with the Plan and the subsequent Bases de Tacubaya. Some sought rectification to suit their own purpose and gain, others to support the government.[24]

Otero, however, saw the revolution as something that was supported "universally," a revolution that would bring a new style of government to the nation. Because of this Otero believed that the Revolución de Jalisco was, at that specific point in time, an acceptable means of moving toward a solution to the nation's malaise as long as the errors that followed independence were not committed again. Otero believed, or at least hoped, at the time that *this* revolution would bring an end to military dominance and signal a new era of political dominance through acceptable political means, a strong constitution, sturdy legislation, and a separation of the Church and the military from the affairs of the government.

Having established why Otero believed that the pronunciamientos in August and September 1841 were acceptable, it is important to ascertain exactly how he felt these differed from all those that had preceded them, successful or otherwise. Otero's causal view of history accepted that everything that had happened to the Mexican nation had been due to the persistent causes, which led to the nation's malaise. The pronunciamientos, revolutions, revolts, uprisings, and other "spontaneous" reactions to national and local problems only ever addressed the immediate causes behind each one.

These causes were then taken at face value as the real expression of the state of society, and because of this, all solutions provided by the outcomes of the pronunciamientos and other revolts were only ever temporary. They addressed only specific concerns, without touching upon the real and persistent causes of the general social malaise. However, although the continuous demonstrations of unrest had never properly addressed these causes, Otero argued that over the years there had been a "slow, radical and irresistible movement" surging unnoticed through the nation, reflecting the human desire for improvement.[25]

This hope that the nation in 1842 was in a better position to improve itself allowed Otero to support the Revolución de Jalisco; it was different from the other pronunciamientos because while it arose from the same basic problems and persistent causes, he believed that the country was ready for change. Only by following faithfully the demands set out by the pronunciamientos and the Bases de Tacubaya, which Otero enumerated as "solely the merger of the parties, the establishment of a new order of things in the sense of liberty and progress, the observance of the sovereign will of the nation and the end of our revolutions," would the country be able to begin the slow process of becoming a truly strong nation.[26]

Otero was optimistic. Once the revolutionary fervor diminished, he felt, a different interest would rise to the fore—that of slow, peaceful reform, which had been forced to take cover because of the prevalence of rapid violent reform as embodied by the pronunciamientos and the military's dominance of the political scene. In the past, Otero argued, all revolutions had worked on the premise that once the immediate demands of the pronunciamientos had been addressed, the immediate causes had been eliminated, and the correct individual was in or out of power, then all had been achieved. This, he said, ignored the depth and complexity of the real and persistent "causes of social discontent."

However, once the persistent causes had been addressed, and this slow peaceful reform process had begun, he believed it would put an immediate end to all pronunciamientos. The military pronunciamientos would no longer be able to hide behind the banner of the will of the nation as the nation's grievances would be addressed in the correct manner, through the appropriate political, constitutional, and judicial channels. As far as he saw it, therefore, the Revolucion de Jalisco had left a blank canvas on which Otero longed to sketch a new state, a political machine that could do away, once and for all, with the *funesta manía de las revoluciones*.

The Mexico that he envisaged emerging from the ashes of the Revolución de Jalisco was a Mexico where all that went before had been destroyed. In its place there was a pristine landscape where all was yet to be decided; "from the first statutory questions to the most essential constitutional principle, all that entailed by the immense whole of the organization of a nation, all is waiting to be resolved."[27]

In order to "to drown the seeds of revolutions" Mexico now needed "obedience to the established laws and to the constituted authorities," but for this to be possible a constitution needed to be drafted that would withstand attack from any front.[28] The support for the Revolución de Jalisco, Otero believed, somewhat idealistically perhaps, showed that something had changed in the country. People had learned in the last twenty years what would and would not work, and Otero felt that these lessons were what had prepared the Mexican people for the task of building a new, strong, unified nation—a task for which he optimistically believed they were finally ready in 1842, and a nation in which the pronunciamiento no longer had a place.

Despite his best attempts at constructing a new constitutional order during the 1842 Congress and in various government positions in the years following the Revolución de Jalisco, pronunciamientos were not to disappear in his lifetime. Indeed, driven by desperation or perhaps due to a change in his views, only five years later Otero not only supported but actively participated in the Rebelión de los Polkos, bringing down the government of Valentín Gómez Farías, when the nation stood on the brink of being overpowered by invading United States forces.

Notes

1. For a detailed account on the Triangular Revolt, see Costeloe, "The Triangular Revolt" and his *The Central Republic*.

2. Bocanegra, *Memorias para la historia*, 2:804–6.

3. Bocanegra, *Memorias para la historia*, 2:804–6.

4. Noriega Elío, *El Constituyente de 1842*, 26.

5. Noriega Elío, *El Constituyente de 1842*, 26.

6. "Manifiesto y Plan del General Paredes (8 de agosto, 1841)," in Vázquez (ed.), *Planes en la nación, Libro cuatro*, 58–60.

7. Jiménez et al. (coords.), *Ensayos histórico-juridicos*, 1–39.

8. Jiménez et al. (coords.), *Ensayos histórico-juridicos*, 1–39.

9. Costeloe, "The Triangular Revolt."

10. "Manifiesto y Plan del General Paredes (8 de agosto, 1841)," "Plan del General Valencia proclamado en la Ciudadela (4 de septiembre, 1841)," and "Manifiesto y Plan de Perote (9 de septiembre, 1841)," in Vázquez (ed.), *Planes en la nación, Libro cuatro*, 58–61, 64–67; Costeloe, "The Triangular Revolt"; Noriega Elío, *El constituyente de 1842.*

11. Otero, *Ensayo sobre el verdadero estado*, 9.

12. Otero, *Ensayo sobre el verdadero estado*, 22.

13. Noriega Elío, *El Constituyente de 1842*, 32.

14. Guerra, "El pronunciamiento en México," 15–26; Vázquez, "El modelo de pronunciamiento"; quote from Costeloe, "The Triangular Revolt."

15. Guerra, "El pronunciamiento en México," 15–26

16. "Manifiesto y Plan del General Paredes (8 de agosto, 1841)," in Vázquez, *Planes en la nación*, Libro cuatro, 58–60.

17. Gaixiola, *Mariano Otero*, 65–66.

18. Otero, *Ensayo sobre el verdadero estado,* 51

19. Otero, *Ensayo sobre el verdadero estado*, 41.

20. Otero, *Ensayo sobre el verdadero estado*, 86.

21. Otero, *Ensayo sobre el verdadero estado*, 49.

22. Otero, *Ensayo sobre el verdadero estado*, 52.

23. Otero, *Ensayo sobre el verdadero estado*, 10.

24. Bustamante, *Apuntes para la historia*, 2.

25. Otero, *Ensayo sobre el verdadero estado,* 53.

26. Otero, *Ensayo sobre el verdadero estado*, 70.

27. Otero, *Ensayo sobre el verdadero estado*, 63.

28. Otero, *Ensayo sobre el verdadero estado*, 86.

REYNALDO SORDO CEDEÑO | *Translated by Victoria Louise Milton*

Nine. Constitution and Congress:
A Pronunciamiento for Legality, December 1844

The *pronunciamiento* of 6 December 1844, in Mexico City, is one of the most atypical in nineteenth-century Mexico. Its speed and effectiveness were astonishing: it succeeded in only three hours, causing the collapse of Valentín Canalizo's government and the most resounding fall of General Antonio López de Santa Anna. Exceptional to this rebellion were that not a single shot was fired and no innocent blood was spilled. The only violence that did occur can be better described as a collective catharsis, like a fiesta. In several parts of the city the jubilant people destroyed the symbols of the "Hero of Tampico" that had been erected by supporters of the *caudillo*: they demolished the plaster statue at the Coliseum, attempted to do likewise to a bronze one in the Plaza del Volador, and dragged Santa Anna's leg—previously amputated and buried in the Santa Paula cemetery—through the streets of the city until the authorities managed to rescue it.

This revolution is also interesting in terms of the participation of Congress, which during 1844 clashed with the government over attempts to organize a constitutional system after more than two years in which a provisional government with full powers had been in place. This pronunciamiento boasts another characteristic shared by very few revolutions of the period: the predominance of civilian participants over members of the military. Without denying the importance of the pronunciamiento of General Mariano Paredes y Arrillaga in Jalisco, there is no doubt that Santa Anna was defeated thanks to the participation of institutions such as Congress, the departmental assemblies, the town councils, and the courts of justice, which joined together and formed a united front in favor of legality.

Last, another decisive element in the fall of the provisional government was the union of the political parties. Usually, the majority of the pronunciamientos of the period arose following the union of one particular faction or political party with sectors of the army in order to instigate a political change in accordance with the ideas of the rebels. In this case the fundamental idea would be to restore the constitutional order, recently founded on the 1843 Constitution, the so-called Bases Orgánicas. Between October and December 1844, centralists from 1836, moderate and radical federalists, honorable men holding conservative beliefs, and high-ranking members of the army put aside their ideological differences and joined forces to overthrow the "colossus with feet of clay," an anarchic government of privilege, disorder, and corruption.

It is clear that this pronunciamiento is understandable only in a wider context. For this reason I have divided this chapter into four sections: the first is a brief summary giving an idea of the provisional government that arose from the 1841 Bases de Tacubaya; in the second I refer to the conflict between Congress and the government during 1844; the third is an analysis of the uprising of the departmental assembly of Jalisco and its consequences; and in the fourth, I discuss the dissolution of Congress and the reaction of 6 December.

The Provisional Government

The Bases de Tacubaya, drafted by a military committee in September 1841, authorized the provisional government that was formed to straighten out the branches of public administration. Its seventh article awarded the provisional executive full powers to govern but with the restriction imposed by the sixth article that he be answerable for his actions before the first Constitutional Congress.[1] This government was in force from October 1841 until December 1843.

Contemporary and subsequent authors have described these years as a military dictatorship. This seems to me an exaggeration. Santa Anna, acting as the provisional president, and Nicolás Bravo and Valentín Canalizo, who temporarily took up the post at different points in time, were not repressors, nor did they cause more or less bloodshed than the other constitutional governments of the period. The excesses of this regime were limited to the short-term imprisonment of certain opposition members and the closing down of newspapers that, in their enthusiasm, crossed the line of what was deemed acceptable.

The real problem of the provisional government was the isolation in which it governed. Overthrowing the centralist government of the 1836 Constitution (the Siete Leyes) and being in conflict with the moderate and radical federalists, Santa Anna had only the support of his followers, businessmen who benefited from governmental business deals, and isolated individuals without any governmental plans to offer. Clearly, from Tacubaya, Santa Anna relied on the support of important military figures such as Mariano Paredes y Arrillaga, Pedro Cortázar, José María Tornel, Gabriel Valencia, and many others.[2]

The weakness of Santa Anna's government required the organization of a constitutional order. First, the government summoned a constituent Congress to draft a new constitution, which they said should be a happy medium between that of 1824 and that of 1836. Santa Anna's expectations were thwarted when the federalists won the elections. The constituent members of the 1842 Congress discussed three different projects with strong inclinations toward a federal system, wearing thin the caudillo's patience. It was during Nicolás Bravo's interim presidency that the pronunciamiento of Huejotzingo in December 1842 put an end to this constituent Congress. On this occasion nobody stuck his neck out to defend it.[3]

The provisional government realized that it was always going to lose through general elections. Therefore it named a junta of worthies (the Junta de Notables) to draw up an ad hoc constitution within a six-month period. The National Legislative Junta did not do a bad job, subsequent criticism notwithstanding. It preserved the fundamental principles of a liberal system, guaranteeing individual rights and the division of powers. It granted more authority to the executive branch than had previous constitutions; it improved the regulation of the departments in comparison to the 1836 Constitution; it preserved its representative character through a system of elections with restrictions on property and introduced a conservative principle by means of a particular organization of the Senate. However, this constitution, known as the Bases Orgánicas, never escaped from its original sin: that of being a charter granted by the provisional government, as opposed to being the product of national sovereignty. The Bases Orgánicas were published and sworn in on 12 June 1843. With this event, the restoration of the constitutional order was prepared for 1 January 1844, after which elections took place in the second half of 1843 to elect the representatives to Congress, members of the departmental assemblies, and the president of the republic.[4]

The provisional government with full powers could organize and systematize the much deteriorated public administration that had been established since the days of independence. However, without any plan whatsoever, it only introduced more disorder and anarchy, especially in the treasury. Space limitations do not allow for a detailed analysis of the chaos at the treasury, but the following were some of the more salient measures taken: the "Pious Fund" of the California Missions was expropriated, as were assets previously owned by Jesuit missionaries; the Banco de Avío credits were sold, as were the nation's stake in the Fresnillo mines and the national salt mines, together with the assets of the Colegio de Santos; the Parián market in Mexico City was destroyed; a low-level customs duty was issued, only to be followed by a higher one; and the payments awarded by previous administrations were suspended at the same time as new arrangements were entered, forced loans were imposed, and a huge increase in moneylending at high interest rates was experienced. The loss of funds could be estimated at around 30 million pesos.[5]

This administrative disorganization, heightened by the comings and goings of Santa Anna as the holder of executive power, meant that they could not deal adequately with two serious problems: the reconquest of Texas and the reincorporation of Yucatán into the Mexican nation. The reconquest of Texas remained on the table and only brought about tax increases, allowing the passage of time to work in favor of the Texans and of the ambitions of the United States. The Yucatán issue was managed with a lack of foresight and responsibility. A disastrous military campaign led to negotiations between Santa Anna and the Yucatán govern-

Sordo Cedeño

ment. The agreement of 14 December 1843 reincorporated Yucatán but granted it so many concessions that the peninsula was almost given full autonomy, causing Mexico serious problems in later years.[6]

Once the Bases had been approved and published, increased restraint was expected on the part of the provisional government. Nevertheless, it was officially arranged for elections to take place during the months of August and September. The government, in spite of its efforts, was incapable of controlling the electoral process. Santa Anna witnessed how a good number of federalists and centralists from 1836 became the new representatives and senators in Congress as well as becoming members of the departmental assemblies.[7] Under the centralist model of the Cádiz system, federalists had always been allowed access to Congress.

Before retiring to his hacienda, Manga de Clavo, Santa Anna published the famous decree of 3 October, which would bring him serious problems in 1844. Through this he declared that the answerability of the provisional executive to the first constitutional Congress was on a merely consultative basis, a mere matter of opinion; as the ministers would explain to the chambers in January of the provisional government's acts and attributes, none of the acts of provisional executive could be overturned; the laws and decrees issued by the provisional government could be repealed, but only as long as the procedures and requirements of the Bases Orgánicas were followed; and finally, the agreements signed by the provisional executive were unbreakable, and the legislative branch had no right to be informed of them.[8] General Santa Anna undoubtedly thought that this decree would save him from the new Congress. In reality what he achieved was to open an irrevocable

rift between a government that was the heir of the provisional regime of 1841 and a new Congress that had emerged as a result of
the 1843 general elections.

Government and Congress in Conflict

On 2 January 1844 Congress registered the votes of the departments
that elected General Santa Anna as the constitutional president.
Different sources from the time declared that Santa Anna won
the elections because they were carried out by the departmental
governments set up by the man himself and controlled by governors who were supporters of the caudillo. Given that Santa Anna
warned Congress he would stay at his hacienda until his health
was restored, the Senate, following the procedures set out in the
Bases Orgánicas, elected Valentín Canalizo as interim president
from the twenty-seventh of that month.[9]

Constitutional order was thus established, but those in power
had different concepts of it. Congress rightly thought the unlim-
ited authority of the government had ceased and that, therefore,
the executive could not legislate. The government, absurdly, tried
to continue legislating, because these powers, it said, had been
granted before the installation of Congress.

The first period of sessions was largely futile, since the government obstructed the proposals of the Congress. It did not send the
necessary documentation or threatened to veto those decisions of
Congress that were contrary to its point of view. Not a single important law was approved. The testimonies of various Congress
members corroborate the fact that the two powers started to clash
with each other.[10]

The first period of sessions, however, enabled the 1836 centralist groups and the moderate federalists to join together in both

Sordo Cedeño

chambers to confront the government. In the Chamber of Deputies, Carlos María de Bustamante, José María Jiménez, and Juan Rodríguez de San Miguel stood out among the old centralists of '36, and Mariano Riva Palacio and Luis de la Rosa among the moderate federalists. In the Senate, among the first to stand out were Cirilo Gómez Anaya and José Ramón Malo, later followed by Manuel Gómez Pedraza, Bernardo Couto, and Juan B. Morales. Other members of Congress were also integrating themselves into the ranks of the opposition, such as José María Llaca, José Ignacio Ormaechea, and Juan Navarrete.[11]

Five months after being named as constitutional president, Santa Anna arrived in Mexico City to take charge of the executive on 4 June 1844. Congress had previously been summoned for special sessions, with three principal aims in mind: to arm themselves with resources with which to wage war on Texas, to increase the number of military troops, and to allow the constitutional president to swear the oath as required in front of the chamber.[12]

The arrival of Santa Anna in Mexico City, instead of pacifying tensions, increased the confrontation between the two powers. The government continued to act as if the Bases Orgánicas did not exist, provoking among the opposition almost outright rejection of Santa Anna's ministers: Manuel Crescencio Rejón (foreign affairs), Ignacio Trigueros (finance), Isidro Reyes (war), and Manuel Baranda (justice).[13]

On 15 June a circular from the treasury stated that the departments should look after their civil lists from then on with the limited means of a poll tax, which was established by going over the heads of Congress. This new tax was not only the subject of further disputes with Congress but was also frowned upon in the regions that saw their income considerably reduced because of it.[14]

Without any doubt, the most controversial issue of those months was that of granting the government resources for the war with Texas. Congress started to work on the issue from June onward. The discussion of the corresponding report lasted until 11 July. On that day the agreement made by the Chamber of Deputies was passed to the Senate. Instead of merely rubber-stamping the agreement made by the lower chamber, as the Bases Orgánicas stipulated, the Senate modified its core contents, converting it into a new initiative. The Senate postponed the issue for longer than it should have done as well. As a consequence, an editorial appeared in the *Diario del Gobierno* criticizing Congress's delay on this vital issue. The newspaper said: "The delays and the legislative processes, the hours of debating time and the slow-moving discussion are bothersome . . . all is proceeding in a sluggish manner. A significant amount of time has been lost; and in war, time and money are the most valuable agents . . . the slowness of proceedings in the Chambers is, to a certain degree, rendering useless the government's willingness."[15]

Well-intentioned enough, the article in the *Diario* might have passed unnoticed, because in reality it was not that offensive toward the chambers; it merely pointed out one fact—the usual formalities and procedures were not the most conducive when problems were foreseen with Texas and the United States. But from this moment on, a duel was sparked between one power and the other, with mutual accusations, legal and legalistic claims against each other, and complete opposition between precisely those two institutions that should have acted as a united force when faced with a powerful external enemy. The conflict lasted more than a month and ended at the beginning of September once the gov-

Sordo Cedeño

ernment agreed to withdraw the documents Congress considered slanderous, while Congress promised not to publish reports that put the government in its place.[16]

Within this tense climate Congress sanctioned, and the government published, the law on resources on 21 August. Thanks to this, an additional direct tax was established, which affected landowners, spinning and weaving factories, tenants, professionals, and various other sectors.[17]

Santa Anna decided to withdraw to his hacienda, and on 8 September Congress granted him the corresponding leave. The Senate went on to elect an interim president. With a divided Congress, General Valentín Canalizo was appointed once more after a second vote count. The government still relied on supporters in the Senate.[18]

Canalizo took up the presidency until 21 September, when he found himself out of town. The interim president kept the same cabinet he had inherited from Santa Anna. The conflicts with the executive continued during the months of September and October. Any action gave rise to confrontation, including an incident involving the French sailor Tessiere in Mazatlán, a government initiative to obtain a loan of 10 million pesos, publicity over the ministry of war's contracts to gain resources for the war with Texas, and the government's accusation against senator Juan B. Morales ("El Gallo Pitagórico") over an article in which he had insulted General Santa Anna, leading to the senator's detention and acquittal by the Grand Jury of his chamber. By this stage, the leading voices of opposition were José María Llaca and Luis de la Rosa in the lower house and Manuel Gómez Pedraza in the upper chamber.[19]

Carlos María de Bustamante said, not without reason, that the

Chamber of Deputies had turned into a "Tower of Babel." In relation to the session of 16 October he commented: "We were dealing with secondary issues when the enemy is at our borders, and when no progress is being made toward discovering whether the government has stolen or acted innocently in its management of funds."[20]

In this climate of passion and imprudence, the approach of the congressmen exceeded reasonable limits. Around the start of October the government presented to Congress an initiative to request a loan of 10 million pesos, with the best possible conditions. This initiative did not have much luck, but the treasury commission reduced the government's request to 3 million pesos. In the session of 15 October José María Llaca and Luis de la Rosa spoke out against the scheme. The former argued that he had no confidence in the ministry, because the money was going to fall into the hands of the moneylenders with no benefit to the nation. The only option would be a complete overhaul of the ministry, given how discredited it was in terms of public opinion. In pressing for refusal to grant the government the requested resources, Luis de la Rosa followed a line of argument that was difficult to sustain. For him, there could be no war between Mexico and the United States; the nations were bound together by mutual benevolence, a product of civilization; great analogies existed between the institutions of the two countries; the two nations were destined by divine Providence to spread civilization and republicanism across the American continent; the American people were very sensible, and there they did not do what President Tyler wanted; the U.S. government was truly popular; Rosa concluded by asking that the government's initiative be turned down. The opposition tri-

Sordo Cedeño

umphed in the vote, and the government's initiative was indeed rejected.[21] By the end of October conditions were right for a pronunciamiento against the government.

The Departmental Assembly of Jalisco

On 30 October the departmental assembly of Jalisco presented a law proposal to Congress, summarized in three points: "One. The national Congress will carry out the provisional government's responsibilities, holding it to the Sixth Article of the Bases de Tacubaya, to which it swore and made the nation swear allegiance. Two. The abolition of the law of 21 August of this year, which saw the imposition of additional monetary contributions. Three. Congress will take over the reform of those constitutional articles that experience has shown to be contrary to the regions' prosperity."[22]

The initiative was presented within a perfectly legal framework, in accordance with article 53 of the Bases Orgánicas. The argument was articulated with impeccable logic. Congress, the statement said, was the only institution that could save the country from the crisis in which it found itself. Implementing the sixth article of the Bases de Tacubaya was an unavoidable duty for the First Constitutional Congress. The decree of 3 October 1843 contradicted the spirit and letter of the Bases de Tacubaya and put at risk the constitutional development of the Bases Orgánicas. The provisional executive—that is, General Santa Anna—was not necessarily going to be condemned. The congressional law of 21 August, concerning additional monetary contributions, had been seen by the public as necessary and urgent and it was thought that the government would invest the money in the national aim of war with Texas. They were mistaken, however, and they watched in amazement as the government hired the resources with large discounts from the usual moneylenders. Finally, the assembly of Jalisco asked that reforms to the Bases Orgánicas be started so that the executive had less predominance and the departments' powers could be increased in branches such as the treasury, police, public education, and justice. The document was signed by the president of the assembly, Pedro Barajas, a prominent member of the Church and a distinguished 1836 constituent member.[23]

The initiative of the departmental assembly of Jalisco was the detonator for a large-scale uprising against Santa Anna's government. This initiative had placed the Constitution and Congress at the center of the process. It was not a matter of breaking the constitutional order that had emerged from the Bases Orgánicas but exactly the opposite, of implementing it. Within a few days Zacatecas, Aguascalientes, and Querétaro gave their support to the initiative. Later Sinaloa, Puebla, Sonora, Nuevo Léon, and Tabasco did the same, while Veracruz, Tamaulipas, and Oaxaca opposed it.[24]

As noted at the start of this chapter, all the pronunciamientos of the period had a combination of civil and military elements. The latter were indispensable for them to succeed. On 1 November the commander-general of Jalisco, Pánfilo Galindo, received the departmental assembly's proposal from the state governor, Antonio Escobedo. With the troops now gathered together, the garrison decided to join them.

The commander-general proposed to General Mariano Paredes y Arrillaga, who happened to be in Guadalajara, that he place himself at the head of the rebellion. On 2 November General Paredes presented a Manifesto to the Nation justifying his pronunciamiento. The most interesting thing about the document is that Paredes, having participated in the rebellion of 1841, considered

Sordo Cedeño

himself as its guarantor and invited all the military to implement the famous sixth article of the Bases de Tacubaya. He finished his declaration: "The acts of General D. Antonio López de Santa Anna's government from 10 October 1841 to 31 December 1843, whatever they may be, remain subject to examination and approval by the current National Congress, in compliance with article 6 of the Bases de Tacubaya and the second Estanzuela agreement: while the trial lasts, Santa Anna will not be allowed to perform his glorious duties as the First Magistrate of the Republic."[25]

The government thought the uprising of the Jalisco garrison, under the orders of a prestigious general, was more dangerous than the assembly's initiatives. On the other hand, although the uprising had begun in Jalisco, the center of opposition had moved to the heart of Mexico City. The call to rebellion started to spread, but it was not difficult to solve: all the executive needed to do was retrace its steps and comply with the Constitution and its laws.

However, the government did not understand the moral dimension of the uprising in Guadalajara and turned to the army to smother a pronunciamiento in which the strength was not military. Paredes's troops were estimated at around two thousand, but he could not convince Pedro Cortázar to join the rebellion, while the government could rely on a force of more than ten thousand, many of whom were considered to be the best troops stationed in Jalapa.[26]

The mistakes made by the government started to pile up one after another. General Santa Anna was named as general-in-chief of the troops sent to bring General Paredes to order, without previous authorization by Congress. On 12 November the Chamber of Deputies asked the minister for war, Isidro Reyes, to let them know whether the command of the army had indeed been given to the constitutional president. Reyes said the Constitution had not been violated because Santa Anna had no active role in the executive branch, and he was going to deploy only part of the navy and army troops. This argument provoked hilarity and created a "ruckus" in the Chamber. Deputy Llaca argued that Santa Anna himself had asked permission from Congress to go to fight in Zacatecas and Texas, by virtue of which he took command of the troops. By not having sought Congress's authorization, he had violated the Bases Orgánicas and snubbed Congress; his appointment was null and void and he could not command the army.[27] The discussion that ensued was very heated. Deputy de la Rosa finished by proposing to the ministry that it revoke Santa Anna's appointment or else accept responsibility for the consequences that such an appointment brought with it.[28]

The government did not back down, and through the month of November the conflict between the two powers reached its peak. In the session of 22 November the Chamber of Deputies, having been converted into the Grand Jury, decreed by 49 votes to 16 that there were grounds for indictment against the minister of war, Isidro Reyes, for having infringed article 89 of the Bases Orgánicas by authorizing the constitutional president to command the army against the rebels. General Reyes consequently had to leave his post and be at the disposal of the corresponding tribunals.[29]

Another serious problem arose between the two powers as a result of the government attempting to conceal from Congress information that was arriving from Guadalajara. The legislature responded with a defiant, unusual, and revolutionary attitude. The Chamber of Deputies resolved that all of the documents, the initiatives of the regional assemblies, and even Paredes's Manifesto should be included in the session's minutes and made public. Inserting the assemblies' initiatives in the congressional minutes posed no legal problem, but that of an armed uprising went beyond the law, I think. Congress was making theirs an act that, although fair, was produced through armed violence and outside legal channels.

The government response was swift: "[the interim president] considers it his obligation to protest as of course he is protesting against the conduct which has been observed in these proceedings by this Chamber, calling the nation to judge whether or not it is legal and to decide which of the proposed plans to be decreed were to be included and published, including both the document concerned as well as others put forward by the revolutionaries, seconding the ideas of Mariano Paredes y Arrillaga."[30] In that same session Deputy Vicente Chico said he had proposed that the documents for and against the uprising in Jalisco be included because the government was at pains to conceal this information. Rodríguez de San Miguel, who initially did not agree with the measure but did support it after Chico's proposal, explained that for him, minutes were just an account of facts, and this reference was far from what he considered to be the actual facts.[31] It was a legalistic argument. Paredes's Manifesto, linked to the law, should never have been included in the congressional minutes.

Santa Anna committed one further error: he was slow to mobilize from Veracruz, giving time for the revolution to grow. On his journey toward Jalisco he arrived at Guadalupe-Hidalgo at the end of November. On the twenty-first he called a meeting that was attended by some deputies and senators. The congressional members present voiced all their complaints about the administrative disorder and the conduct of the government, which was trying to govern above the constitutional order. General Santa Anna assured them that he was in favor of justice and respect for the law; that the Bases Orgánicas would always be respected; and that he would withdraw to private life once Paredes had been defeated, as he had no ambition to govern. The meeting lasted seven hours and in reality no important agreement was reached, only promises and more promises.[32]

Santa Anna left for Querétaro, and things deteriorated. There he committed another error. Instead of carrying out the promises made at the meeting in Guadalupe-Hidalgo he dissolved the departmental assembly for having supported the Jalisco initiative, imprisoned the supporters of the same, and dismissed the constitutional governor. The matter reached Congress at the session of 1 December. The minister of finance appeared before Congress, on behalf of the government. The impassioned deputy José María Llaca, leading voice of the opposition and himself a native of Querétaro, made a vehement speech protesting the events occurring in his home city. Llaca protested against the arbitrariness of Santa Anna: his persecution of legitimately established civil authorities, his violation of individual rights, his violation of the Bases Orgánicas through the denial of the right to initiative of the departmental assemblies, and finally his direct attack on the representative system of government.[33] The violations of Querétaro proved Congress to be right. However, in the heated political atmosphere of Mexico City the idea that Congress was to be dissolved started to circulate.

The Sixth of December

After a stormy session on 1 December Congress decided to meet in the evening. On their return the deputies and senators alike found soldiers guarding the doors of both chambers, preventing them from entering to be in session. The Senate decided to hold its meeting at the house of Juan Navarrete, its president at the time. The following day the government published the decree whereby it dissolved Congress, backdated to 29 November. Congress's sessions were thus suspended, and members of the chambers were unable perform their duties as stipulated in the Bases Orgánicas.[34] According to the decree, the government could now dictate all measures to reestablish order, adopt whatever financial administrative measures it saw fit, and control foreign matters. General Santa Anna continued to be recognized as the constitutional president, in accordance with the Bases Orgánicas. A decree on 2 December stated that the authorities and civil servants must swear allegiance to the decree of 29 November in order to continue in their posts.[35]

The first decree exposed that President Santa Anna and the government wanted to continue governing as they had done between 1841 and 1843. The constitutional order was destroyed, and Santa Anna displayed the same respect for the Bases Orgánicas as he had done for the 1836 Siete Leyes or the 1824 Constitution. The political parties decided that they had to work together in order to overthrow Santa Anna. The Bases Orgánicas immediately turned into the means to salvation, and Congress became the instrument through which the constitutional order could be restored. José María Lafragua remarked on the matter: "In Congress, the *escoceses* and the liberals had united against Santa Anna. A sentiment within the liberal party that was more pronounced was that, as well as overthrowing Santa Anna, they wanted to destroy the political organization. This divided us and in spite of everything, we continued the opposition effort: since suddenly we all shared the same aim. Canalizo carried out his coup d'état, and then we had to support Congress against the military dictatorship."[36]

The government continued compounding its string of errors. The decree of 2 December provoked the opposite effect to that which was intended. The most respectable institutions in Mexico City refused to swear allegiance, were dissolved, and went on to swell the ranks of the opposition: the Supreme Court of Justice, the Mexico City Council, and the Mexican departmental assembly.[37] Puebla heard about the dissolution of Congress on 3 December, protested about what had happened in the capital, and invited the other departmental governments to form a united front in favor of Congress and the restoration of the constitutional order.

Senator José Ramón Malo wrote about 6 December:

> The unrest was already known, the capital found itself in a state of great alarm, and everybody did what they could to oust the most daring and sickening tyranny. At midday, or soon after, we, the generals and heads of the garrison met with Herrera, the division general and the president of the cabinet, representing the voice of the Constitution and Congress. At 3 pm the uprising was accomplished, without a single shot being fired, since both the troops from the barracks and those defending the Palace were united in sentiment with the people and the authorities.[38]

The union of the political parties, the restraint, and the happiness that sources of the time reported was felt everywhere made it a unique day in the political history of the nineteenth century.

The deputies and senators met in the San Francisco Convent, precisely where José Joaquín de Herrera was to be found. The congressional members decided to march to the Palace and that they did, escorted by the people and accompanied by general rejoicing. Carlos María de Bustamante climbed onto the stage to improvise a congratulatory speech to Congress.[39]

In only three hours the constitutional order had been restored in the capital of the republic, but the "tyrant" was still in charge of an army of ten thousand men who could reverse the situation. In the meantime a new government was organized in Mexico City. On the seventh the Senate named as the interim president General Herrera, who made up his Cabinet principally with members of Congress and those of moderate federalist affiliation.[40] Congress announced another two important decrees. The first, on 9 December, authorized the government to make the necessary expenditures to support the bodies named "the voluntary defenders of the law" while the threat of Santa Anna's army existed. The second, on 17 December, stripped General Santa Anna of his title as constitutional president for having rebelled against the constitutional order.[41]

Luck turned its back on the caudillo from Jalapa. Santa Anna continued with his mistakes. He neither attacked Mexico City nor attempted reaching a political deal like those that had favored him so often in the past. He continued toward Puebla, attempted to capture it, spilled blood unnecessarily, withdrew to Amozoc, and resigned as president of the republic. He was finally apprehended in Xico as he tried to continue his way toward the coast.[42]

Seen in perspective, the sixth of December did not signify any key change in nineteenth-century political history. Subsequent events would be a negation of that glorious day: the inability of the government to place Santa Anna on trial, the attempted federalist coup of June 1845; Paredes's uprising and his attempt to establish a monarchy; the return of Santa Anna in 1846, now allied with the radical liberals whom he apparently hated so much; the division of the federalists in the middle of the Mexican-American War and the disastrous loss of territory that the conflict entailed. The sixth of December was a parenthetical moment in the course of Mexican politics of the first half of the nineteenth century, a half century that was neither conciliatory nor law abiding, let alone constructive.

Notes

1. Archivo General de la Nación, Fondo Gobernación, (hereafter cited as AGN FG), 1841, s/c.

2. Cuevas, *Memoria del ministro*, 71–72.

3. For all the vicissitudes of the 1842 Constituent Congress, see an excellent analysis by Cecilia Noriega Elío, *El Constituyente de 1842*.

4. Mayagoitia, "Apuntes sobre las Bases Orgánicas."

5. Cuevas, *Memoria del ministro*, 59–64; Romero, *Memoria de Hacienda y Crédito Público*, 254.

6. AGN FG, s/s, vol. 269, exp. 2, fols. 1–11, 17–23.

7. Copious information about these elections can be found in editions of *Diario del Gobierno de la República Mexicana* (hereafter cited as DGRM) and in *El Siglo XIX* dating from August to December 1843.

8. Government decree, 3 October 1843, Declaration of the answerability of the provisional Ejecutivo, by virtue of the Bases de Tacubaya, in Dublán and Lozano (eds.), *Legislación mexicana*, 4:618.

9. Senate decree, 27 January 1844, Valentín Canalizo declared interim president, in Dublán and Lozano (eds.), *Legislación mexicana*, 4:737.

10. Dublán and Lozano (eds.), *Legislación mexicana*, 4:737–58; Cuevas, *Memoria del ministro*, 76–77; Bustamante, *Diario histórico*, CD 2, January–May 1844; Malo, *Diario de sucesos*, 1:234–41.

11. Mateos, *Historia parlamentaria*, vol. 14; Official section, Sessions of the Senate, DGRM, January–May 1844.

12. Ministry of Foreign Affairs, Government and Police, Official announcement to Congress for special sessions, 13 May 1844, AGN FG, 1844, s/c, c.1.

13. Moreno Valle, *Catálogo de la Colección Lafragua*, 884.

14. Cuevas, *Memoria del ministro*, 77.

15. DGRM, 27 July 1844.

16. Agreement of 22 August 1844, held by a committee of ministers, DGRM, 7 September 1844; Chamber of Deputies, Session of 23 August 1844, DGRM, 8 September 1844.

17. Law, 21 August 1844, Establishment of an additional tax to meet the urgent shortfall in the public treasury, in Dublán and Lozano (eds.), *Legislación mexicana*, 760–66.

18. DGRM, 8 September 1844.

19. Mateos, *Historia parlamentaria*, 17:84–133; *Sessions of the Senate*, DGRM, September and October 1844.

20. Bustamante, *Diario histórico*, CD 2, Wednesday 16 October 1844.

21. Chamber of Deputies, Session of 15 October 1844, *El Siglo XIX*, 17 and 21 October 1844.

22. AGN FG, 1844, s/c, vol. 2.

23. AGN FG, 1844, s/c, vol. 2.

24. AGN FG, 1844, s/c, vol. 2.

25. Agreement of the Jalisco garrison, Guadalajara, 1 November 1844, and Manifesto of General Mariano Paredes to the Nation, Guadalajara, 2 November 1844, both in Bustamante, *Apuntes para la historia del gobierno*, 318–28.

26. Paredes sent commissioners to meet with Cortázar; the latter rejected them, warning that if they attempted to enter the state of Guanajuato, they would be repelled with all possible force. Pedro Cortázar to Excmo. Sr. General Mariano Paredes y Arrillaga, Celaya, 18 November 1844, DGRM, 23 November 1844.

27. Chamber of Deputies, Session of 12 November 1844, in Mateos, *Historia Parlamentaria*, 17:140–51.

28. Chamber of Deputies, Session of 12 November 1844, in Mateos, *Historia parlamentaria*, 17:149.

29. Chamber of Deputies, Session of 22 November 1844, in Mateos, *Historia parlamentaria*, 17:180–81.

30. Chamber of Deputies, Session of 20 November 1844, in Mateos, *Historia parlamentaria*, 17:175–76.

31. Chamber of Deputies, Session of 20 November 1844, *El Siglo XIX*, 28 November 1844.

32. Cuevas, *Memoria del ministro*, 90–93; Bustamante, *Diario histórico*, CD 2, Thursday 21 November 1844; Malo, *Diario de sucesos* 1:254.

33. Chamber of Deputies, Session of 1 December 1844, in Mateos, *Historia parlamentaria*, 17:185–86.

34. Government decree, Congress sessions declared suspended, 29 November 1844, in Dublán and Lozano (eds.), *Legislación mexicana*, 4:767–68.

35. Government decree, Concerning the oath of obedience of the authorities and employees to the 29 November decree, 2 December 1844, in Dublán and Lozano (eds.), *Legislación mexicana*, 4:768.

36. Lafragua, *Miscelánea de política*, 32.

37. AGN FG, 1844, s/s, 278, exp. 1.

38. Malo, *Diario de sucesos*, 257–58.

39. Bustamante, *Diario histórico*, CD 2, 7 December 1844.

40. Decree of the Senate, D. José Joaquín de Herrera declared interim president, 7 December 1844, in Dublán and Lozano (eds.), *Legislación mexicana*, 769.

41. Authorization for the government to make the necessary expenditures to sustain the force raised in defense of constitutional order, 9 December 1844; D. Antonio López de Santa Anna renounced as president of the Republic, 17 December 1844, in Dublán and Lozano (eds.), *Legislación mexicana*, 4:769–70.

42. DGRM, 17 December 1844.

Ten. "The Curious Manner in Which Pronunciamientos Are Got Up in This Country": *The Plan of Blancarte of 26 July 1852*

On 3 October 1852 Percy Doyle, the British plenipotentiary in Mexico, wrote in a letter to the Earl of Malmesbury: "In Guadalajara the Santa Anna Party have quarrelled with the other parties and a complete division has taken place amongst them; what has taken place in that town may be perhaps best explained to your lordship by my sending the translation of a private letter, which will at the same time afford an insight into the curious manner in which 'pronunciamientos' are got up in this country."[1] Enclosed was a translation of a conspiratorial letter between two anonymous parties involved in the preparation of a *pronunciamiento* that took place in Jalisco on 13 September 1852 and formed part of a series of three major pronunciamientos with some *actas* or *planes de adhesión* and *rechazo* (plans seconding or opposing the pronunciamientos) in Guadalajara that year. Also enclosed was a newspaper report from the *Trait de L'Union* giving an account of the Plan of Blancarte of 26 July 1852, the first of the three noted *planes*.

The conspiratorial letter, the article, and the correspondence relating to this series of pronunciamientos do indeed provide insight into how pronunciamientos were "got up" and illustrate a pattern regarding the origins of pronunciamientos in Mexico on several levels. In this chapter I use these documents, the planes themselves, and secondary sources to (1) gain further insight into why the pronunciamiento was such a popular form of political action for individuals and groups, (2) discuss both the process of conspiracy and rumor that was commonly adopted in garnering support for a pronunciamiento and the formalized procedures involved in launching one, (3) demonstrate how a pronunciamiento originating in regional concerns could quickly become co-opted into a movement that targeted the national government, and (4) demonstrate how, as the pronunciamiento became more prevalent, it moved from being a primarily military phenomenon to one in which civilians were increasingly involved.

The analysis uses the few existing definitions of the pronunciamiento and points discussed in this volume to test and refine that definition. The pronunciamiento discussed in the letter, the Plan of Guadalajara or the Segundo Plan de Blancarte of 13 September 1852, was preceded by the Plan of Blancarte on 26 July 1852 and followed by the Plan del Hospicio of 20 October 1852. Several other pronunciamientos and actas opposing, seconding, or reforming these three plans were staged in other areas of Jalisco between July and October.[2] The first addressed local concerns, but subsequent pronunciamientos became nationally targeted, and the movement inspired a series of *planes* (political plans) and pronunciamientos throughout the country in a domino effect that eventually led to the fall of President Mariano Arista.

By 1852 there was great anxiety in the political class about territorial fragmentation after the loss of territory in the U.S-Mexican War and about the threat of social dissolution from the increasing number of agrarian revolts. The first political parties had been formed in an attempt to overcome these problems.[3] But liberal reforms under the moderate governments of José Joaquín de Herrera and Mariano Arista began to alienate both the clergy and the army. As disenchantment grew, so did the political divide between the parties.[4] Some parties believed that democracy and the weak representative system were responsible for regional disunity and loss of territory and that a strong leader was needed. *Santanistas* (members of the Santa Anna party) like Juan Suárez y Navarro put forward the idea of a dictatorship, while conservative Lucas Alamán favored a monarchy under a European prince. By 1852 Alamán and his party began to put aside their monarchist ideals and to see the benefits of uniting with the santanistas.[5] Others, such as Benito Gómez Farías, preferred "intelligent despotism" under Arista rather than a Santa Anna dictatorship, which would lead to "the death, not only of the institutions but also of the nation."[6]

Santanistas Juan Suárez y Navarro and Pedregón Garay saw their opportunity to make their plans for a dictatorship a reality when a regional party dispute in Jalisco led to the Plan de Blancarte of July 1852. This provided the trigger for a series of pronunciamientos through which national leaders realigned in order to overthrow the "weak" moderate government and establish a strong leadership that would overcome the problems of social dissolution and territorial disunity so feared by Mexico's *hombres de bien* (elite political class) and their newly formed political parties.

The first Plan of Blancarte of 26 July was motivated by the divide between the regional moderate and *puro* (radical liberal) parties over the governorship of Jalisco. By 1852 the government of Jalisco had been in the hands of the moderates for six years under Joaquín Angulo and then Jesús López Portillo, who had become governor in March that year. Angulo had been criticized in the local and national press over the poor state of the regional economy, caused in part by a crisis in the textile industry. In 1850 there had been strikes for higher wages in the textile factories. Artisans' unions, some with utopian socialist ideas, had been established. López Portillo had blocked a proposal for free trade in tobacco and an end to the monopoly brought to the table by a local merchant and textile factory owner, José Palomar (the secretary of the Plan del Hospicio). The liberal reforms of the moderate governors had become unpopular with the clergy, whose lands had been sold; with the army, which had seen battalions cut; and with the puros, who saw López Portillo as an ambitious "strongman." The situation came to a head over the broad-ranging powers López Portillo gave to the local police force established by Angulo. The police or *cuicos* had become heavy handed, and their powers were not restricted to Guadalajara; the *jefes políticos* (local political chiefs) in the *cantones* (districts) and many in the capital began to regard the powers awarded to the police as unconstitutional.[7]

The *pronunciados* (participants) in the first Plan of Blancarte were an alliance of regional puros, led by Gregorio Dávila and conservatives. The figurehead was Colonel José María Blancarte, the former commander of a local battalion of the National Guard disbanded by López Portillo. Blancarte took control of the national palace with his troops, some released prisoners, and some members of an artisans' guild. The grievances in the Plan were regional issues. It opposed a decree that had changed the electoral law in the state, rejected the existing state government, and called for a new state constitution under the governorship of Gregorio Dávila. Blancarte, who became captain general, was seconded by Atenógenes Valdivia for the *cuartel número 1* (first barracks), one of the conspirators mentioned in the private letter sent to the Earl of Malmesbury.[8]

In Jalisco there was a *plan de rechazo* opposing the pronunci-amiento.[9] There was also a *plan de adhesión* supporting it.[10] By September this pronunciamiento had developed into a "move-ment," which gained momentum as prominent santanistas from Mexico City became involved. After a realignment of the parties, this plan became a means through which santanistas in alliance with the conservatives could call for the return of Antonio López de Santa Anna to Mexico.

On 13 September Suárez y Navarro and Blancarte issued a sec-ond plan inviting Santa Anna back to restore peace and order. This plan combined national and regional grievances. It rejected the ex-isting government of the republic, ratified the executive and legis-lative powers established in Jalisco by the Plan of Blancarte of 26 July, and called for the appointment of an interim president un-til the states could create a provisional government. This plan put forward a temporary dictatorship and promised all states second-ing the Plan powers to defend the frontier states and protect the republic.[11] Blancarte took the governorship of Jalisco for ten days before santanista José María Yañez took over. Pronunciamientos in Michoacán and Sinaloa seconded the plan.[12] The conspiracies leading up to this pronunciamiento are the subject of the private letter sent by Percy Doyle to the Earl of Malmesbury illustrating how pronunciamientos were "got up."

The third plan, the Plan del Hospicio of 20 October, was signed primarily by civilian actors. The support base had broadened to include santanistas, conservatives, federalists, anti-federalists, and crucially, the clergy and merchants. This plan would make Gen-eral José López Uraga captain general of Jalisco. He was a mem-ber of the moderate party who, despite having rebelled against Arista, was sent to Jalisco to restore order.[13] However, he joined the pronunciados after negotiations mediated by Lázaro J. Gallardo, a well-connected *tapatío* (citizen of Jalisco), over the setting up of a *junta de notables* (temporary council of worthies) in exchange for financing. Yáñez remained governor. The demands in the Plan del Hospicio were primarily national concerns. It declared in favor of the federal system, promoted a limited dictatorship, and ruled that a congress would be called to reform the Constitution, reorganize the army, and declare an amnesty for all political crimes. It demanded that states provide half their income to the national government to help defend the borders, repealed taxes (*capitación*), and called for Santa Anna to return to the executive in recognition of his services to the republic.[14] The extent of the civilian involvement in this Plan—almost all of the Guadalajara clergy and several powerful merchants, including Palomar, signed—illustrates how, as pronunciamientos became more established and accepted, they moved from being a primarily military phenomena to attracting the ever more overt involvement of civilian actors.

On 20 October the national Congress finally agreed to send five thousand members of the National Guard to Jalisco, Veracruz, Michoacán, and any areas with uprisings. However, the troops commanded by Vicente Miñón arrived late in Guadalajara as they stopped at the *feria* in San Juan de los Lagos. Gradually the santanistas, in alliance first with the puros and then with all the other parties, had won the governorship of Jalisco, and by January 1853 pronunciamientos seconding one or other Plan had been staged in Tepic, Michoacán, Sinaloa, Durango, Chihuahua, Veracruz, Mexico, Coahuila, Oaxaca, and San Luis Potosí.[15] The movement ultimately led to General Arista's resignation from the presidency on 6 January 1853 and—after the interim presidency of Juán Bautista

Ceballos, the agreements of Arroyo Zarco signed in February by López Uraga, and a second interim presidency of Manuel María Lombardini—paved the way for the return of Santa Anna to power in a highly centralist, republican, military-style dictatorship.[16] The Jalisco state government considered this "revolution" to be complete on 19 March 1853, since "the plan of 20 October of the previous year has been adopted throughout the republic."[17]

What light do the conspiratorial letter and the related documents shed on the participants' motivations for using the pronunciamiento as a form of political expression? What information can be gained from the letter regarding how the second Plan de Blancarte of 13 September was got up, and how does this fit with what has been written about pronunciamientos?

The letter Percy Doyle sent to the Earl of Malmesbury is evidence of the conspiracy and action following the *compromisos* (agreements) stage of a pronunciamiento. In this compromisos stage, agreements would have been made among politicians, sergeants, and officers offering promotions, increases in pay, etc., and then the plan would have been drawn up in a formal meeting. The letter relates the events of the day before the pronunciamiento of 13 September. It shows the final stage of garnering support, in which the pronunciados move from garrison to garrison in an attempt either to win over the troops or, in the case of the governor, Dávila, to discourage the troops from supporting the Plan: "Dávila came at 9 o'clock at night of the same day, Sunday, went to Carmen, and harangued the troops commanded by Tolsa, hurried to San Agustin and did the same with those of Valdivia— he . . . gained much ground. The Santa Annaites Blancarte and others said that their cause was lost."[18]

Percy Doyle's conspiratorial letter provides an insight not only into what made certain actors choose to pronounce but also what made others choose to avoid overt association with pronunciamientos. Atenógenes Valdivia, commander of the second *cuartel* (barracks) in Jalisco and Blancarte's second in the Plan of 26 July, told his troops that he would neither adhere to the plan nor oppose Blancarte and "that those soldiers who might think it proper to adhere to the new 'pronunciamiento' were to step forward three paces, and those who would not remain firm should give up their arms and accoutrements, as he himself was going to deliver up his sword, that for the rest he would follow the fortunes of Blancarte."[19]

One conclusion to be drawn from this would be that Valdivia was loyal to Blancarte but was not a santanista. This, however, does not explain why he would not discourage his troops from backing a santanista pronunciamiento. For some reason not evident from the letter, he clearly did not want to be seen as publicly supporting the plan. This was certainly the case of Ronaldo Tolsa, the commander of the troops at Carmen who, according to the letter, "said that notwithstanding his decided opinion in favour of Sr Santa Anna and of having offered $3,000 for them to pronounce, he would not do it, nor admit to it, in order to be consistent in his conduct towards the Governor Dávila, who had resigned."[20]

One motivation for involvement in a pronunciamiento may have been to use it as a form of "social networking" and "self-publicity" to gain promotion or prestige (see chapter 12). It would therefore have been important, publicly at least, to show some consistency to political allies. It would also have been important to be associated with successful movements, which would explain why some participants waited until the pronunciamiento was a success to

Doyle

pronounce openly in favor. Julián Villabaso, the commander of the artillery, according to the letter, "kept aloof until the result was known and he then declared in favour."[21]

Being associated with successful movements would also be less dangerous and could lead to military promotion, which has been identified as a primary motivation for involvement in pronunciamientos.[22] Through participating in the Plan del Hospicio, López Uraga not only became captain general of the State of Jalisco but was later given the honorary title of *benemérito del Estado* (worthy hero of the state).[23]

Pronunciados or financial backers of pronunciamientos may also have been protecting their already important position in society by avoiding overt association with a plan. The bishop of Guadalajara, Diego Aranda y Carpintero, was one of the few members of the Jalisco clergy not to have signed the third pronunciamiento, the Plan del Hospicio. However, according to newspaper reports he was prepared to give four thousand pesos to fund it.[24] The success of the Plan del Hospicio could be attributed partly to the backing of the majority of the clergy, a powerful force in Jalisco, who joined the movement to protect their privileges in the face of liberal reforms. Yet supporting a potentially violent movement associated with the military was evidently a delicate matter for a representative of the Church.

While the letter sheds new light on the detail of events leading up to a pronunciamiento and the ostensible inconsistencies in support for a plan, it is difficult to find definitive answers regarding individual motivations without access to further private correspondence. These documents highlight the ambiguity of individual motivations in the complex political climate of shifting allegiances.

Existing definitions of the pronunciamiento have indicated a contrast between the grandiose claims about the "good of the nation" or the "will of the people" and the underlying personal goals of promotion and financial gain participants were hoping to achieve.[25] This creates a metatext by which the grievances in the text refer to high ideals and call governments to account for injustices suffered, but reading between the lines, it is possible to see the various practical or personal demands of a sometimes disparate group of individuals or groups "represented" in the texts (see chapter 5). If the reports are to be believed, this contrast is particularly marked in the Blancarte series. The reports suggest that the participants were motivated by personal or financial gain rather than "higher" political ideals. The *Monitor Republicano* claimed that Blancarte had been seduced by Suárez Navarro and the *agiotista* (moneylender) Luis Rivas. The *Trait de L'Union* newspaper reported that he had received 50,000 pesos and the title of general and that Valdivia, his second, received 25,000 pesos.[26]

In addition to financial gain or promotion another motivation for pronouncing could have been vengeance and the settling of personal arguments. Lázaro J. Gallardo claimed that López Uraga, who was the main fundraiser of the Plan del Hospicio and influenced the plan's content, pronounced to settle a personal argument with Arista.[27] The *Trait de L'Union* hinted at personal rancor among the principal pronunciados of the Plan de Blancarte. It reported that Blancarte had been dismissed by the governor and, shortly before the pronunciamiento, had been arrested for assaulting a policeman. Julián Villabaso, the commander of artillery, had also been dismissed. Blancarte's involvement in the initial plan could be explained by his personal argument with López Portillo over the disbanding of his garrison, especially since two years previously, in 1851, Blancarte had supported López Portillo.[28]

It has been suggested that a "favourable climate of unrest" was an essential element in the instigation of pronunciamientos.[29] A disgruntled minority has been identified as essential as well.[30] The July Plan of Blancarte was framed in the climate of discontent over the governorship of López Portillo. The report in the *Trait de L'Union* suggested that the participants in the July pronunciamiento were just such a disgruntled minority. It highlighted the class origins of the pronunciados, mentioning their trades as milliners and artisans, and drew attention to their dubious morality or lack of "respectability." The pronunciados' social status and lack of respectability were no doubt linked, betraying the anxiety of the hombres de bien over social unrest among the workers and the "dangerous classes." The newspaper reported that the pronunciados and their troops were "joined by a multitude of *léperos* and a considerable number of thieves who had been released from prison crying 'death to . . . the . . . chief of police,'" and together they took the government palace by jumping the palace guard.[31] If the *Trait de L'Union* is correct, there is an interesting metatext to the opening of the second Plan of Blancarte, displaying a stark contrast between the grandiose claims of the plan and the personal goals of the pronunciados. The Plan proclaimed in favor of the rights of Jalisco's citizens to the "protection of their person" and to be ruled by those who respected the "will of the people."[32]

The opposition to the police force was a key factor allowing the disgruntled minority of army officers, puros, and conservatives to garner support from the artisans and their union. Pronunciados often exploited the discontent of minorities to garner support. They included articles in their plans expressing grievances and demands of an increasingly broad and sometimes disparate range of actors. The Blancarte series started as a movement of a few liberals, conservatives, and army officers and gradually gained the support of most of the Guadalajara clergy and merchants. As it did so, the plans became longer, including articles to benefit all their supporters. In this sense the pronunciamiento could be likened to coalition building in opposition. Groups brought separate demands to the table and joined forces with others, who may have shared some but not all of their ideas, in order to influence the government from outside the electoral process.[33]

The pronunciamiento has been interpreted as a political tool of military officers who sought civilian backing to finance their plans.[34] However, as the practice became more commonplace, the opposite was also true. Military actors were sought and used by civilian politicians to lend force to the negotiations they aimed to initiate through their pronunciamientos. Dávila, a civilian politician, sought the backing of Colonel Blancarte for his plan. As the mix of civilian and military financiers, secretaries, backers, and pronunciados in the Blancarte series shows, by 1852 the civilian-military divide in pronunciamientos was not clear-cut. If civilian actors provided financing, they could strongly influence the content of a plan. There is also ambiguity regarding which actors could be considered civilian and which actors were military and whether their concerns would be different. Suárez y Navarro, the main instigator of the second plan, was a politician general rather than an active member of the army. Blancarte, as the commander of a battalion, may have "pronounced" to defend military *fueros* (privileges), but "politicians in uniform" like Suárez y Navarro did not necessarily promote the interests of the army. Their intervention in politics was more often motivated by the constitutional crisis.[35]

The social networking, coalition building aspect of pronunciamientos involved appealing to all the powerful potential supporters, military and civilian, in the state and neighboring states to ensure the success of the plan. However pronunciamientos were not exactly nascent nineteenth-century social movements or pressure groups. Despite the rhetoric of representation a strong element of coercion was involved, and the negotiations were forceful, as the title of this volume suggests.

A paradox of the pronunciamiento was that it was legitimized insubordination with great potential for violence. Pronunciados were simultaneously breaking the constitutional order and calling the government to account for failing to govern according to the Constitution. The threatened use of force, in general not resorted to in action, was a key element of pronunciamientos.[36] Article 9 of the Segundo Plan de Blancarte read: "Any corporation or individual who opposes the present plan . . . is responsible for their person and goods and will be treated as enemies of the independence and unity of the republic."[37] This does not sit comfortably with the ideals of liberty and protection of "sacred rights." However, a pronunciamiento that resorted to force was considered an aberration.[38] The period of conspiracy preceding the pronunciamiento was designed to garner sufficient support to achieve the stated aims without resorting to force. Many participants themselves saw pronunciamientos as a cause of instability, detrimental to the constitutional process, yet they would justify the pronunciamientos they backed as a necessary evil (see chapter 8). Due to the existence of the *derecho de insurrección* (right to insurrection) in Mexico, many pronunciados may not have considered pronunciamientos as wholly unlawful.[39] In a militarized society with a politicized military, force was a vital element of political leverage and a part of the negotiation process. While in many pronunciamientos it remained merely a threat, accounts of the Blancarte series suggest that force was used, at least in the first Plan of Blancarte, when the pronunciados took the government palace.

While most pronunciados aimed to avoid overt use of force in the achievement of their goals, peripheral violence of banditry and looting was often involved and, as the letter shows, there was also an element of coercion in garnering support for pronunciamientos. If the troops needed to be "harangued," as was the case with the second Plan of Blancarte, pronunciamientos were perhaps not exercises in representative politics, as the texts often claimed them to be. If pronunciamientos aimed to win the approval rather than just the backing of others, violence should not have been a factor.

Individual actors may have been forced to join pronunciamientos, making it difficult to prove that they became involved purely for personal gain. The documents relating to the Blancarte series suggest that analysis of the networking aspect of pronunciamientos may be more important than inquiring into personal motivations. Some definitions have suggested that pronunciamientos represented the interests of the corporate bodies within society: the clergy, merchants, soldiery, and regional elites.[40] The collaboration between seemingly opposed political parties in the Blancarte series, as in many series' of pronunciamientos, points to a continually shifting process of coalition building among different factions and parties of the elite.

It has been suggested that puros and conservatives were "unlikely" allies in the first Plan of Blancarte, and conservatives and santanistas were "strange allies" in the second, and that the Plan del Hospicio was "designed to unite moderates, conservatives, monarchists, and discontented soldiers in joint opposition to Arista."[41] Yet puros and conservatives, in Jalisco at least, were not such strange allies in calling for the return of Santa Anna since in 1846, before the parties were formed, the individual actors involved had joined forces to support Santa Anna against Paredes y Arrillaga.[42] These "unlikely" alliances could be explained better by the fact that the hombres de bien, irrespective of party affiliation, needed to protect their class interests and limit democracy to avoid the much-feared social dissolution and preserve territorial unity in the face of increased unrest among the peasant and working majority. Article 8 of the Plan del Hospicio refers to "savages" threatening the frontier states.[43]

These "strange" or "unlikely" allegiances suggest that the puros, moderates, conservatives, monarchists, and santanistas were prepared to ignore their political differences in the interests of the state of Jalisco or the nation of Mexico they wanted to create. While perhaps not truly representing the "will of the people," the hombres de bien represented *their* people through preserving stability, constructing a liberal system and a limited democracy, representative of *their* interests and retaining power in the hands of the privileged, educated, moneyed, and mainly creole elite.[44] If pronunciamientos were primarily a political tool of the hombres de bien, their continued popularity indicates a failure to come to a consensus as late as 1852.

The pronunciamiento stemmed from a context in which constitutional authority was contested due to the lack of consensus. The phenomenon endured due to the inability of the powerful groups in society—the Church, the army, the states, and the wealthy—

to solve the fiscal and constitutional crisis.[45] Therefore the legitimacy of governments and governors, local and national, was not perceived to be superior to that of the pronunciados. Most significant political changes in the period were preceded by a pronunciamiento.[46] Thus it was probable that this was the means by which the existing president, state governor, or legislative assembly had gained those positions. In this case, why should generals, politicians, priests, and citizens who believed they could solve the nation's ills not use the pronunciamiento to put forward their proposal for a system of government that would better suit their (or the nation's) interests? If the frequency and formality of the pronunciamiento meant that it was a meta-constitutional but accepted form of political action, and the participants truly felt themselves and their ideals to be above those of the constitutional powers of the time, then the metatexts—dubious self-interested aims of the individual actors and changing "coalitions" involved—should not be treated with more skepticism than we would treat the motivations and actions of politicians today.

The appeal to ideals such as the will of the people and the good of the nation and the allusion to the breaking of the social pact was one way in which pronunciados justified their claims to legitimacy. The first Plan of Blancarte railed against the Jalisco government's attacks on the "sacred rights" of its citizens, and the second Plan of Blancarte blamed the political crisis on "immorality" and "lack of respect for the constitution and the law."[47]

Pronunciados also used formalized, legalistic procedures to claim the authority to challenge the constitutional order. Pronunciamientos became part of the maneuvering and factional intrigue at a time when congressional and parliamentary procedures were being invented, and pronunciados imitated those procedures to claim equal legitimacy. They followed pseudo-legal procedures involving a series of formal meetings, some voting procedures, and the drawing up of a text. This elaborate bureaucracy and these normative procedures served to make the unlawful lawful.

These pseudo-legal procedures are evident in the documents related to the Blancarte series. One element of the procedure was the staging of a formal meeting to approve the plan, as shown in Doyle's letter: "A council of war was held this morning at 8 o'clock, at which by a unanimity of votes, they approved of the plan."[48]

Another vital part of the form was the oral element. A pronunciamiento was not a pronunciamiento without the *grito* (proclamation): "At 11 o'clock today the act was sent to Valdivia by an 'aide,' as soon as Valdivia had read it, he ordered his troops to form in order and read it to them."[49]

Arguably the defining feature differentiating the pronunciamiento from other forms of revolt was the text. A pronunciamiento had to have a text. The bureaucratic record was the ultimate symbol of legality, and the text created a "mock bureaucracy" in imitation of constitutional procedures. The signatures following the text, like the signatures on a petition, added weight to the pronunciados' claims to legitimate representation of the will of the people.

A large number of planes de adhesión gathered by a pronunciamiento also provided a legitimizing element and "evidence" that the grievances expressed were the will of the majority. Moreover, many of the planes de adhesión came from the legitimate regional authorities. In this series the Ayuntamiento de Guadalajara officially backed the July plan and the Plan del Hospicio.[50] Pseudo-legal language and procedures were also features of the *actas de adhesión* or *rechazo*, which had their own specific form and procedure. These documents are important to consider in their own right, but were they pronunciamientos? It could be argued that there is a difference between a pronunciamiento, which was proactive and aspired to something new, and an acta de adhesión, which was reactive. The signatories of the actas, often civilians, were perhaps more likely to have been coerced into supporting the movement so should not be considered as proactive political actors, meaning that actas had less potential to effect change. In reality, a movement, as was the case with the Blancarte series, needed a combination of pronunciamientos and actas de adhesión to achieve its desired effect, and many contemporaries and signatories of actas called their documents pronunciamientos. While some actas de adhesión reiterated the pronunciamiento word for word, many "cut and pasted," adding grievances of their own so that their signatories could benefit from involvement in the movement. For these reasons the actas de adhesión are worthy of consideration as pronunciamientos.

The typical acta de adhesión included an account of how the events had become known and a description of the meeting and decision-making process.[51] An acta opposing the first Plan of Blancarte, the pronunciamiento of the ayuntamiento of Colotlán, was got up by a local council. It opened with a classic preamble: "In the city of Colotlán, on the third day of the month of August 1852, the local council gathered in special session, and heard the official communication of their local governor . . . regarding the events that took place in the state capital on 26 July and his resolution to not recognize the authorities established in said altercation . . . [as it was his duty to] preserve the constitutional order."[52]

The ayuntamiento of Colotlán considered itself to be above the pronunciados. The language in the text refers to the constitutional order to highlight the fact that the pronunciamiento had broken that order. Many contemporaries, even regular pronunciados, saw the pronunciamiento as dangerous for that very reason. However, pronunciamientos were such a popular form of political action precisely because the constitutional order was not sufficiently established to command the automatic respect of all actors in the political class. While many pronunciamientos did not achieve their stated aims, those that were able to garner sufficient support regionally or nationally, as was the case with the Blancarte series, were in a position to effect real political change.[53] By dint of having such broad-based support, pronunciados were able to claim legitimacy equal if not superior to that of the existing constitutional order. The formulaic introduction of an acta de adhesión to the Plan of Guadalajara of 13 September reflects this. After recording the place and date of the meeting and the officers present, it proclaimed that the persons gathered considered that "the program initiated in Guadalajara on 13 September and modified on 30 October last, accepted by the states of Jalisco, Aguascalientes, Michoacán, Sinaloa, Veracruz, Tamaulipas, the territory of Colima and various towns in the state of México, is the expression of a considerable majority of the nation."[54]

This acta de adhesión illustrates the extent to which the movement triggered by regional concerns became co-opted to target national concerns and spread throughout the country. The interface between the regional and the national is a feature of the pronunciamiento, which in Mexico became a regionally led practice and a favorite of provincial elites. Jalisco elites in tandem with army officers frequently resorted to pronunciamientos. However, as was the case with the Blancarte series, national elites also used regional discontent to develop nationally targeted movements. Geopolitically important states like Guadalajara, with their customs houses and ports, were popular places from which to pronounce, and movements launched from those states were more likely to be successful than those launched from Mexico City.[55] The Blancarte series is an example of one such successful movement. It achieved a large number of planes de adhesión, eventually leading to the end of Arista's government and the dictatorship of Santa Anna, as called for in the second Plan of Blancarte and the Plan del Hospicio. All three pronunciamientos achieved their stated aims. The first won the governorship of Jalisco, and the movement as a whole changed the form of government and the presidency.

The letter from Percy Doyle to the Earl of Malmesbury provides insight into the origins of the second Plan of Blancarte in particular and the conspiracy, maneuvering, and procedures involved in pronunciamientos in Mexico in general. The documents relating to these plans illustrate what has been written about the procedure behind a pronunciamiento and the form of the texts themselves. They also provide some insight into the motivations of the pronunciados and highlight the complexity of individual motivations and political allegiances in the rapidly changing political climate, suggesting that the pronunciamiento should not be considered an exclusively military phenomenon. Further study of the pronunciamiento will help to explain the popularity of the pronunciamiento as the chosen form of political action of the elites and other actors. Finally, the Blancarte series provides an example of how pronunciamientos originating in regional concerns could be co-opted into a national movement by prominent politicians and, with sufficient planes de adhesión, effect real political change. This highlights the need for the further study of the origins of pronunciamientos from a regional perspective to see why certain regions were chosen as bases by national actors and how regional elites exploited national politics for their own ends.

Notes

1. Percy Doyle to the Earl of Malmesbury, Mexico City, 3 October 1852, Public Record Office, Foreign Office Papers (hereafter cited as FO), FO 50/253, fol. 230.

2. The Pronunciamiento del Ayuntamiento de Colotlán (3 August 1852) opposed the Plan de Guadalajara of 26 July. See "Proyecto de reformas al Plan de Guadalajara aprobado por el gobierno y la Guarnición, proclamado el 13 de octubre," in Vázquez (ed.), *Planes en la nación, Libro cuatro*, 402.

3. Fowler, *Mexico in the Age of Proposals*, 29–30.

4. Johnson, *Mexican Revolution of Ayutla*, 8–9, and Guardino, *Peasants, Politics*, 180.

5. Fowler, *Santa Anna of Mexico*, 292, and Fowler, *Tornel and Santa Anna*, 262.

6. Benito Gómez Farías to Valentín Gómez Farías, London, 30 November 1852, Nettie Lee Benson Latin American Collection, University of Texas at Austin (hereafter abbreviated as BLAC), Valentín Gómez Farías Papers 3560.

7. Muría, *Historia de Jalisco*, 3:85–88.

8. "Plan de Blancarte," in Vázquez (ed.), *Planes en la nación, Libro cuatro*, 398.

9. "Plan de Blancarte," in Vázquez (ed.), *Planes en la nación, Libro cuatro*, 399

10. González Navarro, *Anatomía del poder*, 292.

11. "Segundo Plan de Blancarte," in Vázquez (ed.), *Planes en la nación, Libro cuatro*, 400.

12. González Navarro, *Anatomía del poder*, 296.

13. The rumor that he rebelled came from an anonymous letter. See González Navarro, *Anatomía del poder*, 306.

14. "Plan del Hospicio," in Vázquez (ed.), *Planes en la nación, Libro cuatro*, 401.

15. Farías to Farías, London, 30 November 1852, BLAC, Valentín Gómez Farías Papers 3560; Mariano Arista to Jose Vicente Miñon, Mexico, 11 October 1852, BLAC, Ignacio Comonfort Papers.

16. This is not to be understood on twentieth-century terms as in the military authoritarian regimes of the Southern Cone.

17. *La Voz de Jalisco: Periodico oficial del Estado de Jalisco*, 19 March 1953, Hemeroteca Nacional de México (hereafter abbreviated as HNM), Impresos/ document code HRI 95.

18. Percy Doyle to the Earl of Malmesbury, Mexico City, 3 October 1852, FO 5O/253, fols. 230–32.

19. Percy Doyle to the Earl of Malmesbury, 3 October 1852.

20. Percy Doyle to the Earl of Malmesbury, 3 October 1852.

21. Percy Doyle to the Earl of Malmesbury, 3 October 1852.

22. Costeloe, "A *Pronunciamiento*," 245.

23. *La Voz de Jalisco*, 19 March 1853, HNM, HRI 95.

24. González Navarro, *Anatomía del poder*, 304.

25. Costeloe, "A *Pronunciamiento*," 245; Guerra, "El pronunciamiento," 17.

26. González Navarro, *Anatomía del poder*, 300.

27. González Navarro, *Anatomía del poder*, 307.

28. González Navarro, *Anatomía del poder*, 290.

29. Vázquez, "Political Plans and Collaboration," 21.

30. Comellas, *Los primeros pronunciamientos*.

31. *Trait de L'Union*, 2 September 1852.

32. "Segundo Plan de Blancarte," in Vázquez (ed.), *Planes en la nación, Libro cuatro*, 400 (my translation).

33. Rodriguez O., "Origins of the 1832 Rebellion," 146–62.

34. Vázquez, "Political Plans and Collaboration," 21.

35. Hamnett, "Partidos políticos," 574.

36. Costeloe, "A *Pronunciamiento*," 245; Fowler, introduction, this volume, xvi.

37. Vázquez (ed.), *Planes en la nación, Libro cuatro*, 398–99, 401–2.

38. See chapter 12, this volume.

39. Fowler, "Civil Conflict," 64.

40. Tenenbaum, "'They Went Thataway,'" and Guerra, "El pronunciamiento," 17.

41. Johnson, *Mexican Revolution of Ayutla*, 8–9.

42. González Navarro, *Anatomía del poder*, 292.

43. "Plan del Hospicio," in Vázquez (ed.), *Planes en la nación, Libro cuatro*, 401.

44. Fowler, "Civil Conflict," 70.

45. Tenenbaum, "'They Went Thataway,'" 187–205.

46. Guerra, "El pronunciamiento," 15.

47. "Plan de Blancarte" and "Segundo Plan de Blancarte," in Vázquez (ed.), *Planes en la nación, Libro cuatro*, 399–400 (my translation).

48. Percy Doyle to the Earl of Malmesbury, Mexico City, 3 October 1852, FO 50/253, fols. 230–32.

49. Percy Doyle to the Earl of Malmesbury, 3 October 1852.

50. Actas de Cabildo 1852, Sessions of 27 July 1852 and 24 December 1852, Archivo Municipal de Guadalajara, Legajo 38.

51. Guerra, "El pronunciamiento," 17.

52. "Pronunciamiento del Ayuntamiento de Colotlán," in Vázquez (ed.), *Planes en la nación, Libro cuatro*, 399–400 (my translation).

53. Vázquez, "Political Plans and Collaboration," 19, 21–22.

54. Vázquez, "Political Plans and Collaboration," 23.

55. Vázquez, "Political Plans and Collaboration," 23.

Eleven. Inventing the Nation:
The Pronunciamiento and the Construction of Mexican National Identity, 1821–1876

P ronunciamientos were a constant in everyday life in Mexico following independence and throughout much of the nineteenth century. It is because of this that the pronunciamiento phenomenon can be studied not only from a historical perspective but from one that employs cultural or discourse analysis, especially since this practice became a constitutive part in the birth of the incipient country's distinctive culture. In analyzing the cultural dimension of the pronunciamiento it is possible to follow the process through which this practice served as one of the contributing factors in shaping a sense of national identity. This chapter aims, therefore, to broaden the focus of the study of the pronunciamiento, privileging its function as a source for cultural analysis and focusing on it as a building block in the construction of Mexican national identity.[1]

The pronunciamiento is understood here primarily as a written text. These texts were not meant to appear as the work of an individual author but rather as official records of proceedings and meetings. The pronunciamiento intended to involve a community as a whole, or at least the key figures of a given site or group. The launch of a pronunciamiento included several steps. There was a process of preparation of the final meeting, which involved securing support for the pronunciamiento. The meeting in which the pronunciamiento was drafted was conducted as a discussion that led to the conclusions written in the document. The pronunciamiento was then signed, and it was not infrequent that a celebration would follow. Once the pronunciamiento ritual was over, its political and social consequences could be extremely varied, from practically not being taken into account by the significant political actors of the day to leading to meaningful political negotiations or, exceptionally, to sanguinary revolts.[2] The pronunciamiento, therefore, claimed from its inception to have collective legitimacy; that is, it claimed to go beyond the political aims of its authors and primary supporters and instead purported to represent the collective will.

Even though it sometimes seemed to stand for the will of its community, as voting was mentioned in some of the texts, the pronunciamiento did not acquire its debatable representative legitimacy through the kind of established electoral procedures associated with contemporary democracies. Instead, the text frequently claimed that the people attending the pronunciamiento meeting had unanimously reached the decision to "pronounce." Therefore in these documents a source of legitimacy other than what today is understood as democracy can be discerned. In the pronunciamiento it was not unusual for a gathering of just a few people—all of whom bore some form of power and in this sense belonged to the elites of their respective communities—to come out, from a remote and small town, with a document that was openly declared to represent the will not only of their community but of the entire nation.

The pronunciamiento was therefore a written document in close interaction with social events, before and after its drafting. The reasons for studying the pronunciamiento as a cultural text are twofold. On the one hand, the pronunciamiento phenomenon lasted for several decades, and throughout that time its texts were produced constantly and in significant numbers. On the other hand, regardless of the region or time of the nineteenth century in which it was produced, the pronunciamiento retained a number of distinctive characteristics.

Let us consider the pronunciamientos that unfolded from 1821, with the pronunciamiento that led to the independence of Mexico, to 1876, the year in which Porfirio Diaz's Plan of Tuxtepec gave way to his long spell in power. It is a period that spans fifty-five years. During these five and half decades there were hundreds of pronunciamientos, produced almost every month and drafted in all the regions and under all kinds of circumstances.[3] The *Dictamen de la comisión especial de la Excma. asamblea departamental de Sinaloa* (5 January 1846), provides us with newspaper evidence of how the pronunciamiento came to be seen as a very common event, perhaps even too frequent, belonging to a seemingly endless chain of pronunciamientos, as it quoted a journalist's adverse reaction to a pronunciamiento's attempt to "legalize rebellion," since in the journalist's mind, it would just be followed by other similar attempts one after another. That this practice extended over half a century and all over the country, and was depicted as a recurrent feature in the political landscape of the republic, enables us to consider the pronunciamiento as an element that was present in people's life and culture and, more specifically, that was part of the political culture of the military, intellectual, and political elites of the time.

Many documents, even though they were not specifically termed pronunciamientos (i.e., *proclamas, actas, manifiestos,* etc.), were actually produced in the same way and read just like pronunciamientos. There is also evidence from the time that nineteenth-century Mexicans viewed many of these documents as part of the pronunciamiento phenomenon and even called them pronunciamientos regardless of whether their authors had not. In this sense a document like the "Proclama del comandante general de Jalisco a las tropas de su mando" (1 November 1844) gives us an important clue about the way in which Mexicans in the mid-1840s regarded the pronunciamientos. The document labels itself a *proclama* (proclamation or address), and nevertheless within its text the following statement is made: "if you want this to be a pronunciamiento, so be it; never was there a more beautiful one [than this]."[4] Similarly, the Acta de Copayula (31 January 1846), ends its account of the town council meeting saying that: "having concluded this pronunciamiento," assuming, therefore, that the proceedings and the resulting acta were in themselves part of a pronunciamiento. Another example comes from the document entitled "Se declara subversivo el Plan de San Luis" (23 December 1845). In it, the earlier Manifiesto y plan de San Luis (14 December 1845), was referred to without hesitation as a pronunciamiento.[5] This indicates that both for its supporters and for the rest of the political actors, regardless of the titles used, the shared perceived category of many documents was that they were indeed pronunciamientos in as much as they followed the pronunciamiento logic.

The pronunciamiento could be regarded as a particular cultural-textual expression of that time and space since it tended to follow established patterns rather than having distinctive individual features. The pronunciamiento is, therefore, defined here as any document that adhered to the aforementioned practices and had characteristics like those now to be described. In terms of style both structurally and rhetorically speaking, the many and different pronunciamientos resembled one another. In view of this it can be stated that the pronunciamiento was a distinctive literary genre. Structurally, the pronunciamiento usually made a description of the meeting that issued the call to arms or negotiation. This was commonly followed by denunciations of a certain state of affairs; a presentation of grievances. The climax of the pronunciamiento was its advancement of often punctual proposals to solve the problems that had been described. Finally, the conclusion of the text contained a clear legalistic dimension in that those who attended the meeting signed the document. It was not rare for the literate to sign on behalf of the illiterate or even for those who had been unable to attend. Moreover, the language employed in the pronunciamiento texts was not significantly different from that used in other legal documents. Nevertheless, the practice and rhetoric of the pronunciamiento had a political and cultural meaning that went beyond that of other "legal" documents. This could be seen in the peculiar rhetoric of the pronunciamiento.

The pronunciamiento rhetoric was a form of utterance that had a meaning in itself and contributed to the construction of a discourse, that of the political logic of pronunciamiento. This rhetoric is analyzed in the following section, in particular the element within it that relates to building a sense of national identity, accepting at the same time that there are several other issues to be analyzed when studying the pronunciamiento, for instance, the aforementioned concept of legitimacy. So how did the pronunciamiento genre actually contribute to the construction of Mexican national identity?

It is possible to rely on Ernesto Laclau and Chantal Mouffe's views, and their "concept of discourse that includes all the practices and

Martínez Martínez

meanings shaping a particular community of social actors," to analyze the struggle toward the definition of a Mexican national identity in the pronunciamiento.[6] In the nineteenth century the pronunciamiento was clearly one such practice. A discourse, as understood by Mouffe and Laclau, shapes the way in which a society understands events, when such a discourse is hegemonic.[7] This is not to imply that the discourse on national identity was defined by the pronunciamiento alone. Of several ways of studying identity, this one tackles the participation of the elites in the definition of such a discourse. The pronunciamiento is thus interpreted here as one of the constitutive parts of identity discourse.

At least one other theory has a concurrent logic. Benedict Anderson's vision on the development of nationalism went through a stage in which scholars were widely receptive to it. This phase has been followed by criticisms of Anderson's descriptions, particularly from historians of the Spanish American nations.[8] Such a debate, however, is not strictly relevant to the present discussion. Of interest here is Anderson's suggestion that the sense of existence of a nation is a process constructed upon imaginary means. Anderson's argument that the debate should not revolve around communities being false or true, but on how they have been imagined, is endorsed here.[9] When talking about communities in which people do not know one another, particularly in a country with the geographical diversity of Mexico, in which different regional circumstances generate diverse senses of identification, we should analyze why and how not only different regional communities but also dissimilar social classes, religious communities, and ethnic and other groups come to share a sense of belonging to a nation. In this sense the analysis provided here does not attempt to describe the historical process through which Mexican national identity became fully fleshed. It does, however, point to the pronunciamiento as one of the building blocks that contributed to such a process.

The pronunciamiento provides an important piece of analysis for this topic in as much as it was produced directly by the elites, reduced groups of people bearing some form of power within their communities, to mobilize broader sectors of society. For that reason pronunciamientos were circulated widely for the public to be aware of their contents. However, the relevance of the pronunciamiento to the analysis of the formation of a national identity discourse has another dimension that goes beyond illustrating the elites' views of the time and how these were disseminated. The contents and the political significance of the pronunciamiento have to be understood as a struggle for hegemony.

The pronunciamiento was a hybrid creation, as is expressed even in its name. The pronunciamiento was a written document, and it seemed to be important for its leaders and participants for it to be so and for them to sign it, to signify a distinctly legalistic commitment. However, the word *pronunciamiento* itself refers to the oral dimension as its literal meaning is that of enunciating something—*pronouncing*. This could be linked to some reflections of Martin Lienhard regarding the imposition of writing systems in the Americas after the Conquest.

This author points out that throughout Latin America the writing systems of the pre-Columbian societies were mostly for the purpose of registering data and sometimes events and myths. Even where they were elaborate, these systems were not for creating literature, or philosophy, as it is currently understood; practices such as poetry and theater were fundamentally based on orality

Martínez Martínez

and memory rather than on writing.[10] In this context the "imposition of European writing" was an action that founded a novel cultural practice in the Americas, one that created a new sense of what was official, and a privileged form for political communication.[11] This was not only a technical change but a radically different way of doing things. In other words, what today seems "natural," namely the official character of writing, was not always inevitable, and a culture other than Western culture could view writing in a different way. The imposition of writing in Mexico and the rest of Latin America led to what Lienhard called "writing's fetishism," the centrality in official affairs of a cultural practice that was not that of the pre-Columbian communities or that of large segments of the population thereafter.[12] For the purpose of this chapter, even though this leads to the complex and broad debate of the level of westernization that the Mexican people had undergone by that time, suffice it to say that literacy was a commodity of a minority. In the nineteenth century the majority of the population was thus excluded from full political participation in what for nearly three centuries had been imposed as the new official way of dealing with affairs. The leaders of the pronunciamientos were allegedly literate people. They conducted the pronunciamiento meeting and spread it orally. But these same leaders made a point of having a written document, signed even by illiterate people. This shows that the elites were fully aware of the logic of the hegemonic official culture in which they moved, regardless of the groups of people they were leading. This is important for the analysis of political culture. Regardless of all the rhetoric about the communities, the pronunciamiento was one of the practices demonstrating that in independent Mexico the elites tended to make politics in a way that did not include many social groups. The pronunciamiento leaders exercised this exclusion while simultaneously claiming to speak for the people.

A few years after independence, to be Mexican amounted to learning to be one, acquiring a sense of political identification; at least many pronunciamiento leaders would appear to have hoped this was the case. In the "Acta firmada en Tepic" (10 February 1838), the incipient nationalistic sentiment was called upon as a reason to redirect social mobilization. This pronunciamiento argued that the internal debates around what political system should govern the country needed to be abandoned and that instead, people should unite in the common cause of "losing life in defense of the honor and territorial integrity of the republic."[13] The closing statements of this text noted even more clearly that a "good Mexican sacrifices his opinions to save his country."[14] Another perspective emerges in the context of opposing the established administration and keeping control of a key port.[15] The "Pronunciamiento de la guarnición y autoridades de Mazatlán" (7 May 1846), in contrast, spoke of "bogus Mexicans."[16] And the "Acta suscrita en San Luis Potosí" (18 November 1844) went as far as to state that "all Mexicans must sacrifice themselves" for their nation.[17] The aforementioned documents and statements such as "Mexicans who deserve such a name," as expressed in the "Exposición de la junta departamental de Puebla" (5 January 1838), constitute pieces of evidence of the political meanings pronunciamiento leaders gave to individuals when being identified, or not, as Mexican.[18] They show the political implications of national identification: when a nation is fully imagined by a community, then individual obligations exist toward such an entity together with the rights it grants.

Martínez Martínez

This rhetoric also included elements of the ideas that had contributed to the atmosphere leading to independence. The process of the independence of Texas shows that by 1836, the interpretations of creole patriots such as Servando Teresa de Mier or Carlos María de Bustamante had been disseminated enough to be used in the remonstrances that were made against the possibility of Texas seceding from Mexico. The "Acta firmada en la villa de Cunduacán" (18 August 1836) stated that the Texans wanted "to break apart the land of the Aztecs," thus associating the indigenous past of Mexico with the Aztec civilization, suggesting with this assertion that before the Conquest there was one indivisible Aztec nation, when in fact several indigenous nations with different cultures existed.[19] Likewise, the "Plan del capitán Mariano Olarte" (20 December 1836) described Mexico as "the fatherland of the ancient Aztecs."[20] What the pronunciamientos enable us to appreciate is that throughout the nineteenth century the political use of this version of history became well known and was adopted by the elites drafting these documents. Given the diffusion of the pronunciamiento, these images of history were also making their way into the imaginary of the general population.

Anderson argues that print-capitalism was a source of identification as people living far away from one another and in diverse circumstances could feel through it that they were also part of the larger imagined community.[21] It was a constant characteristic and aim of the pronunciamiento to be published and disseminated by the authorities and communities. That the intellectual, military, and political elites of nineteenth-century Mexico were aware of the power of newspapers is unquestionable. For instance, in the *Decreto de la asamblea de Yucatán* (1 January 1846), one of its proposals was to establish two publicly funded newspapers, in different cities, "exclusively dedicated" to "shaping the opinion" of the readers, in the hope of persuading them of the "need" to ask for the protection of a foreign nation. Remarkably, the same fragment of the pronunciamiento called for all "influential people" to spread the same ideas.[22] Thus the diffusion of certain conceptions about Mexican identity, paired with other political issues, was an aim shared by the elites. While this does not mean that such stances came to be part of the hegemonic discourse, they were part of a complex series of events purposely and inadvertently contributing to the creation of an understanding of Mexican identity.

One of the issues that repeatedly appeared in the pronunciamientos was that of Mexico's Spanish heritage, which acquired a number of divergent manifestations. Evidence perhaps of the divide that separated the pronunciamiento leaders from the population at large was their unnoted use of the Spanish language in all official practices as well as in the pronunciamientos: a tangible example of their Spanish heritage that does not appear ever to have been mentioned. One document that came close to taking this into account, by showing some awareness of the linguistic conflicts taking place among the communities, was the "Planteamiento de la solución al levantamiento del sur" (15 May 1843). The language issue, which must have been an everyday reality for the pronunciamiento leaders of nineteenth-century Mexico, was at least considered in this pronunciamiento, since Mexico's language diversity is alluded to and the difficulties posed by translation are pointed out. There is even a hint at the official character of the pronunciamiento, and its dissociation from ordinary people, in its expression of the need to send messages to different towns, "not written in office-speak (*estilo de oficina*), which they do not understand, and which does not speak to their hearts."[23] This tends to support the assertion that the pronunciamiento was an expression of "writing's fetishism" by the social and political leaders of the country.

The reality of a monarchical past of more than two hundred years is one of the concrete contents of the Spanish heritage referred to in some pronunciamientos. Some nineteenth-century leaders seemed to assume that such a background would influence people's political behavior. For example, in the "Exposición de la junta departamental de Puebla" (5 January 1838), reflections upon the possibility of implementing a democratic republican system in Mexico conclude that after having experienced a monarchical system, "we are incapable of adopting" a democracy.[24] While this argument, given in 1838, could also be related to a defense of the centralist republic, the political conclusion of this and other pronunciamientos suggested that by having a monarchical past Mexicans were incapable of living in a democracy and implied, by default, that Mexico had inherited a monarchical identity from Spain.

The aspect of Spanish heritage alluded to more frequently in a number of pronunciamientos is Catholicism. This appears to have been regarded as the most significant legacy of the colonial period. The statements in favor of the Catholic Church seemed to have been both an echo of the foundational Plan of Iguala and a way of not alienating or of even aligning themselves with the factual power represented by such a Church, the only legal one in independent Mexico. However, these mentions also hint at the possibility that there was a crucial matter beyond considerations of power—that several pronunciamiento authors were inclined to emphasize the union of communities around the Catholic Church, as that might have been the main element linking otherwise very diverse groups into a coherent imagined community; further research into this needs to be undertaken. Catholicism was mentioned in a positive way equally in pronunciamientos signed by priests and others where there was no obvious clerical presence, in documents where there was a clear mingling between political and religious issues, and in others devoid of such interests. It would, of course, be naïve not to consider the element of power when talking about the Catholic Church in nineteenth-century Mexico. For example, in the context of the reforms implemented throughout the previous two years by Valentín Gómez Farías and his allies, the "Plan de varios vecinos de la ciudad de México para declarar que su apoyo a la religión es incompatible con el sistema republicano federal" (12 June 1835), represented a movement that was simultaneously opposed to federalism and religious freedom and made reference to the "sacrosanct religion we inherited from our elders."[25] Together with the reality of existing power games, the fact remains that people have beliefs and that in many circumstances it is precisely these beliefs that flesh out a sense of identity.

There were, thus, references to the Spanish heritage in the pronunciamiento. What is not clear is what the overall appreciation of such a legacy was. What the pronunciamiento seems to provide so far is the confirmation that there were different and contested versions of Mexican national identity among the elites in this period. In this sense, within the 1820s there were both expressions that emphasized the links with Spain and statements favoring the dissolution of any such links. The Plan of Iguala (24 February 1821), spoke about Spain educating people and making Mexico great.[26] But the Plan of Perote (16 September 1828) included a declaration in favor of the "total expulsion" of Spaniards from Mexico. These contrasts attest to how no discourse on national identity was yet hegemonic.

Martínez Martínez

The presence of the neighboring United States as an issue for Mexican national identity can also be seen to have been noted from the outset. It is possible to find expressions of admiration toward the United States in the pronunciamientos, which continued the identification that Mexican political elites had expressed toward the United States from before and particularly in the aftermath of Mexican independence.[27] In this regard the "Acta del pronunciamiento de las autoridades y pueblo de Culiacán" (13 January 1838) contained praise for Washington as a visionary hero and praise for the federal system that had "created happiness for that nation."[28] This was meant to nudge Mexico toward a similar federal system. Some historians of our time would argue that the source of inspiration for the 1824 Mexican Constitution was not that of the United States.[29] Yet several pronunciamiento authors seem to have thought otherwise, as it is possible to read repeated statements like the one in the "Representación de los militares y empleados del departamento de Aguascalientes para que el congreso constituyente se aleje de las cartas de 1824 y 1836" (25 August 1842), which argued that "imitating" the United States had led to Mexico's early problems.[30]

Another aspect of interest involving the United States is that in the pronunciamientos one can find opposed points of view concerning the similarities and differences between the cultures of the two nations and the relation of these cultures to their ability to adopt certain political systems. On the one hand, it is possible to read a centralist argument that stressed differences between the two countries and blamed Mexico's problems in Mexico on having imitated the United States political model, as evidenced in the "Exposición y plan de la ciudad de Toluca sobre que se establezca en la nación el sistema popular, representativo y central" (29 May

1835), which describes adoption of federalism "without anticipating the disgraceful consequences" it would have. On the other hand, taking the "Representación de 528 vecinos de la ciudad de Toluca por el restablecimiento del sistema federal" (21 November 1837) as an example, it is equally possible to find a text pointing out that the differences between the United States and Mexico in terms of political practices and behaviors merely constituted an excuse to achieve certain political aims, and it denounced the "pretext of our habits not being similar to those of North America."[31] This representación therefore dismissed the notion that the cultural differences between Mexican and U.S. citizens would make it impossible for Mexico to be a federation. Again this points toward a still undefined identity discourse, in which the accepted and acceptable models to be followed had not yet been established.

It was perhaps because of the lack of consensus exemplified in the documents cited that in some pronunciamientos one gets the impression of the authors realizing that they could, in fact, impact the consolidation of Mexico as a nation as they watched the events unfold before their very eyes. For example, disappointment with the centralist system provoked the federalist mobilization of the time.[32] In this setting the "Proclama y plan de José Urrea y pronunciamiento de la guarnición de Arizpe" (26 December 1837) called for Mexico to take its place among "the powerful countries of the world."[33] Leaders like Urrea clearly had the creation of a national identity as an aim that should be pursued by the Mexican administrations, as in the same pronunciamiento he also said that the government should provide the means for the people to be educated and for "the national character to be formed."[34] Other examples of projects for the Mexican nation relate to what in the twentieth century would be referred to as *mestizaje*. In the Plan of Iguala (24 February 1821) the union of "Europeans and Americans, Indians and Indigenous people" is advocated as "the only solid base" for the welfare of the country.[35]

A final example within this review of pronunciamientos comes from the "Plan de la monarquía indígena" (2 February 1834). This case serves as a reminder that these examples form a display of sorts; their presentation is not aimed at suggesting that the pronunciamientos quoted were especially significant for Mexican culture. Instead, those selected serve the purpose of showing that the pronunciamiento phenomenon seen as a whole contributed toward the creation of a national identity. The "Plan de la monarquía indígena" is not even mentioned in the major works of historiography on the period to which it belongs, as it did not have widespread political consequences. This pronunciamiento proposed the creation of a monarchy with an emperor who was to be married to a white woman if he was an Indian man, or to a "pure Indian woman" if he was white, thus engendering a royal family of mixed ancestry, representative of a *mestizo* race, as such miscegenation would subsequently be defined.[36] This pronunciamiento could be seen as a call for the creation of something new, an identity materialized in a royal family that was neither pre-Columbian nor Spanish. This and all the contested visions noted in the examples analyzed so far show that the pronunciamiento bore elements of a national culture and identity in formation, conscious of its legacies and aspirations, its roots and routes.

The process of construction of a Mexican national identity discourse had the pronunciamiento phenomenon as one of its elements. The pronunciamiento provides a significant source for the analysis of Mexican political culture in the nineteenth century, and it may be possible to see similarities between the politics of that time and contemporary events. Lienhard argues that in Latin America not only are there "asymmetries" in the sociopolitical interaction between the "hegemonic sectors" and the rest of the social groups but that the holders of power even "fix the rules of the game."[37] This relates both to political control and, more important, to a virtual monopoly over the possibility of defining what constitutes official life in a given country. The pronunciamiento culture shows, in its authors' attempts at legitimizing their movements, that pronunciamiento leaders were competing fiercely to establish the rules of the political game in Mexico by means of acquiring legitimacy.

The pronunciamiento as a literary genre has specific characteristics and is surrounded by a variety of social events; it is not only a source for historians but a suite of documents worthy of cultural analysis. Examining the pronunciamiento in such a way reveals that it played a part in the debate surrounding construction of a hegemonic discourse of Mexican national identity. The pronunciamiento phenomenon itself was an expression of the identity under construction in as much as the pronunciamiento was a political-cultural tool employed by the social actors of the day in their struggle for power. This confrontation for power seems to suggest, in the pronunciamiento culture, a severe dissociation between the elites and the rest of the Mexican people. It is a practice that resembles a game in which official life—that is to say, effective control of society—tended to be in the hands of the leaders, to the radical exclusion of the rest of the communities. Besides indicating that the people were manipulated by the elites, this was a much more complex context, in which the elites, through pronunciamientos, sought legitimacy precisely by way of claiming to represent the nation and the people, while acting in ways that placed the contention for power strictly among the elites and out of the reach of most people. The question that inevitably arises is whether the dissociation between the sociopolitical leaders and the people, incarnated in the pronunciamiento culture, still persists in today's Mexico. Meanwhile, the pronunciamiento phenomenon provides fertile ground for the study of Mexican political culture in the nineteenth century and of the manner in which its texts contributed, both consciously and unintentionally, to constructing an incipient sense of nationhood and national identity in postcolonial Mexico during its early national period.

Notes

This chapter has benefited from the comments made by Timothy Anna and Michael Ducey at the "Forceful Negotiations" conference and from the notes of the anonymous reviewer appointed by the University of Nebraska Press.

1. This chapter's approach is part of a book project on Mexican national identity.

2. Vázquez, "El modelo de pronunciamiento"; Guerra, "El pronunciamiento."

3. Within the first year of the pronunciamientos project over one thousand pronunciamientos were added to its database.

4. "Proclama del comandante general de Jalisco a las tropas de su mando (1 November 1844)," in Vázquez (ed.), *Planes en la nación, Libro cuatro*, 225.

5. "Acta de Copayula (31 January 1846)," and "Manifiesto y plan de San Luis (14 December 1845)," in Vázquez (ed.), *Planes en la nación, Libro cuatro*, 309, 289–90.

6. Howarth, *Discourse*, 5.

7. Laclau and Mouffe, *Hegemony and Socialist Strategy*.

8. Guerra, "Forms of Communication." I thank Natasha Picôt for advice on bibliography on nationalism and the critiques to Anderson's theory.

9. Anderson, *Imagined Communities*, 6.

10. Lienhard, *La voz y su huella*, 21.

11. Lienhard, *La voz y su huella*, 12.

12. Lienhard, *La voz y su huella*, 12.

13. "Acta firmada en Tepic (10 February 1838)," in Vázquez (ed.), *Planes en la nación, Libro tres*, 150.

14. "Acta firmada en Tepic (10 February 1838)."

15. Santoni, *Mexicans at Arms*, 126.

16. "Pronunciamiento de la guarnición y autoridades de Mazatlán (7 May 1846)," in Vázquez (ed.), *Planes en la nación, Libro cuatro*, 315–16.

17. "Acta suscrita en San Luis Potosí (18 November 1844)," in Vázquez (ed.), *Planes en la nación, Libro cuatro*, 232.

18. "Exposición de la junta departamental de Puebla (5 January 1838)," in Vázquez (ed.), *Planes en la nación, Libro tres*, 143.

19. "Acta firmada en la villa de Cunduacán (18 August 1836)," in Vázquez (ed.), *Planes en la nación, Libro tres*, 87–88.

20. "Plan del capitán Mariano Olarte (20 December 1836)," in Vázquez (ed.), *Planes en la nación, Libro tres*, 96–98.

21. Anderson, *Imagined Communities*, 44–46.

22. "Decreto de la asamblea de Yucatán (1 January 1846)," in Vázquez (ed.), *Planes en la nación, Libro cuatro*, 296.

23. "Planteamiento de la solución al levantamiento del sur (15 May 1843)," in Vázquez (ed.), *Planes en la nación, Libro cuatro*, 219.

24. "Exposición de la junta departamental de Puebla (5 January 1838)," in Vázquez (ed.), *Planes en la nación, Libro tres*, 141–43.

25. "Plan de varios vecinos de la ciudad de México para declarar que su apoyo a la religión es incompatible con el sistema republicano federal (12 June 1835)," in Vázquez (ed.), *Planes en la nación, Libro cuatro*, 44.

26. "Plan de Iguala (24 February 1821)," Jiménez Codinach (ed.), *Planes en la nación, Libro uno*, 123–24.

27. Brack, *Mexico Views Manifest Destiny*, 15–25.

28. "Acta del pronunciamiento de las autoridades y pueblo de Culiacán (13 January 1838)," in Vázquez (ed.), *Planes en la nación, Libro tres*, 145–47.

29. Rodríguez O., "Constitution of 1824." An interpretation of Mexico's federal system as the outcome of domestic developments can be found in Anna, *Forging Mexico*, 109–10, and Benson, *Provincial Deputation*, 65–66.

30. "Representación de los militares y empleados del departamento de Aguascalientes para que el congreso constituyente se aleje de las cartas de 1824 y 1836 (25 August 1842)," Archivo Histórico de la Secretaría de la Defensa Nacional, Mexico City, XI/481.3/1780, fols. 48–55.

Martínez Martínez

31. "Exposición y plan de la ciudad de Toluca sobre que se establezca en la nación el sistema popular, representivo y central" (29 May 1835), Archivo General de la Nación, Mexico City, Historia, vol. 283; "Representación de 528 vecinos de la ciudad de Toluca por el restablecimiento del sistema federal" (21 November 1837), Colegio de México, Mexico City, J. Z. Vázquez Planes y documentos, Caja 16, Exp. 2, fol. 9.

32. Costeloe, *The Central Republic*, 137–38.

33. "Proclama y plan de José Urrea y pronunciamiento de la guarnición de Arizpe (26 December 1837)," in Vázquez (ed.), *Planes en la nación, Libro tres*, 135–36.

34. "Proclama y plan de José Urrea y pronunciamiento de la guarnición de Arizpe."

35. "Plan de Iguala (24 February 1821)," in Jiménez Codinach (ed.), *Planes en la nación, Libro uno*, 123–24.

36. "Plan de la monarquía indígena (2 February 1834)," in Vázquez (ed.), *Planes en la nación, Libro dos*, 208–9.

37. Lienhard, *La voz y su huella*, 98.

Twelve. "I Pronounce Thus I Exist": *Redefining the Pronunciamiento in Independent Mexico, 1821–1876*

François-Xavier Guerra rightly noted that the phenomenon of the *pronunciamiento* should be considered one of the most important political practices of nineteenth-century Mexico because of its recurrence.[1] From the achievement of independence in 1821 to the Plan of Tuxtepec that brought Porfirio Díaz to power in 1876 more than fifteen hundred pronunciamientos were plotted, launched, circulated, and negotiated across the country, both at a national and at a regional level. Albeit originally instigated by army officers, this particular Hispano-Mexican exercise in petitioning or lobbying, did not take long to become widespread and popularized.[2] It was endorsed and adopted by soldiers and civilians alike, with its robust attempt to force negotiation or significant concessions through a public statement of defiance and/or disobedience, and with the threat of violence (at times explicitly noted, at other times implicitly assumed). Although only a handful of pronunciamientos were actually successful in effecting political change, most of the major shifts at a national level in government policy and personnel were nonetheless brought about as a result of this typically paradoxical practice, which could be unlawful yet legitimate, revolutionary and at the same time tiresomely bureaucratic, openly aggressive yet not always violent, and which defied the government while hoping to negotiate with it.

The groundbreaking model was forged in the trendsetting and ultimately successful pronunciamientos of Rafael del Riego (Cabezas de San Juan, Spain, 1 January 1820), Iguala (24 February 1821), and Veracruz and Casa Mata (2 December 1822 and 1 February 1823).[3] Adopting the model, disgruntled officers, town council members, priests, businessmen, and villagers found themselves resorting to this curiously idiosyncratic form of forceful petitioning to the extent that by the 1830s there were years in which more than three hundred communities or corporate bodies "pronounced" in the ostensible hope of seeing their grievances addressed—pueblos, *guarniciones* (garrisons), *ayuntamientos* (town councils), *parroquias* (parish churches), *barrios* and *vecinos* (neighborhoods), and *tribus* (Indian tribes). Whether calling for the removal of an unpopular president, minister, governor, or local official; a shift in policy; the reversal of a controversial law; or a change in political system (to name but a sample of common demands), the pronunciamiento became the extra-constitutional yet commonly accepted way of making representations to the local and national governments. The domino format of the pronunciamiento, whereby people expected that the successful *grito* would be backed by a series of *actas* or *planes de adhesión* (declarations of allegiance) no doubt contributed in transforming this practice into one that was used extensively, turning the original act of insubordination, usually perpetrated by a small group of restless armed men, into potentially widespread petitioning movements with popular appeal and significant support.

In this final chapter I review the origins of this intriguing practice to attempt to establish what purposes the pronunciamiento served and, in so doing, to come to an understanding of its relevance and importance in the political and cultural life of Mexico during the early national period. This entails redefining the complex and multifaceted pronunciamiento phenomenon, given that conventional wisdom would still have us believe it was nothing more than a "revolt, insurrection, [or] military rising."[4]

The Pronunciamiento: An Established Means of Seeking Change in Nineteenth-Century Mexico

The pronunciamiento, from very early on, became a ritualistic and pseudo-legal practice that, albeit meta-constitutional and unlawful, served the main purpose of allowing a broad range of actors, both enfranchised *and* disenfranchised, to attempt to influence, inform, participate in, and engage with local and national politics. The fact that pronunciamientos became an established way of seeking to effect change is certainly worthy of note. It highlights one of the key purposes of this widely used practice: to force those in positions of power to listen to the demands that the *pronunciados* made and, through intimidation, to ensure that these were met. It is also noteworthy in terms of what can be inferred about the society and context in which the pronunciamiento arose, developed, and evolved as a way of "doing politics."

Although there were significant variations and the style and content of the pronunciamiento changed over the years, the broad pattern of this exercise in aggressive complaining remained interestingly the same. Generally a conspiracy led to a gathering of disgruntled people in a garrison, *ayuntamiento*, or church, where a formal meeting was held to discuss the grievance at hand. A secretary was appointed to take the minutes, which in turn and somewhat bureaucratically became the *acta* of the pronunciamiento once it was launched. The pronunciamiento text itself developed into a genre in its own right, with a characteristically formal register and an awkward legalistic style. A preamble was often included in its opening paragraphs outlining the nature of the grievances that had brought the community together on that day and at that time before the "unanimous" decision to "pronounce" had been reached, typically after a lengthy discussion. As became the norm, a numbered petition ensued in which the aggrieved collective listed the actions they believed needed to be taken to remedy their critical situation. It was here that the explicit or veiled threat was included, noting that people would resort to violence should the requested demands not be met. The representative nature of the pronunciamiento or plan was enhanced by including the signatures of all those present (who could read and write). The said document was then launched with the corresponding *grito*, pealing of church bells, and fanfare of festive music and fireworks; copies of it were sent to all the relevant authorities, including both those being publicly challenged in the hope that they would be intimidated into implementing the pronunciados' demands and those the pronunciados hoped would come out in support by launching their own *pronunciamientos de adhesión* in a copycat fashion, mimicking the steps outlined.[5]

In a context of contested authority and questioned (as well as questionable) legitimacy—and with the enduring legacy of violence hanging over from an eleven-year-long civil war of independence that had resulted in the emergence of a politicized army and, to a certain degree, a militarized society—it is perhaps not surprising that this threatening, ritualized, and deliberately bureaucratic practice became so popular.[6] It was a natural response to a context of turbulence and change, in which power structures were unclear and contested, and the institutional mechanisms for reform were perceived as being weak, ineffective, and unrepresentative.

The power vacuum resulting from the dissolution of the Spanish monarchy in 1808, paired with the generation-long constitutional crisis it engendered in the Hispanic world, undoubtedly generated a context in which nobody and everybody could claim to be the legitimate representative of the nation's sovereignty or the so-called general will. The fact that the first pronunciamientos erupted in Spain following Ferdinand VII's return to the throne and his refusal to recognize the constitutional institutions that had emerged in his absence (i.e., abolishing the liberal 1812 Cádiz charter) indicates how the said constitutional crisis informed and justified this practice. Against a backdrop in which long-established governmental figures and institutions were shown to have no authority or enduring legitimacy, and were replaced randomly or arbitrarily by a plethora of contesting and contested rulers and juntas at both local and national levels, it is not surprising that the pronunciamiento became an acceptable way of seeking change. People were faced with institutional breakdown in which an absolutist monarch found himself vying for power alongside and against improvised juntas, an elected yet disbanded Cortes, powerful military governors, constituted and then abolished provincial deputations, and insurgent warlords with a popular following. In this context the pronunciamiento offered a way of giving forceful representations legitimacy and a fledgling institutional sense. In the absence of institutions with legitimacy and authority recognized and respected by society at large, the pronunciamiento's form evidences a quest for legitimizing through bureaucratic formalism in what was otherwise an arguably revolutionary exercise.

The fact that the pronunciamiento could be successful in effecting major political change—and almost bloodlessly, as was evidenced following Riego's surprising ability to garner the kind of support in 1820 that forced the monarch to restore the 1812 Constitution—made the pronunciamiento all the more appealing as a way of seeking to bring about change in a time of contested authority and questioned legitimacy.[7] Bearing in mind that in Mexico, Agustín de Iturbide's Plan of Iguala resulted in an essentially consensual declaration of independence and eventually made a disgruntled royalist officer the emperor of a sovereign nation, it is obvious that the pronunciamiento would prove worthy of emulation (see introduction and chapters 1 and 2). Conditions following independence involved the absence of a long-established state or a clearly defined representative political system, constitutions that ultimately disenfranchised the popular classes, governments that were either unconstitutional or perceived as despotic, and institutional channels of effecting change becoming exhausted or proving unworkable. In these circumstances it is not difficult to appreciate how it came to pass that the pronunciamiento became the most common and popular means for urban and rural communities, soldiers and civilians alike, to try to inform and influence local and national politics, especially when the pronunciamientos of Cabezas de San Juan, Iguala, and Casa Mata had demonstrated that significant change could be negotiated this way.

In one sense the pronunciamiento could almost be depicted as a representative form of seeking popular participation through the consultative nature of the demands made and the expectation that the plans of allegiance it received would allow the disenfranchised a say in the way they were governed.[8] In another sense it was obviously a force of chaos. The practice generated instability, preventing any government or system from ever having the time and space to take root properly or acquire the kind of authority and legitimacy that would have made the pronunciamiento redundant with its claim to stem from the people's right to petition or even insurrection. Moreover, as evidenced in chapter 4, the pronunciamiento's potential for violence must not be underplayed, understated, or underestimated.

From what has been noted so far and the success of the precursors Riego, Iturbide, Antonio López de Santa Anna, and the rebels of Casa Mata, it is evident that the pronunciamiento was endowed with an aura of prestige that proved worthy of emulation at a time when the legitimacy of every government was questioned, and government authority was notoriously weak.[9]

However, beyond its major and obvious purpose of seeking to effect change forcefully in a revolutionary age, there were other aspects to the experience of the pronunciamiento that deserve consideration and may help explain the resonance this practice acquired in Mexico at the time. This pertains especially if we accept that not all pronunciamientos were instigated by army officers and that the *actas de adhesión* or *rechazo* launched by a range of civilian actors were pronunciamientos in their own right (see introduction). A closer look at the texts that were circulated and the circumstances in which they were launched demonstrates that the pronunciamiento was an extremely versatile and multifaceted practice with multiple political and cultural dimensions and purposes. As discussed later, although a pronunciamiento was primarily a means of effecting change, it was also an exercise whereby individuals and above all communities and corporate bodies could express their political beliefs and publicize their affinities vis-à-vis other pronunciados and the government. In this sense it became like a marker of identity at a time when notions of nationhood or provincehood were fluid and contested and the beliefs of particular political factions were malleable. Furthermore, it was a practice that allowed pueblos, ayuntamientos, parroquias, and barrios to make national trends work for local needs, legitimizing the unlawful and providing a bureaucratic means for civilizing or institutionalizing the *barbarie* (barbarism) of provincial independent Spanish America, to use Domingo F. Sarmiento's term.[10] In broader cultural terms, rethinking the pronunciamiento as an *experience*, from the perspective of the gathered community it could also be an act of communion, an excuse for a fiesta, and a space in which organic democracy could flourish—where the people could participate in politics and exercise their perceived right of petition regardless of whether they were disenfranchised. Last but not least, the pronunciamiento became an expected if not a necessary career move for any aspiring political actor. A quick survey of the careers of the leading general-presidents of nineteenth-century Mexico highlights the obvious fact that all of them, invariably, participated in, actively supported, benefited from, or led a pronunciamiento at some point in their careers.

The Pronunciamiento's Many Uses

Inherently associated with the forceful demand for change was the pronunciamiento's voicing or "pronouncing" of an opinion. As a result, regardless of whether the pronunciamiento succeeded in influencing the political scene, it served the purpose of making known what a given community believed in.[11] This in turn had two clear and distinct uses. First, it offered the community the opportunity to engage with the analysis of a particular problem and provide a public statement in which people publicized their views on remedies. Second, it allowed the community to articulate a communal sense of identity on the basis of their standpoint vis-à-vis "other" people or communities with whom they wanted to be associated or from whom they disassociated themselves.

If we take the preamble of the Plan of Cuernavaca of 25 May 1834 as a representative opening statement, it allows us to appreciate that the pronunciamiento created a textual space in which political analysis could be vocalized and circulated:

> Submerged in the most dreadful confusion and disorder as a result of the violent measures our legislative bodies have inflicted on the Mexican Republic, filling this period with blood and tears, allowing absolute demagoguery to assault criminally our foundational Constitution which took so many sacrifices to draft, it is indispensable for us to make known expressly the real meaning of the votes of our pueblos, so that positive and precise measures are taken to remedy these ills and destroy the existence of the Masonic lodges that have planted the seed of our internal divisions.[12]

On the periphery of early institutional spaces such as national or state congresses, the pronunciamiento afforded pueblos, vecinos, and guarniciones a chance to disseminate their understanding of the political problems they faced. In many cases such expressions of discontent were broadly rhetorical, prone to overdosing on adjectives, verging on the melodramatic, and devoid of any serious analytical depth. In others, however, the points were carefully thought out and structured along a clear argumentative thread. In the case of the Plan of Orizaba of 19 May 1835, for instance, the call for a change in the political system with the demand that the 1824 federal charter be replaced with a constitution that was "more analogous to [our] needs, demands, and customs, and that may guarantee better our independence, domestic peace, and the Catholic faith we profess" was made following a particularly sophisticated interpretation of how "the federal system is not conducive to [bringing about] the Mexicans' happiness."[13]

In this sense a pronunciamiento provided the perfect vehicle for professions of faith to be made. A study of the numerous pronunciamientos the 1834 Plan of Cuernavaca and the 1835 Plan of Orizaba inspired, both for and against them, demonstrates the extent to which this practice became the accepted way for communities to publicize their viewpoint. The pronunciamiento, and in particular that of *adhesión*, and the *despronunciamiento* (launched after a given corporate body had changed its mind) was often more a statement than a petition, designed for the public arena and officialdom, adorned as it was in legalistic language.[14] Taking as an example the numerous *actas de adhesión* the 1834 Plan of Cuernavaca received, they offered a whole range of political actors a way of saying publicly not only that they supported the said pronunciamiento but that they were devout Roman Catholics, did not want to tolerate any other religion, condemned the anti-clerical reforms of the 1833–34 Congress as well as the figure of Vice President Valentín Gómez Farías, and were prepared to entrust Santa Anna with whatever powers he might consider necessary to protect their religion.[15] To put it differently, above and beyond being a forceful petition the pronunciamiento was a robust way of disseminating one's credo, especially at a volatile time when it was important for public figures and communities to come out and declare whose side they were on or what they believed in, showing support or opposition to a particular government or preceding pronunciamiento.

The pronunciamiento was thus as much about publicizing a view, a cause, or a person (in those cases where it backed or condemned a particular individual) as it was about seeking to negotiate change. It was an exercise in public relations at a time of upheaval and uncertainty, which served to place the individual and the community, or the individual as part of the community (garrison, pueblo, barrio, etc.) on the political map.

Consequently the pronunciamiento served as a marker of identity. With its forthright references to what the pronunciados' garrison or town council stood for, faced with issues such as the legality of a particular government, social injustice, the popular will, sovereignty, federalism, centralism, and the like, it was possible for an aggrieved group of people to project an idea of who they were. Unsurprisingly, the texts are full of allusions to collective codes of behavior and notions of communal identity vis-à-vis the "other," whether another group of pronunciados or the government. Two examples to illustrate this point are the 1832 pronunciamientos of Tarecuato and Seris. The Plan of Tarecuato of 26 January 1832 started by declaring that "these Pueblos are free of dependence, and are sovereign, and [reject] royal patrimony, the English and Santa Anna. We live according to God's will." In other words, the first point these pronunciados wanted to make and publicize was that they were God-fearing, free, and sovereign and would not bow before kings, Englishmen, or Santa Anna, thus distancing and differentiating themselves from monarchists, foreigners, and the notorious caudillo of Veracruz. In a similar fashion the Plan of Seris of 3 June 1832 opened with the statement that the villagers of Seris were "true lovers of the patria, idolaters of liberty," and were resolved to "oppose the evils that afflict the patria as a result of the ministries' despotism and tyranny," defending their plan "with our weapons in our hands." They were thus telling other Mexicans that the people of Seris were patriotic, freedom-loving, brave, and committed to backing Santa Anna's Plan of Veracruz of 2 January 1832, while refraining from "assaulting properties or private persons" and ensuring that they obeyed "the

Fowler

Constitution and general laws."[16] As suggested by Germán Martínez Martínez in the previous chapter, the pronunciamiento not only served to vocalize a sense of local-communal identity; it contributed to forging a sense of nationhood.

It also provided a vehicle for town councils, villages, and regional elites to use preceding pronunciamientos to suit local needs. In most pronunciamientos de adhesión the different ayuntamientos and/or guarniciones repeated the articles of the pronunciamiento they were backing but did not miss the opportunity to add demands that were of a strictly local nature. To note just one example, the Acta of Jonacatepec of 2 June 1835 implicitly supported the plans of Orizaba and Toluca, *and* appended to the original pronunciamientos' demand for the creation of a "central representative popular government" the request that one Francisco Saldívar be made commander general of the district.[17] As evidenced in Kerry McDonald's chapter, the elites of San Luis Potosí clearly became quite adept at making national pronunciamientos conform with and aid local interests.

The pronunciamiento served the further important purpose of legitimizing the unlawful, and in so doing, empowering the disempowered and the marginalized through the written (and spoken) word. The importance of the word deserves to be highlighted. There was no pronunciamiento without a plan or acta. In this sense pronunciamientos relied more on words than on guns. The text gave legal, moral, and political meaning to the original act of insubordination or insurrection. Without it, those involved would be criminals, unruly rebels, rioters, mutineers, and bandits. Thus the acta with its plan, by its very existence, served to justify an action that was outside the law and could have recourse to violence. What is more, it enshrined the unlawful in legality through its bureaucratic formalism, ensuring that the text, again by its very existence, transformed a criminal action according to the established authorities into a rightful and pseudo-legal one according to its own alternative logic and aspiring or self-proclaimed authority.

The Plan of Iguala, as seen repeatedly throughout this volume, presented Mexico with an incredibly resonant and resilient prototype. Its text, with its preamble, demands, and petitioned articles, converted an act of insubordination against New Spain's colonial government into a foundational pact of its own accord. Thus the pronunciamiento text enabled the broken pact to be replaced by an alternative one, ensuring, at least in theory, that a negotiated resolution reached between government and pronunciados was both possible and "legally" binding.

It also empowered the disempowered by creating a means whereby, eventually, an illegal and potentially violent political action, exercised or perpetrated by disenfranchised actors, could become a legitimate set of demands upon which a new order was forged. In the most extreme cases the pronunciamiento legitimized the overthrow of a given constitutional order and government (e.g., the closure of the elected 1833–34 Congress or the abolition of the 1824 Constitution in 1835). In the less dramatic cases, to quote Michael P. Costeloe, it enabled "the poor to augment their income with loot, and bandits to legitimize their trade."[18] The pronunciamiento thus served the paradoxical needs of those who used this practice as a means of institutionalizing the wilderness, civilizing barbarism, as well as of those who gave bureaucratic form to angry protests and mob rule.

When it spread beyond the officers' barracks or the priests' parish church, the pronunciamiento could certainly be construed as an act of communion in the manner in which it brought a community together and provided people with an established albeit unlawful practice that allowed the collective to act and participate in the political arena as a corporate body. In this respect the pronunciamiento offers yet another instance of how traditional corporate practices defied, resisted, or continued to prosper alongside the individualist tenets of trendy liberalism and modernity. As Guerra observed when providing a typology of the Mexican pronunciamiento model, it was undoubtedly a collective practice, representative of colonial or traditionalist corporative political norms of conduct.[19]

Associated with the pronunciamiento's relevance to communal practices and identity was the festive element that accompanied some of its manifestations (see chapter 9). Taking the Acta of the Ayuntamiento de la Villa de San Andrés Tuxtla of 2 June 1834 as an example, it concluded by noting, like so many others did, that the pueblo rejoiced with "pealing of church bells, fireworks, music, and a Te Deum to thank the Almighty" at the ayuntamiento's decision to pronounce in favor of Santa Anna using his powers to guarantee that the Roman Catholic religion be preserved in all its purity and vigor as stated in articles 30 and 171 of the 1824 Constitution.[20] The excuse the pronunciamiento offered the community to hold a fiesta with bands and parades was too good to be ignored. Perhaps more significant, the fact that the pronunciamiento could be equated with celebrations and happy times highlights the extent to which this practice was not just about intimidating others into negotiating change. It was a cause for communal rejoicing and merrymaking, which in turn and by association meant it could be equated with other sacralized occasions, such as annual religious fiestas in honor of saints or civic celebrations commemorating independence or the 1829 victory of Tampico. Apart from the fact that the pronunciamiento could be endowed with a festive character (an aspect usually ignored in the historiography in favor of its potentially violent and destabilizing character), its celebration served to give the community's pronounced act of communion greater resonance. It also resulted in a legitimization and institutionalization of this extra-constitutional practice through the rituals of pealing church bells, religious ceremonial practices such as Te Deum), and the traditional fiesta merriment of cheers, gunshots, fireworks, processions, and music.

Last but not least, the pronunciamiento offered the leading pronunciados the definite chance of improving their career prospects. Again the trendsetting cases of Riego and Iturbide gave rise to the generalized view that if you wanted to climb the social and political hierarchy fast and furiously, the easiest option was to lead or join a pronunciamiento. In ways that only the pronunciamiento made possible, both Riego and Iturbide enhanced their prestige and status as warriors and heroes of outstanding courage and liberal or liberating merits, respectively. In the case of Iturbide, thanks to Iguala and the coup of 1822, he even succeeded in becoming emperor.

Faced with a context of upheaval and uncertainty that lent itself to what Max Weber defined as "charismatic domination" (i.e., the perceived need on the part of a group for a messianic leader or hero), the pronunciamiento provided the aspiring caudillo with the perfect medium with which to establish himself as a redeemer.[21] Given that, as noted by Miguel Alonso Baquer, for the leading pronunciado to be successful it was essential that he had the kind of prestige capable of inspiring men to defy the government publicly and mobilize, the pronunciamiento offered one obvious way for him to acquire revolutionary prestige and kudos.[22] The paradox remains that while the incipient general-president needed to pronounce to obtain that prestige, to garner support he needed to have the prestige of a veteran pronunciado. One way or another, it is clear that it was a practice many interpreted and adopted as a necessary career move. If you wanted to go somewhere in life, you made sure you could add some pronunciamientos to your *hoja de servicios* or figurative curriculum vitae. Perhaps not surprisingly, even civilian presidents such as José Justo Corro were at one stage or another involved in the staging of a pronunciamiento.[23]

Consequently, it could be said that in nineteenth-century Mexico there was the perception that you did not exist politically if you did not or had not at some stage pronounced. It could be said, therefore, that most Mexicans believed in the motto: "I pronounce thus I exist." If you did not pronounce, you ran the risk that people would not know who you were, what you stood for, or how resourceful and successful you were at summoning support or effecting shifts in government policy. To cite just one example, Santa Anna's Plan of San Luis Potosí of 5 June 1823, as I have argued elsewhere, could certainly be interpreted more as a publicity stunt staged to draw attention to his persona and federalist credentials than as a serious attempt to influence the government's choice of political system.[24]

Conclusion

The pronunciamiento might have been a widespread practice because of the noted context of contested authority, questioned legitimacy, and fiscal disarray. However, it also becomes evident that by the 1830s—the practice having become part of the cultural scene and life of so many Mexicans as an accepted and even expected way of expressing an opinion and making oneself known—it is not surprising that it was appropriated and used by a wealth of actors regardless of whether there were genuine grievances demanding to be addressed. In other words, it could be argued that the pronunciamiento was a widespread practice because of its many functions, and that as a result we cannot or should not view it as necessarily indicative of a context of acute instability. While instability accounts for the origin of this phenomenon, its durability and widespread appeal developed and acquired other motivational causes. Thus we should not necessarily view the pronunciamiento as an expression of, or a reaction to, institutional meltdown but rather as a cultural political custom that, with time, cultivated and forged its own internal logic and satisfied a wide range of needs, not all of which were related to seeking political change.

A closer study of the pronunciamientos, their texts, pretexts, contexts, and metatexts therefore serves not only to help us understand the nature of the grievances that afflicted Mexico for the greater part of the nineteenth century; it allows us to appreciate a whole range of cultural as well as political aspects of the period, enabling us to decipher behavioral norms and patterns that until relatively recently were simplistically depicted as the ugly symptoms of a so-called age of chaos. The pronunciamiento, which originated in the barracks, spearheaded by Masonic conspiracies in opposition to Ferdinand VII's absolutism, and which was initially used to negotiate political change forcefully, became a practice whereby Mexicans, at a time of constitutional turmoil or uncertainty, could express and publicize their views, commune with their fellow soldiers, villagers, and parishioners, party late into the night, and advance their careers. It was a practice and it was also an experience. It became part of everyday life, accepted, used, and endorsed by almost everybody regardless of the fact that it was outside the law. Like bribes, *mordidas*, and other illegal yet accepted ways of daily oiling the cumbersome or irritating bureaucratic machinery of the established law, the pronunciamiento became a cultural norm and expression of nineteenth-century Mexican society, not just a political practice. The day we fully understand what the pronunciamiento meant and how it was used we will be in a position truly to appreciate the subtle and multilayered political shifts and changes of independent Mexico as well as the nature of the transitional society in which the phenomenon flourished.

Notes

1. Guerra, "El pronunciamiento," 15.

2. In Spain the original precursors of the pronunciamiento model were the following conspiring or insubordinate liberal officers: Juan Díaz Porlier (La Coruña, September 1815), Vicente Richart and Baltasar Gutiérrez (Conjura del Triángulo, February 1816), Luis de Lacy and Miláns del Bosch (Catalonia, April 1817), Joaquín Vidal (Valencia, January 1819), and Rafael del Riego (Cabezas de San Juan, 1820). In Mexico they were Agustín de Iturbide and Vicente Guerrero (Iguala, February 1821), Felipe de la Garza (September 1822), Antonio López de Santa Anna and Guadalupe Victoria (Veracruz, December 1822), and José Antonio Echávarri (Casa Mata, February 1823).

3. They resulted in the reinstatement of the 1812 Constitution, Mexican independence, and the demise of Agustín de Iturbide's Mexican Empire (1822–23). See chapters by Timothy E. Anna and Ivana Frasquet and Manuel Chust in this volume. Also see Vázquez, "El modelo de pronunciamiento."

4. Colin Smith, in collaboration with Manuel Bermejo Marcos and Eugenio Chang-Rodríguez, *Collins Spanish-English English-Spanish Dictionary* (Glasgow: HarperCollins, 1991), 544.

5. As may be observed in chapter 7 there were also cases where the actual pronunciamiento text was drafted after the given community had risen up in arms.

6. Archer, "Politicization of the Army."

7. For Riego's pronunciamiento see Comellas, *Los primeros pronunciamientos*, and Gil Novales, *Rafael del Riego*.

8. Although Guerra notes that the pronunciamiento amounted to a form of direct consultation, "a plebiscite of sorts" or "democracy of corporate bodies," like Barbara A. Tenenbaum he arrives at the conclusion that the democratic nature of this practice was flawed and ultimately unrepresentative. See Guerra, "El pronunciamiento," 24, and Tenenbaum, "'They Went Thataway,'" 199.

9. As Miguel Alonso Baquer noted in his seminal study on the pronunciamiento model in Spain, for a pronunciamiento to garner support and prove successful the government needed to be weak, not unbearable. See his *El modelo español*, 20.

10. Sarmiento, *Facundo*.

11. This is not dissimilar to present-day email petitions, which generally fail to bring about change in government policy but enable those who add their names to circulate them to publicize on the Internet their opposition to or support of a given idea/person.

12. The Plan of Cuernavaca is reproduced in Bocanegra, *Memorias para la historia*, 2:573–74.

13. The complete version of the "Pronunciamiento de la Villa de Orizaba" is reproduced in Vázquez (ed.), *Planes en la nación, Libro tres*, 17–19.

14. Generally the *despronunciamiento* arose when communities had been initially coerced into "pronouncing" for or against a given plan either by government forces or by marauding rebels. It offered the community the opportunity to renege publicly on an original pronunciamiento they claimed had been launched under duress. For characteristic despronunciamientos, see those of Tancahuitz (1 June 1832), Zacualtipan (17 June 1832), Zacapu (24 September 1832), Zacualpan (21 July 1836), Camargo (13 May 1840), Ciudad Guerrero (17 May 1840), Mier (17 May 1840), and San Fernando de Rosas (30 May 1840).

15. Over two hundred related pronunciamientos can be found in Vázquez (ed.), *Planes en la nación, Libro dos*, 214–450.

16. The "Plan reformador de Tarecuato con su capital Tangamandapío" and "Pronunciamiento del Pueblo de Seris" are both in Vázquez (ed.), *Planes en la nación, Libro dos*, 82 and 124, respectively.

17. "Acta de Jonatepec" is in Vázquez (ed.), *Planes en la nación, Libro tres*, 40–41.

18. Costeloe, "A Pronunciamiento," 245.

19. Guerra, "El pronunciamiento," 18.

20. "Acta del Ayuntamiento de la Villa de San Andrés Tuxtla, 2 June 1834," in Vázquez (ed.), *Planes en la nación, Libro dos*, 236.

21. See Runciman (ed.), *Weber*, 235–36.

22. Baquer, *El modelo español*, 63.

23. Corro assisted with the promotion of the "Acta celebrada por la guarnición de la capital del estado de Jalisco" of 24 December 1829.

24. Fowler, *Santa Anna of Mexico*, 73–75.

Bibliography

Abbreviations

AGI   Archivo General de Indias (Spain)
AGN   Archivo General de la Nación
AGENL Archivo General del Estado de Nuevo León
AHN   Archivo Histórico Nacional (Spain)
AHSDN Archivo Histórico de la Secretaría de la Defensa Nacional
AHEM Archivo Histórico del Estado de México
AJH   Archivo Judicial Huejutla
AJP   Archivo Judicial Puebla
AMG   Archivo Municipal de Guadalajara
BCEM   Biblioteca del Congreso del Estado de México
BNAH   Biblioteca Nacional de Antropología e Historia, Mexico City
CIESAS Centro de Investigaciones y Estudios Superiores en
        Antropología Social
HNM   Hemeroteca Nacional de México, Mexico City
BLAC   Benson Latin American Collection (Texas)
INAH   Instituto Nacional de Antropología e Historia
UNAM Universidad Nacional Autónoma de México

Libraries, Archives, and Collections
Britain
British Library, London
National Archives at Kew, London
Public Record Office, Foreign Office Papers, London

Mexico
Archivo General de la Nación, Mexico City
Archivo General del Estado de Nuevo León, Monterrey

Archivo Histórico de la Secretaría de la Defensa Nacional, Mexico City
Archivo Histórico del Estado de México, Toluca
Archivo Judicial Huejutla, Huejutla, Hidalgo
Archivo Judicial Puebla, Instituto Nacional de Antropología e Historia,
    Puebla, Puebla
Archivo Municipal de Guadalajara, Guadalajara
Biblioteca del Congreso del Estado de México, Toluca
Biblioteca Nacional, Colección Lafragua, Mexico City
Centro de Estudios de Historia de México CONDUMEX, Mexico City
Hemeroteca Nacional de México, Mexico City

Spain
Archivo General de Indias, Seville
Archivo Histórico Nacional, Madrid

United States
Latin American Manuscript Collection, Lilly Library, Indiana University,
    Bloomington
Nettie Lee Benson Latin American Collection, University of Texas at Austin
Sutro Collection, California State Library, San Francisco

Books, Pamphlets, and Articles

Acereto, Albino. *Evolución histórica de las relaciones políticas entre México y Yucatán.* Mexico City: Gobierno de Yucatán, 1904.
Actas del congreso constituyente del estado libre de México. 10 vols. Mexico City: Imprenta a cargo de Martín Rivera, 1824–31.
Actas del congreso constituyente mexicano. 4 vols. Mexico City: Alejandro Valdés, 1822–23.
Actas del congreso constituyente mexicano. Mexico City: UNAM, 1980.
Aguirre Costilla, Virgilio. *Primeros ensayos constitucionales del México independiente.* Mexico City: Facultad de derecho de la UNAM, Seminario de derecho constitucional, 1962.
Alamán, Lucas. *Examen imparcial de la administración de Bustamante.* Mexico City: CONACULTA, 2008.
———. *Historia de Méjico desde los primeros movimientos que prepararon su independencia en el año de 1808 hasta la época presente.* 5 vols. Mexico City: José María Lara, 1849–52.
———. *Historia de México desde los primeros movimientos que prepararon su*

independencia en el año de 1808 hasta la época presente. 5 vols. Mexico City: Fondo de Cultura Económica, 1985.

———. *Obras de D. Lucas Alamán: Documentos diversos (inéditos y muy raros).* 4 vols. Mexico City: Editorial Jus, 1947.

Alcalá Galiano, Antonio. *Recuerdos de un anciano.* Biblioteca de Autores Españoles. Madrid: Ediciones Atlas, 1955.

Aldana Rendón, Mario. "La privatización de los terrenos comunales en Jalisco: Los primeros pasos 1821–1833." In Alejandra García Quintanilla and Abel Juárez (eds.), *Los lugares y los tiempos: Ensayos sobre las estructuras regionales del siglo XIX en México.* Mexico City: Editorial Nuestro Tiempo, 1989. 50–82.

Ancona, Eligio. *Historia de Yucatán: Desde la época más remota hasta nuestros días.* 4 vols. Barcelona: Jaime Jepús Roviralta, 1917.

Anderson, Benedict. *Imagined Communities: Reflections on the Origin and Spread of Nationalism.* New York: Verso, 1996.

Anderson, Rodney D. *Guadalajara a la consumación de su independencia: estudio de su población según los padrones de 1821–1822.* Guadalajara: Gobierno de Jalisco, 1983.

———. "Race and Social Stratification: A Comparison of Working-Class Spaniards, Indians, and Castas in Guadalajara, Mexico in 1821." *Hispanic American Historical Review* 68, no. 2 (May 1988): 209–43.

Andrade, Aníbal. *Huaxtecapan, el estado Huaxteco.* Mexico City: N.p., 1955.

Andrews, Catherine. "Discusiones en torno de la reforma de la Constitución Federal de 1824, durante el primer gobierno de Anastasio Bustamante (1830–1832)." *Historia Mexicana* 56, no. 1 (July–September 2006): 71–115.

Anna, Timothy E. "Demystifying Early Nineteenth-Century Mexico." *Mexican Studies* 9, no. 1 (Winter 1993): 119–37.

———. *The Fall of the Royal Government in Mexico City.* Lincoln: University of Nebraska Press, 1978.

———. *Forging Mexico 1821–1835.* Lincoln: University of Nebraska Press, 1998.

———. "Francisco Novella and the Last Stand of the Royal Army in New Spain." *Hispanic American Historical Review* 51, no. 1 (February 1971): 97–111.

———. *El imperio de Iturbide.* Mexico City: Consejo Nacional para la Cultura y las Artes–Alianza Editorial, 1991.

———. "The Independence of Mexico and Central America." In Leslie

Bethell (ed.), *The Cambridge History of Latin America*, vol. 3. Cambridge: Cambridge University Press, 1985. 51–94.

———. "Inventing Mexico: Provincehood and Nationhood after Independence." *Bulletin of Latin American Research* 15, no. 1 (January 1996): 7–17.

———. "Iturbide, Congress, and Constitutional Monarchy in Mexico." In Kenneth J. Andrien and Lyman L. Johnson (eds.), *The Political Economy of Spanish America in the Age of Revolution, 1750–1850*. Albuquerque: University of New Mexico Press, 1994. 17–38.

———. "The Iturbide Interregnum." In Jaime E. Rodríguez O. (ed.), *The Independence of Mexico and the Creation of the New Nation*. Los Angeles: UCLA Latin American Center, 1989. 185–99.

———. *The Mexican Empire of Iturbide*. Lincoln: University of Nebraska Press, 1990.

———. "Modelos de continuidad y ruptura, Nueva España y Capitanía General de Guatemala." In Germán Carrera Damas and John V. Lombardi (eds.), Vol. 5, UNESCO *Historia General de América Latina*. Paris: UNESCO, 2003. 207–38.

———. "The Rule of Agustín de Iturbide: A Reappraisal." *Journal of Latin American Studies*, 17, no. 1 (May 1985): 79–110.

———. "Spain and the Breakdown of the Imperial Ethos: The Problem of Equality." *Hispanic American Historical Review* 62:2 (May 1982): 254–72.

———. *Spain and the Loss of America*. Lincoln: University of Nebraska Press, 1983.

Annino, Antonio. "Cádiz y la revolución territorial de los pueblos mexicanos 1812–1821." In Antonio Annino (ed.), *Historia de las elecciones en iberoamérica: Siglo XIX de la fromación del espacio político nacional*. Mexico City: Fondo de Cultura Económica 1995.

———. "Otras naciones: Sincretismo político en el México decimonónico." In *Imaginar la nación: Cuadernos de Historia Latinoamericana*, no. 2 (1994), 215–55.

———. "Nuevas perspectivas para una vieja pregunta." In Maricel Fonseca (ed.), *El primer liberalismo mexicano, 1808–1855*. Mexico City: INAH 1995. 45–91.

———. "Some Reflections on Spanish American Constitutional and Political History." *Itinerario* 19, no. 2 (1995): 26–47.

———. "The Two-Faced Janus: The Pueblos and the Origins of Mexican Liberalism." In Elisa Servin, Leticia Reina, John Tutino (eds.), *Cycles of Conflict, Centuries of Change: Crisis, Reform and Revolution in Mexico*. Durham NC: Duke University Press, 2007. 60–90.

Annino, Antonio, and Alberto Filippi. "Las formas del poder: Proyecto político y efectividad." In Antonio Annino et al. (eds.), *America Latina: Dallo stato coloniale allo stato nazione*. Milan: Franco Angeli, 1987. 2:415–26.

Annino, Antonio, Marcello Carmagnani, Gabriella Chiaramonti, Alberto Filippi, Flavio Fiorani, Alberto Gallo, and Giovanni Marchetti (eds.). *América Latina: Dallo stato coloniale allo stato nazione*. 2 vols. Milan: Franco Angeli, 1987.

Archer, Christon I. "'La Causa Buena': The Counterinsurgency Army of New Spain and the Ten Years' War." In Jaime E. Rodríguez O. (ed.), *The Independence of Mexico and the Creation of the New Nation*. Los Angeles: UCLA Latin American Center, 1989. 85–108.

———. "Insurrection—Reaction—Revolution—Fragmentation: Reconstructing the Choreography of Meltdown in New Spain during the Independence Era." *Mexican Studies/Estudios Mexicanos* 10, no. 1 (Winter 1994): 63–98.

———. "The Key to the Kingdom: The Defense of Veracruz, 1780–1810," *The Americas* 27, no. 4 (1971): 426–49.

———. "The Militarization of Mexican Politics: The Role of the Army, 1815–1821." In Virginia Guedea and Jaime E. Rodríguez O. (eds.), *Five Centuries of Mexican History*. 2 vols. Mexico City: Instituto de Investigaciones Dr. José María Luis Mora–University of California, Irvine, 1992. 1:285–302.

———. "Politicization of the Army of New Spain during the War of Independence, 1810–1821." In Jaime E. Rodríguez O. (ed.), *The Evolution of the Mexican Political System*. Wilmington DE: SR Books, 1993. 17–38.

———. "Where Did All the Royalists Go? New Light on the Military Collapse of New Spain, 1810–1822." In Jaime E. Rodríguez O. (ed.), *The Mexican and Mexican American Experience in the 19th Century*. Tempe AZ: Bilingual Press, 1989. 24–43.

Arista, M. *Reseña histórica de la revolución que tuvo lugar en la república el año de 1833*. Mexico City: Impresa por Mariano Arévalo, 1835.

Arnold, Linda. "La administración, la ajudicación y la política en la rama judicial en México, 1825 a 1835." In Beatriz Bernal (ed.), *Memoria del IV Con-*

greso de historia del derecho mexicano (1986). 2 vols. Mexico City: UNAM, 1988. 59–69.

———. *Bureaucracy and Bureaucrats in Mexico City, 1742–1835*. Tucson: University of Arizona Press, 1988.

———. José Ramón García Ugarte: Patriot, Federalist, or Malcontent. Paper given at the international conference on Politics, Conflict, and Insurrection: The Experience of the *Pronunciamiento* in Nineteenth-Century Mexico, University of St. Andrews, June 2009.

Arrangoíz y Berzabal, F. de P. *México desde 1808 hasta 1867*. Mexico City: Editorial Porrúa, 1971.

Arrom, Silvia M. "Popular Politics in Mexico City: The Parián Riot, 1828." *Hispanic American Historical Review* 68, no. 2 (May 1988): 245–68.

———. *The Women of Mexico City, 1790–1857*. Stanford: Stanford University Press, 1985.

Artola, Miguel. *La España de Fernando VII: Historia de España de R. Menéndez Pidal, vol. XXXII*. Madrid: Espasa, 1978.

———. *La guerra de independencia*. Madrid: Espasa, 2007.

———. *Los orígenes de la España contemporánea*. 2 vols. Madrid: Centro de Estudios Políticos y Constitucionales, 1975; reprint 2000.

Augusta cámara de diputados. *Dictamen de la comisión especial nombrada por la augusta cámara de diputados para el asunto de independencia, de 1 de octubre 1841*. Mérida: Imprenta del Boletín Comercial, 1841.

Ávila, Alfredo. *En nombre de la nación: La formación del gobierno representativo en México (1808–1824)*. Mexico City: Taurus–CIDE, 2002.

Aymes, J. R. *La guerra de independencia en España (1808–1814)*. Madrid: Siglo XXI, 1986.

Baquer, Miguel Alonso. *El modelo español de pronunciamiento*. Madrid: Rialp, 1983.

Baqueiro, Serapio. *Ensayo histórico sobre las revoluciones de Yucatán desde el año 1840 hasta 1864*, vol. 1. Mérida: Universidad Autónoma de Yucatán, 1878–79.

Baranda, Joaquín. *Recordaciones históricas*, vol. 1. N.p., 1907.

Barker, Nancy Nichols. *The French Experience in Mexico 1821–1861: A History of Constant Misunderstanding*. Chapel Hill: University of North Carolina Press, 1979.

Barragán Barragán, José. *Introducción al federalismo (la formación de los poderes en 1824)*. Mexico City: UNAM, 1978.

———. "La legislación gaditana como derecho patrio." In José Luis Soberanes Fernández (ed.), *Memoria del II Congreso de historia del derecho mexicano (1980)*. Mexico City: UNAM, 1981. 377–92.

———. *Principios sobre el federalismo mexicano: 1824*. Mexico City: Departamento del Distrito Federal, 1984.

Bastian, Jean-Pierre. "Una ausencia notoria: La francmasonería en la historiografía mexicanista." *Historia Mexicana* 44, no. 3 (January–March 1995): 439–60.

Baur, John E. "The Evolution of a Mexican Foreign Trade Policy, 1821–1828." *The Americas* 19, no. 3 (January 1963): 225–61.

Bazant, Jan. *Alienation of Church Wealth in Mexico*. New York: Cambridge University Press, 1971.

Bazant, Jan. *Antonio Haro y Tamariz y sus aventuras políticas, 1811–1869*. Mexico City: El Colegio de México, 1985.

———. "Evolución de la industria textil poblana (1554–1845)." *Historia Mexicana* 13, no. 4 (April–June 1964): 473–516.

———. *Historia de la deuda exterior de México (1823–1946)*. Mexico City: El Colegio de México, 1968.

———. "Industria algodonera poblana de 1800–1843 en números." *Historia Mexicana* 14, no. 1 (July–September 1964): 131–43.

Bazant, Mílada (ed.). *175 años de historia del Estado de México y perspectivas para el tercer milenio*. Mexico City: El Colegio Mexiquense, 1999.

Benavides, Artemio y Pedro Torres Estrada. *La Constitución de 1857 y el noreste mexicano*. Monterrey: Archivo General del Estado de Nuevo León, 2007.

Benson, Nettie Lee, *La diputación provincial y el federalismo mexicano*. Mexico City: El Colegio de México, 1994.

———. "The Plan of Casa Mata." *Hispanic American Historical Review* 25, no. 1 (February 1945): 45–56.

———. *The Provincial Deputation in Mexico, Harbinger of Provincial Autonomy, Independence, and Federalism*. Austin: University of Texas Press, 1992.

———. "Servando Teresa de Mier, Federalist." *Hispanic American Historical Review* 28 (1948): 514–25.

———. "Territorial Integrity in Mexican Politics, 1821–1833." In Jaime E. Rodríguez O. (ed.), *The Independence of Mexico and the Creation of the New Nation*. Los Angeles: UCLA Latin American Center, 1989. 275–307.

Benson, Nettie Lee (ed.). *Mexico and the Spanish Cortes, 1810–1822: Eight Essays*. Austin: University of Texas Press, 1966.

Bernecker, Walther L. "Comercio y comerciantes extranjeros en las primeras décadas de la independencia mexicana." In Reinhard Liehr (ed.), *América Latina en la época de Simón Bolívar: La formación de las economías nacionales y los intereses europeos 1800–1850*. Berlin: Colloquium Verlag, 1989. 87–114.

Bertola, Elisabetta, Marcello Carmagnani, and Paolo Riguzzi. "Federación y estados: Espacios políticos y relaciones de poder en México (Siglo XIX)." In Pedro Pérez Herrero (ed.), *Región e historia en México (1700–1850): Métodos de análisis regional*. Mexico City: Instituto de Investigaciones Dr. José María Luis Mora/Universidad Autónoma Metropolitana, 1991. 237–59.

Black, Lawrence. "Conflict among the Elites: The Overthrow of Viceroy Iturrigaray." Unpublished PhD thesis, Department of History, Tulane University, New Orleans LA, 1980.

Bocanegra, José María. *Memorias para la historia de México independiente, 1822–46*. 2 vols. Mexico City: Imprenta del Gobierno Federal, 1892–97; reprint., 3 vols, Mexico City: Fondo de Cultura Económica, 1987.

Booker, Jackie R. *Veracruz Merchants, 1770–1829: A Mercantile Elite in Late Bourbon and Early Independent Mexico*. Boulder CO: Westview Press, 1992.

Brack, Gene M. *Mexico Views Manifest Destiny, 1821–1846: An Essay on the Origins of the Mexican War*. Albuquerque: University of New Mexico Press, 1975.

Brading, David A. *The First America: The Spanish Monarchy, Creole Patriots, and the Liberal State, 1492–1867*. Cambridge: Cambridge University Press, 1991.

———. "Creole Nationalism and Mexican Liberalism." *Journal of Interamerican Studies and World Affairs* 15 (May 1973): 139–90.

———. *Los orígenes del nacionalismo mexicano*. Mexico City: Secretaría de Educación Pública, 1973.

———. *The Origins of Mexican Nationalism*. Cambridge: Centre of Latin American Studies, 1985.

———. "El patriotismo liberal y la Reforma Mexicana." In Cecilia Noriega Elío (ed.), *El Nacionalismo en México*. Zamora: El Colegio de Michoacán, 1992. 179–204.

Bravo Ugarte, José. *Historia de México: Independencia, caracterización política e integración social*. 2nd ed. rev. Mexico City: Editorial Jus, 1953.

———. "Independencia de las Provincias Unidas del Centro de América y adhesión definitiva de Chiapas a México." *Memorias de la Academia Mexicana de la Historia* 14, no. 1 (January–March 1955): 43–48.

———. *Periodistas y periódicos mexicanas (hasta 1935, selección)*. Mexico City: Editorial Jus, 1966.

Breña, Roberto. *El primer liberalismo español y los procesos de emancipación en América, 1808–1824: Una revision historiográfica del liberalismo hispánico.* Mexico City: El Colegio de México, 2006.

Buldain Jaca, Blanca E. *Régimen político y preparación de Cortes en 1820.* Madrid: Congreso de los Diputados, 1988.

Bustamante, Carlos María de. *Apuntes para la historia del gobierno del general don Antonio López de Santa Anna. 1845; facsimile ed.,* Mexico City: Instituto Cultural Helénico-Fondo de Cultura Económica, 1986.

———. *Continuación del cuadro histórico: Historia del emperador D. Agustín de Iturbide hasta su muerte, y sus consecuencias, establecimiento de la república popular federal.* Mexico City: Imprenta de I. Cumplido, 1846.

———. *Continuación del cuadro histórico de la Revolución Mexicana.* Mexico: INAH, 1963.

———. *Cuadro histórico de la revolución mexicana comenzada en 15 de Septiembre de 1810 por el ciudadano Miguel Hidalgo y Costilla, cura del pueblo de Los Dolores en el obispado de Michoacán.* Mexico City: Imprenta de J. Mariano Lara, 1846.

———. *Diario histórico de México.* 2 vols. Mexico City: INAH, 1980–81.

———. *Diario histórico de México, 1822–1848.* 2 CDs. Edited by Josefina Vázquez and Cuauhtémoc Hernández. Mexico City: Centro de Investigaciones y Estudios Superiores en Antropología Social–El Colegio de México, 2001.

Calderón, Francisco. "El pensamiento económico de Lucas Alamán." *Historia Mexicana* 34, no. 3 (January–March 1985): 435–59.

Calvillo Unna, Tomás, and María Isabel Monroy Castillo. "Las apuestas de una región: San Luis Potosí y la República Federal." In Josefina Zoraida Vázquez (ed.), *El establecimiento del federalismo en México, 1821–1827.* Mexico City: Colegio de México, 2003. 319–50.

Camp, Roderic A. "La cuestión chiapaneca: Revisión de una polémica territorial." *Historia Mexicana* 24, no. 4 (April–June 1975): 579–606.

Campos García, Melchor, *De provincia a estado de la república mexicana: La península de Yucatán, 1786–1835.* Mérida: Universidad Autónoma de Yucatán, Consejo Nacional de Ciencia y Tecnología, 2004.

———. *"Que los yucatecos todos proclamen su independencia": Historia del secesionismo en Yucatán, 1821–1849.* Mérida: Universidad Autónoma de Yucatán, 2002.

Cañeque, Alejandro. *The King's Living Image: The Culture and Politics of Viceregal Power in Colonial Mexico.* New York: Routledge, 2004.

Carmagnani, Marcello. "Del territorio a la región: Líneas de un proceso en la primera mitad del siglo XIX." In Alicia Hernández Chávez and Manuel Miño Grijalva (eds.), *Cincuenta años de historia en México.* 2 vols. Mexico City: Centro de Estudios Históricos, El Colegio de México, 1991. 2:221–41.

———. "El federalismo, historia de una forma de gobierno." In Marcello Carmagnani (ed.), *Federalismos latinoamericanos: México/Brasil/Argentina.* Mexico City: El Colegio de México–Fondo de Cultura Económica, 1993. 16–29.

———. "Finanzas y estado en Mexico, 1820–1880." *Ibero-Amerikanisches Archiv* 9, nos. 3–4 (1983): 279–317.

———. "Territorialidad y federalismo en la formación del estado mexicano." In Inge Buisson et al. (eds.), *Problemas de la formación del estado y de la nación en Hispanoamérica.* Cologne: Bohlau Verlag, 1984. 289–304.

———. "Territorios, provincias y estados: Las transformaciones de los espacios políticos en México, 1750–1850." In Josefina Zoraida Vázquez (ed.), *La fundación del estado mexicano, 1821–1855.* Mexico City: Nueva Imagen, 1994. 39–73.

Carr, Raymond. *Spain 1808–1939.* Oxford: Clarendon Press, 1966.

Castells, Irene. "El liberalismo insurreccional español (1815–1833)." In Xosé Ramón Barreiro Fernández (ed.), *O liberalismo nos seus contextos: Un estado da cuestion.* Santiago de Compostela: Universidade de Santiago de Compostela, 2008. 71–87.

———. *La utopía insurreccional del liberalismo: Torrijos y las conspiraciones liberales de la década ominosa.* Barcelona: Crítica, 1989.

Castro Morales, Efraín. *El federalismo en Puebla.* Puebla: Gobierno del Estado de Puebla, 1987.

Censo general de la república mexicana: Verificado el 20 de octubre de 1895, censo del estado de Nuevo León. Mexico City: Ministerio de Fomento, Dirección General de Estadística, 1897.

Chowning, Barbara, *Wealth and Power in Provincial Mexico: Michoacán from the Late Colony to the Revolution.* Stanford CA: Stanford University Press, 1999.

Chust, Manuel. "Armed Citizens: The Civic Militia in the Origins of the Mexican National State, 1812–1827." In Jaime E. Rodríguez O. (ed.), *The Divine Charter: Constitutionalism and Liberalism in Nineteenth-Century Mexico.* Lanham: Rowman and Littlefield Publishers, 2005. 235–52.

———. *La cuestión nacional americana en las Cortes de Cádiz.* Valencia: Fundación Instituto Historia Social–UNAM, 1999.

———. "Milicia e independencia en México: De la Nacional a la Cívica, 1812–1827." In S. Broseta, C. Corona, y M. Chust et al. (eds.), *Las ciudades y la guerra, 1750–1898.* Castellón: Universitat Jaume I, 2002. 361–80.

———. *La cuestión nacional americana en las Cortes de Cádiz.* Valencia: Fundación Instituto Historia Social–UNAM, 1999.

Chust, Manuel, and Ivana Frasquet. "Soberanía hispana, soberanía mexicana: 1810–1824." In Manuel Chust (ed.), *Doceañismos, constituciones e independencias: La constitución de 1812 y América.* Madrid: Mapfre–Instituto de Cultura, 2006. 169–236.

Cline, Howard F. "Regionalism and Society in Yucatan, 1825–1847: A Study of 'Progressivism' and the Origins of the Caste War." Unpubl. PhD diss., University of Harvard, 1947.

Coatsworth, John H. "Los orígenes sociales del autoritarismo en México." In John H. Coatsworth (ed.), *Los orígenes del atraso: Nueve ensayos de historia económica de México en los siglos XVIII y XIX.* Mexico City: Alianza Editorial Mexicana, 1990. 209–37.

Coatsworth, John H. "The Decline of the Mexican Economy, 1800–1860." In Reinhard Liehr (ed.). *América Latina en la época de Simón Bolívar: La formación de las economías nacionales y los intereses económicas europeos 1800–1850.* Berlin: Colloquium Verlag, 1989. 27–53.

———. "Obstacles to Economic Growth in Nineteenth Century Mexico." *American Historical Review* 83, no. 1 (February 1978): 80–100.

Cockburn, H. *Memorials of His Time.* Edinburgh: Adams and Charles Black, 1856.

Colín, Mario (ed.). *Constituciones del Estado de México 1827, 1861, 1870, 1917.* Mexico City: Biblioteca Enciclopédica del Estado de México, 1974.

Comellas, José Luis. *Los primeros pronunciamientos en España, 1814–1820.* Madrid: CSIC, 1958.

Compilación de leyes y reglamentos del Estado de México. Toluca: Gobierno del Estado de México, 1980.

Connaughton, Brian. *Ideología y sociedad en Guadalajara (1788–1853)*. Mexico City: Consejo Nacional para la Cultura y las Artes, 1992.

Corbett, Barbara M. "Las fibras del poder: La guerra contra Texas (1835–36) y la construcción de un estado fisco-militar en San Luis Potosí." In Jorge Silva Riquer, Juan Carlos Grosso, and Carmen Yuste (eds.), *Circuitos mercantiles y mercados en Latinoamérica siglos XVIII–XIX*. Mexico City: Instituto de Investigaciones Dr. José María Luis Mora, 1995. 362–94.

———. "Republican Hacienda and Federalist Politics: The Making of 'Liberal' Oligarchy in San Luis Potosí 1787–1853". Unpubl. PhD thesis, Princeton University, November 1997.

Costeloe, Michael P. "The Administration, Collection, and Distribution of Tithes in the Archbishopric of Mexico, 1800–1860." *The Americas* 23, no. 1 (July 1966): 3–27.

———. *Bonds and Bondholders: British Investors and Mexico's Foreign Debt, 1824–1888*. Westport CT: Praeger, 2003.

———. *The Central Republic in Mexico, 1835–1846: Hombres de bien in the Age of Santa Anna*. Cambridge: Cambridge University Press, 1993.

———. *Church and State in Independent Mexico: A Study of the Patronage Debate 1821–1857*. London: Royal Historical Society, 1978.

———. "Federalism to Centralism in Mexico: The Conservative Case for Change, 1834–1835." *The Americas* 45, no. 2 (October 1988): 173–85.

———. "*Hombres de bien*" in the Age of Santa Anna." In Jaime E. Rodríguez O. (ed.), *Mexico in the Age of Democratic Revolutions, 1750–1850*. Boulder CO: Lynne Rienner Publishers, 1994. 243–57.

———. *La primera república federal de México (1824–1835): Un estudio de los partidos políticos en el México independiente*. Trans. Manuel Fernández Gasalla. Mexico City: Fondo de Cultura Económica, 1975.

———. "A *Pronunciamiento* in Nineteenth Century Mexico: '15 de Julio de 1840,'" *Mexican Studies/Estudios Mexicanos* 4, no. 2 (Summer 1988): 245–64.

———. "Santa Anna and the Gómez Farías Administration in Mexico, 1833–1834." *The Americas* 31, no. 1 (July 1974): 18–50.

———. "The Triangular Revolt in Mexico and the Fall of Anastasio Bustamante, August–October 1841." *Journal of Latin American Studies* 20 (1988): 337–60.

Crónicas: Constitución federal de 1824. 2 vols. Mexico City: Secretaría de Gobernación, 1974.

Cue Cánovas, Agustín. *El federalismo mexicano*. Mexico City: Libro Mex, 1960.

———. *Historia social y económica de México (1521–1854)*. 3rd ed. Mexico City: Editorial F. Trillas, 1963.

Cuevas, Luis G. *Memoria del ministro de relaciones exteriores y gobernación, leída en el senado el 11 y en la cámara de diputados el 12 Marzo de 1845*. Mexico City: Imprenta de Ignacio Cumplido, 1845.

———. *El porvenir de México, o juicio sobre su estado político en 1821 y 1851*. Mexico City: Editorial Jus, 1954.

Cuevas, Mariano. *El libertador: Documentos selectos de don Agustín de Iturbide*. Mexico City: Ed. Patria, 1947.

David, Thomas B., and Amado Ricon Virulegio (eds.). *The Political Plans of Mexico*. Lanham MD: University Press of America, 1987.

Davies, Keith A. "Tendencias demográficas urbanas durante el siglo XIX en México." *Historia Mexicana* 21, no. 3 (January–March 1972): 481–524.

De Diego, Emilio. *España, el infierno de Napoleón, 1808–1814: Una historia de la guerra de la independencia*. Madrid: La esfera de los libros, 2008.

De la Portilla, Anselmo. *Historia de la revolución de México contra la dictadura del general Santa-Anna, 1853–1855*. Mexico City: Biblioteca de México-Fundación Miguel Alemán, A.C.–Fondo de Cultura Económica, 1993.

Deans-Smith, Susan. "State Enterprise, Work, and Workers in Mexico: The Case of the Tobacco Monopoly, 1750–1850." In Kenneth J. Andrien and Lyman L. Johnson (eds.), *The Political Economy of Spanish America in the Age of Revolution, 1750–1850*. Albuquerque: University of New Mexico Press, 1994. 63–93.

Diario de sesiones de Cortes Generales, 1820–1823 (Madrid: Publicaciones de las Cortes, 2000) 5 CD-ROM.

Di Tella, Torcuato S. "Ciclos políticos en la primera mitad del siglo XIX." In Josefina Zoraida Vázquez (ed.), *La fundación del estado mexicano, 1821–1855*. Mexico City: Nueva Imagen, 1994. 111–33.

———. "The Dangerous Classes in Early Nineteenth Century Mexico." *Journal of Latin American Studies* 5, no. 1 (May 1973): 79–105.

———. "Las huelgas en la minería mexicana, 1826–1828." *Desarrollo Económico* 26 (January–March 1987): 579–608.

———. *National Popular Politics in Early Independent Mexico, 1820–1847*. Albuquerque: University of New Mexico Press, 1996.

————. *Política nacional y popular en México, 1820–1847*. Mexico City: FCE, 1994.

Díaz Díaz, Fernando. *Caudillos y caciques: Antonio López de Santa Anna y Juan Alvarez*. Mexico City: El Colegio de México, 1972.

Díaz y Díaz, Martín. "Las relaciones de propiedad en el proceso de constitución nacional." In Cecilia Noriega Elío (ed.), *El nacionalismo en México*. Zamora: El Colegio de Michoacán, 1992. 519–49.

Diccionario Porrúa de historia, biografía y geografía de México. 3rd ed. corrected and augmented. 2 vols. Mexico City: Editorial Porrúa, 1976.

Dublán, Manuel, and José María Lozano (eds.). *Legislación mexicana, o colección completa de las disposiciones legislativas expedidas desde la independencia de la república*. 34 vols. Mexico City: Imprenta del Comercio, 1876–1914.

Ducey, Michael T. *A Nation of Villages: Riot and Rebellion in the Mexican Huasteca, 1750–1850*. Tucson: University Arizona Press, 2004.

Echánove Trujillo, Carlos A., *La vida pasional e inquieta de don Crecencio Rejón*. Mexico: Sociedad Mexicana de Geografía y Estadística, 1941.

El que despeja la incógnita ¿Es el Ministerio quién dirige los planes de Yucatán? (27 August 1830). Mexico City: Imprenta de Galván a cargo de Mariano Arévalo, 1831.

Enciclopedia parlamentaria de México. México City: Instituto de Investigaciones Legislativas–LVI Legislatura del Congreso de la Unión, 1997.

Escobar, Manuel María. "Campaña de Tampico de Tamaulipas, año de 1829." *Historia Mexicana* 9, no. 1 (July–September 1959): 44–96.

Escobar Ohmstede, Antonio. "'Vil venganza': Movimientos político-sociales en la Huasteca potosina, 1845–1851." In José Alfredo Rangel and Carlos R. Ruiz Medrano (eds.), *Discursos públicos, negociaciones y estrategias de lucha colectiva*. San Luis Potosí: El Colegio de San Luis–AHESLP, 2006. 81–122.

————. "La conformación y las luchas por el poder en las Huastecas, 1821–53," *Secuencia* 36, nueva época (1996): 5–32.

————. "Las Huastecas para los huastecos: Los intentos para conformar un estado huasteco durante la primera mitad del siglo XIX." *Vetas: Revista de El Colegio de San Luis* 2, no. 4 (2000): 117–50.

————. "Movimientos socio-rurales en las actuales Huastecas hidalguense y veracruzana (México) en la primera mitad del siglo XIX." *Jahrbuch für Geschichte Lateinamerikas* 38 (2001): 157–81.

————. *De la costa a la sierra: Las Huastecas, 1750–1900*. Mexico City: CIESAS-INI, 1998.

Escobar Ohmstede, Antonio, and Luz Carregha (coords.). *El siglo XIX en las Huastecas.* Mexico City: CIESAS–El Colegio de San Luis, 2002.

Escobar Ohmstede, Antonio, and Romana Falcón (eds.). *Los ejes de la disputa: Movimientos sociales y actores colectivos en América Latina, siglo XIX.* Madrid: Iberoamericana–AHILA–Vervuert, 2002.

Escobar Ohmstede, Antonio, Raúl Mandrini, and Sara Ortelli (eds.). *Sociedades en movimiento: Los pueblos indígenas de América Latina en el siglo XIX.* Buenos Aires: Instituto de Estudios Histórico-Sociales FCH/UNCPBA, 2007.

Estep, Raymond. *Lorenzo de Zavala, profeta del liberalismo mexicano.* Trans. Carlos E. Echanove Trujillo. Mexico City: Libreria de M. Porrúa, 1952.

Facio, José Antonio. *Memoria que sobre los sucesos del tiempo de su ministerio, y sobre la causa intentada contra los cuatro ministros del Excmo. señor vicepresidente D. Anastasio Bustamante, presenta a los mexicanos el general ex ministro de la guerra y marina, D. José Antonio Facio.* Paris: Imprenta de Moqueo, 1835.

Falcón, Romana. *México descalzo: Estrategias de sobrevivencia ante la modernización liberal.* Mexico City: Plaza y Janés, 2002.

———. "Poderes y razones de las jefaturas políticas: Coahuila en el primer siglo de vida independiente." In Jaime E. Rodríguez O. (ed.), *The Evolution of the Mexican Political System.* Wilmington DE: SR Books, 1993. 137–62.

Falcón, Romana (ed.). *Culturas de pobreza y resistencia: Estudios de marginados, proscritos y descontentos en México, 1804–1910.* Mexico City: El Colegio de México–Universidad Autónoma de Querétaro, 2005.

Filippi, Alberto. *Instituciones e ideologías en la independencia hispanoamericana.* Buenos Aires: Alianza Editorial, 1988.

Flores Caballero, Romeo. *La contra-revolución en la independencia: Los españoles en la vida política, social, y económica de México (1804–1838).* Mexico City: El Colegio de México, 1969.

———. "Del libre cambio al proteccionismo." *Historia Mexicana* 19, no. 4 (April–June 1970): 492–512.

———. *Protección y libre cambio: El debate entre 1821 y 1836.* Mexico City: Banco Nacional de Comercio Exterior, 1971.

Flores Escalante, Justo Miguel, "Proyectos de gobierno y procesos electorales en la península de Yucatán, 1829–1839." Mérida: Unpubl. BA thesis, Universidad Autónoma de Yucatán, 2002.

———. "El primer experimento centralista en Yucatán: El proyecto de gobierno de José Segundo Carvajal (1829–1831)." *Secuencia* 62 (May–August 2005): 50.

Florstedt, Robert F. "Mora contra Bustamante." *Historia Mexicana* 12, no. 1 (July–September 1962): 26–51.

———. "Mora y la génesis del liberalismo burgués." *Historia Mexicana* 11, no. 2 (October–December 1961): 207–23.

Fontana, Josep. *La crisis del Antiguo Régimen, 1808–1833*. Barcelona: Ariel, 1971.

Fowler, Will. "Civil Conflict in Independent Mexico, 1821–57: An Overview." In Rebecca Earle (ed.), *Rumours of Wars: Civil Conflict in Nineteenth-Century Latin America*. London: University of London, Institute of Latin American Studies, 2000. 49–86.

———. "Fiestas Santanistas: La celebración de Santa Anna en la villa de Jalapa, 1821–1855." *Historia Mexicana* 52, no. 2 (October–December 2002): 391–447.

———. "The Origins of the Nineteenth-Century Mexican *Pronunciamiento*: From Rafael de Riego's *Pronunciamiento* of January 1, 1820 to the Women of Zacatlán de las Manzanas' *Pronunciamiento* of July 29, 1833." Paper given at the Research Seminar of the Department of Spanish, University of St. Andrews, 15 February 2008.

———. *Mexico in the Age of Proposals, 1821–1853*, Westport CT: Greenwood Press, 1998.

———. "El pronunciamiento mexicano: Hacia una nueva tipología," *Estudios de Historia Moderna y Contemporánea de México* 32 (October–December 2009): 5–34.

———. *Santa Anna of Mexico*. Lincoln: University of Nebraska Press, 2007.

———. *Tornel and Santa Anna, the Writer and the Caudillo (Mexico 1795–1853)*. Westport CT: Greenwood Press, 2000.

Fowler, Will, and Juan Ortiz Escamilla. "La revuelta de 2 de diciembre de 1822: Una perspectiva regional." *Historias* 47 (September–December 2000): 19–37.

Frasquet, Ivana. "Alteza *versus* Majestad: El poder de la legitimidad en el Estado-nación mexicano, 1810–1824." In Víctor Mínguez and Manuel Chust (eds.), *El imperio sublevado: Monarquía y nación en España e Hispanoamérica*. Madrid: CSIC, 2004. 255–76.

———. *Las caras del águila: Del liberalismo gaditano a la república federal mexicana, 1820–1823*. Castellón: Universitat Jaume I, 2008.

———. "Ciudadanos ya tenéis Cortes: La convocatoria de 1820 y la representación americana." In Jaime E. Rodríguez O. (ed.), *México y España, 1750–1850*. Madrid: Fundación Mapfre, 2008. 145–67.

———. "El estado armado o la nación en armas: Ejército versus milicia cívica en México, 1821–1823." In Manuel Chust and Juan Marchena (eds.), *Las armas de la nación: Independencia y ciudadanía en Hispanoamérica, 1750–1850*. Madrid: Iberoamericana Vervuert, 2007. 111–35.

———. "La senda revolucionaria del liberalismo doceañista en España y México, 1820–1824." *Revista de Indias*, 68, no. 242 (January–April 2008): 153–80.

———. "Se obedece y se cumple: La jura de la Constitución de Cádiz en México en 1820." In Izaskun Álvarez and Julio Sánchez (eds.), *Visiones y revisiones de la independencia Americana: La independencia de América, la Constitución de Cádiz y las constituciones iberoamericanas*. Salamanca: Universidad de Salamanca, 2007. 217–45.

Gaixiola F., Jorge. *Mariano Otero, creador del Juicio de Amparo*. Mexico City: Editorial Cultura, 1937.

García Cubas, Antonio. *Atlas geográfico, estadística e histórico mexicano*. Mexico City: Imprenta J. M. Fernández de Lara, 1858.

García Fuertes, Arsenio. *Dos de mayo de 1808: El grito de una nación*. Barcelona: Inedita Ediciones, 2007.

García Mora, Carlos, and Martín Villalobos (eds.). *La antropología en México: Panorama histórico*. Vol 4. Mexico City: INAH, 1988).

García Quintanilla, Alejandra. "En busca de la prosperidad y la riqueza: Yucatán a la hora de la independencia." In Alejandra García Quintanilla and Abel Juárez (eds.), *Los lugares y los tiempos: Ensayos sobre las estructuras regionales del siglo XIX en México*. Mexico City: Editorial Nuestro Tiempo, 1989. 83–108.

García Quintanilla, Alejandra, and Abel Juárez (eds). *Los lugares y los tiempos: Ensayos sobre las estructuras regionales del siglo XIX en México*. Mexico City: Editorial Nuestro Tiempo, 1989.

Garza, Luis Alberto de la. "La transición del imperio a la república o la participación indiscriminada (1821–1823)." *Estudios de historia moderna y contemporánea de México* 11 (1988): 21–57.

———. "Una visión historiográfica errónea: La idea de nacionalidad." In *Evolución del estado mexicano*, Tomo 1: *Formación, 1810–1910*. Mexico City: Ediciones El Caballito, 1986. 21–54.

Gayón Córdova, María. *Condiciones de vida y de trabajo en la ciudad de México en el siglo XIX.* Mexico City: INAH, 1988.

Gil Novales, Alberto (ed.). *Rafael del Riego: La revolución de 1820 día a día.* Madrid: E. Tecnos, 1976.

Gómez Pedraza, Manuel. *Manifiesto que Manuel Gómez Pedraza, ciudadano de la república de Méjico dedica a sus compatriotas, o sea una reseña de su vida pública.* New Orleans: Imprenta de Benjamín Levy, 1831.

González de la Vara, Martín. "La política del federalismo en Nuevo México, 1821–1836." *Historia Mexicana* 36, no. 1 (July–September 1986): 49–80.

González Navarro, Moisés. *Anatomía del poder en México (1848–1853).* Mexico City: El Colegio de México, 1977.

———. "La independencia, el yorkinato y la libertad." In *Extremos de México: Homenaje a don Daniel Cosío Villegas.* Mexico City: El Colegio de México, 1971. 151–80.

———. *El pensamiento político de Lucas Alamán.* Mexico City: El Colegio de México, 1952.

———. "La venganza del sur." *Historia Mexicana* 21, no. 4 (April–June 1972): 677–92.

———. "Tipología del conservadurismo mexicano." In Solange Alberro, Alicia Hernández Chávez, and Elías Trabulse (eds.), *La revolución francesa en México.* Mexico City: El Colegio de México, 1991. 215–34.

———. "Tipología del liberalismo mexicano." *Historia Mexicana* 32, no. 2 (October–December 1982): 198–225.

González Oropeza, Manuel. "Características iniciales del federalismo mexicano (1823–1837)." In Cecilia Noriega Elío (ed.), *El nacionalismo en México.* Zamora: El Colegio de Michoacán, 1992. 413–32.

———. *El Federalismo.* Mexico City: UNAM, 1995.

González Pedrero, Enrique. *País de un solo hombre: El México de Santa Anna,* vol. 1: *La ronda de los contrarios.* Mexico City: Fondo de Cultura Económica, 1993.

———. *País de un solo hombre: El México de Santa Anna,* vol. 2. Mexico City: Fondo de Cultura Económica, 2003.

González y González, Luis. "Patriotismo y matriotismo: Cara y Cruz de México." In Cecilia Noriega Elío (ed.), *El nacionalismo en México.* Zamora: El Colegio de Michoacán, 1992. 477–95.

González, María del Refugio. "Ilustrados, regalistas y liberales." In Jaime E.

Rodríguez O. (ed.), *The Independence of Mexico and the Creation of the New Nation*. Los Angeles: UCLA Latin American Center, 1989. 247–63.

———. "El pensamiento de los conservadores mexicanos." In Jaime E. Rodríguez O. (ed.), *The Mexican and Mexican American Experience in the 19th Century*. Tempe: Bilingual Press, 1989. 55–67.

González, María del Refugio (ed.). *La formación del estado mexicano*. Mexico City: Editorial Porrúa, 1984.

Gortari Rabiela, Hira de. "El federalismo en la construcción de los estados." In Jaime E. Rodríguez O. (ed.), *Mexico in the Age of Democratic Revolutions, 1750–1850*. Boulder: Lynne Rienner Publishers, 1994. 209–22.

———. "La minería durante la guerra de independencia y los primeros años del México independiente, 1810–1824." In Jaime E. Rodríguez O. (ed.), *The Independence of Mexico and the Creation of the New Nation*. Los Angeles: UCLA Latin American Center, 1989. 129–61.

———. "Realidad ecónomica y proyectos políticos: Los primeros años del México independiente." In Cecilia Noriega Elío (ed.), *El nacionalismo en México*. Zamora: El Colegio de Michoacán, 1992. 163–78.

———. "El territorio y las identidades en la construcción de la nación." In Alicia Hernández Chávez and Manuel Mioño (eds.), *Cincuenta años de historia en México*. 2 vols. Mexico City: Centro de Estudios Históricos, El Colegio de México, 1991. 2:199–220.

Green, Stanley C. *The Mexican Republic: The First Decade, 1823–1832*. Pittsburgh: University of Pittsburgh Press, 1987.

Guardino, Peter F. "Barbarism or Republican Law? Guerrero's Peasants and National Politics, 1820–1846." *Hispanic American Historical Review* 75, no. 2 (May 1995): 185–213.

———. *Peasants, Politics, and the Formation of Mexico's National State: Guerrero, 1800–1857*. Stanford: Stanford University Press, 1996.

———. *The Time of Liberty: Popular Political Culture in Oaxaca, 1750–1850*. Durham NC: Duke University Press, 2005.

Guardino, Peter, and Charles Walker. "The State, Society, and Politics in Peru and Mexico in the Late Colonial and Early Republican Periods." *Latin American Perspectives* 19, no. 2 (Spring 1992): 10–43.

Güemez Pineda, Arturo. *Liberalismo en tierras del caminante Yucatán 1812–1840*. Zamora: El Colegio de Michoacán, 1994.

Guerra, Francois-Xavier. "Forms of Communication, Political Spaces, and

Cultural Identities in the Creation of Spanish American Nations." In John Charles Chasteen and Sara Castro-Klarén (eds.), *Beyond Imagined Communities: Reading and Writing the Nation in Nineteenth-Century Latin America*. Washington DC: Woodrow Wilson Center Press and Johns Hopkins University Press, 2003. 3–32.

———. "Identidades e independencia: La excepción americana." *Imaginar la nación: Cuadernos de Historia Latinoamericana*, no. 2 (1994): 93–134.

———. "Introducción, Epifanías de la Nación." *Imaginar la nación: Cuadernos de Historia Latinoamericana*, no. 2 (1994): 7–14.

———. *México: Del Antiguo Régimen a la Revolución*. 2 vols. Mexico City: Fondo de Cultura Económica, 1988.

———. *Modernidad e independencias: Ensayos sobre las revoluciones hispánicas*. Mexico City: Editorial Mapfre–Fondo de Cultura Económica, 1993.

———. "El pronunciamiento en México: Prácticas e imaginarios." *Travaux et Recherches dans les Amériques du Centre* 37 (June 2000): 15–26.

———. "The Spanish-American Tradition of Representation, and Its European Roots." *Journal of Latin American Studies* 26. no. 1 (February 1994): 1–35.

Guzmán, Fernando. *Catecismo político*. Managua: Tipografía Nacional, 1887.

Hale, Charles A. "Alamán, Antuñano, y la continuidad del liberalismo." *Historia Mexicana* 11, no. 2 (October–December 1961): 224–45.

———. *Mexican Liberalism in the Age of Mora, 1821–1853*. New Haven: Yale University Press, 1968.

———. "José María Luis Mora and the Structure of Mexican Liberalism." *Hispanic American Historical Review* 45, no. 2 (May 1965): 196–227.

———. "Liberalismo mexicano." *Historia Mexicana* 12, no. 3 (January–March 1963): 456–63.

———. "The Reconstruction of 19th Century Politics in Spanish America: A Case for the History of Ideas." *Latin American Research Review* 8 (Summer 1973): 53–73.

———. *The Transformation of Liberalism in Late-Nineteenth Century Mexico*. Princeton: Princeton University Press, 1989.

Hamill, Hugh M. Jr. "Caudillismo and Independence: A Symbiosis?" In Jaime E. Rodríguez O. (ed.), *The Independence of Mexico and the Creation of the New Nation*. Los Angeles: UCLA Latin American Center, 1989. 163–74.

Hamnett, Brian R. "Anastasio Bustamante y la guerra de independencia, 1810–1821." *Historia Mexicana* 28, no. 4 (April–June 1979): 515–45.

———. "Between Bourbon Reforms and Liberal Reforma: The Political Economy of a Mexican Province—Oaxaca, 1750–1850." In Kenneth J. Andrien and Lyman L. Johnson (eds.), *The Political Economy of Spanish America in the Age of Revolution, 1750–1850*. Albuquerque: University of New Mexico Press, 1994. 39–62.

———. "The Economic and Social Dimension of the Revolution of Independence in Mexico, 1800–1824." *Ibero-Amerikanisches Archiv* 6, no. 1 (1980): 1–27.

———. "Faccionalismo, constitución y poder personal en la política mexicana, 1821–1854: Un ensayo interpretativo." In Josefina Zoraida Vázquez (ed.), *La fundación del estado mexicano, 1821–1855*. Mexico City: Nueva Imagen, 1994. 75–109.

———. "Factores regionales en la desintegración del regimen colonial en la Nueva España: El federalismo de 1823–1824." In Inge Buisson et al. (eds.), *Problemas de la formación del estado y de la nación en Hispanoamérica*. Cologne: Bohlau Verlag, 1984. 305–17.

———. *Juárez*. London: Longman, 1994.

———. "Liberal Politics and Spanish Freemasonry, 1814–1820." *History* 69, no. 226 (June 1984): 222–37.

———. "Oaxaca: Las principales familias y el federalismo de 1823." In María Angeles Romero Frizzi (ed.), *Lecturas históricas del Estado de Oaxaca*. Colección Regiones de México, vol. 3. Mexico City: INAH, 1990. 51–69.

———. "Partidos políticos mexicanos e intervención militar, 1823–1855." In Antonio Annino (ed.), *América Latina: Dallo stato coloniale allo state nazione*. 2 vols. Milan: Franco Angeli, 1987. 2:573–91.

———. *Roots of Insurgency: Mexican Regions, 1750–1824*. Cambridge: Cambridge University Press, 1986.

———. "Social Structure and Regional Elites in Late Colonial Mexico, 1750–1824." Glasgow: University of Glasgow, Occasional Papers, 1984.

Hanson, Victor Davies. *Matanza y cultura: Batallas decisivas en el auge de la civilización occidental*. Mexico City: Fondo de Cultura Económica–Turner, 2006.

Hart, John. "La guerra de los campesinos del suroeste mexicano en los años de 1840: Conflicto en una sociedad transicional." In Friedrich Katz (ed.), *Revuelta, rebelión y revolución*. 2 vols. Mexico City: Ed. ERA, 1988. 1:225–41.

Heath, Hilarie J. "British Merchant Houses in Mexico, 1821–1860: Conforming Business Practices and Ethics." *Hispanic American Historical Review* 73, no. 2 (May 1993): 261–90.

Hernández Chávez, Alicia, and Manuel Miño Grijalva (eds). *Cincuenta años de historia en México*. 2 vols. Mexico City: Centro de Estudios Históricos, El Colegio de México, 1991.

Hernández Chávez, Alicia. "La Guardia Nacional y mobilización política de los pueblos." In Jaime E. Rodríguez O. (ed.), *Patterns of Contention in Mexican History*. Wilmington DE: SR Books, 1992. 207–25.

———. *La tradición republicana del buen gobierno*. Mexico City: El Colegio de México–Fondo de Cultura Económica, 1993.

Herrera Canales, Inés. *El Comercio exterior de México—1821–1875*. Mexico City: El Colegio de México, 1977.

Howarth, David. *Discourse*. Milton Keynes, U.K.: Open University Press, 2000.

Hutchinson, C. A. *Valentín Gómez Farías: La vida de un republicano*. Guadalajara: Gobierno de Jalisco, 1983.

Ibarra Bellon, Araceli. *El comercio y el poder en México, 1821–1864: La lucha por las fuentes financieras entre el Estado central y las regiones*. Mexico City: Fondo de Cultura Económica–Universidad de Guadalajara, 1998.

Jiménez, Armando Alfonzo, Óscar Cruz Barney, and Emmanuel Roa Ortiz (coords.), *Ensayos histórico-juridicos: Mejico y Michoacán*. México City: UNAM, Universidad Latina de América, Supremo Tribunal de Justicia del Estado de Michoacán, 2006.

Jiménez Codinach, Guadalupe. *La Gran Bretaña y la independencia de México 1808–1821*. Mexico City: Fondo de Cultura Económica, 1991.

———. "Veracruz, almacén de plata en el Atlántico: La Casa Gordon y Murphy, 1805–1824." *Historia Mexicana* 38, no. 2 (October–December 1988): 325–53.

Jiménez Codinach, Guadalupe (ed.). *Planes en la nación Mexicana. Libro uno: 1808–1830*. Mexico City: Senado de la República–El Colegio de México, 1987.

Jiménez, Fernández Manuel. "Las doctrinas populistas en la independencia de Hispano-América." *Anuario de Estudios Americanos* 3 (1964): 517–666.

Johnson, Richard A. *The Mexican Revolution of Ayutla, 1854–1855: An Analysis of the Evolution and Destruction of Santa Anna's Last Dictatorship*. Westport CT: Greenwood, 1974.

Kahle, Gunter. *Militar und Staatsbildung in den Anfangen der Unabhangigkeit Mexicos.* Cologne: Bohlau Verlag, 1969.

Katz, Friedrich (ed.). *Revuelta, rebelión y revolución.* 2 vols. Mexico City: Ed. ERA, 1988.

Kenyon, Gordon. "Mexican Influence in Central America, 1821–1823." *Hispanic American Historical Review* 41, no. 2 (May 1961): 175–205.

Knight, Alan. "Continuidades históricas en los movimientos sociales." In Jane-Dale Lloyd and Laura Pérez (eds.), *Paisajes rebeldes.* Mexico City: Universidad Iberoamericana, 1995. 14–52.

———. "Mexican National Identity." In Susan Deans-Smith and Eric Van Young (eds.), *Mexican Soundings: Essays in Honour of David A. Brading.* London: Institute for the Study of the Americas, 2007. 192–214.

———. "Peasants into Patriots: Thoughts on the Making of the Mexican Nation." *Mexican Studies/Estudios Mexicanos* 10, no. 1 (Winter 1994): 135–61.

Krauze, Enrique. *Siglo de caudillos: Biografía política de México (1810–1910).* Mexico City: Tusquets Editores, 1994.

Kuethe, Allan J., and Juan Marchena Fernández (eds.). *Soldados del rey: El ejército borbónico en América colonial en vísperas de la independencia.* Castellón: Universitat Jaume I, 2005.

Laclau, Ernesto, and Chantal Mouffe. *Hegemony and Socialist Strategy: Towards a Radical Democratic Politics.* London: Verso, 1999.

Lafragua, José María. *Miscelánea de política.* México City: Instituto Nacional de Estudios Históricos de la Revolución Mexicana, 1987.

Landázuri Benítez, Gisela, and Verónica Vázquez Mantecón. *Azúcar y Estado, 1750–1880.* Mexico City: Fondo de Cultura Económica, 1988.

Libro de Actas del Honorable Congreso del Estado de Jalisco (1 de enero–31 de mayo de 1824). Guadalajara: Poderes de Jalisco, 1975.

Lienhard, Martin. *La voz y su huella: Escritura y conflicto étnico-social en América Latina, 1492–1988.* Hanover: Ediciones del Norte, 1991.

Lira, Andrés. *Comunidades indígenas frente a la ciudad de México: Tenochtitlan y Tlatelolco, sus pueblos y barrios, 1812–1919.* Zamora: El Colegio de México–El Colegio de Michoacán, 1983.

Lira González, Andrés. "Mier y la Constitución de México." In Jaime E. Rodríguez O. (ed.), *Mexico in the Age of Democratic Revolutions, 1750–1850.* Boulder CO: Lynne Rienner Publishers, 1994. 161–76.

Lloyd, Jane-Dale, and Laura Pérez (eds.). *Paisajes rebeldes.* Mexico City: Universidad Iberoamericana, 1995.

Lovett, Gabriel H. *La guerra de la independencia y el nacimiento de la España contemporánea.* 2 vols. Barcelona: Península, 1975.

Macune, Charles W. Jr. "Conflictos entre el gobierno nacional y el estado de México—1823–1835." *Historia Mexicana* 26, no. 2 (October–December 1976): 216–37.

——. *El Estado de México y la federación mexicana.* Mexico City: Fondo de Cultura Económica, 1978.

——. "The Expropriation of Mexico City—Regional Antipathy in Newly Independent Mexico." *Proceedings of the Pacific Coast Council on Latin American Studies* 2 (1973): 117–42.

——. "The Impact of Federalism on Mexican Church-State Relations, 1824–1835: The Case of the State of Mexico." *The Americas* 40, no. 4 (April 1984): 505–29.

Malamud, Carlos D. "Acerca del concepto de 'Estado colonial' en la América hispana." *Revista de Occidente* 116 (January 1991): 114–27.

Mallon, Florencia E. *Campesino y Nación: La construcción de México y Perú poscoloniales.* Mexico City: CIESAS–El Colegio de Michoacán–El Colegio de San Luis, 2003.

Mallon, Florencia E. "Peasants and State Formation in Nineteenth-Century Mexico: Morelos, 1848–1858." *Political Power and Social Theory* 7 (1988): 1–54.

Malo, José Ramón. *Diario de sucesos notables 1832–1853.* 2 vols. Mexico City: Editorial Patria, 1948.

Marchena Fernández, Juan. *El ejército de América antes de la Independencia: Ejército regular y milicias americanas, 1750–1815.* Madrid: Fundación Mapfre–Tavera, 2005.

——. *Oficiales y soldados en el ejército de América.* Sevilla: Escuela de Estudios Hispanoamericanos, 1983.

——. "Reformas borbónicas y poder popular en la América de las luces": El temor al pueblo en armas a fines del periodo colonial." *Anales de Historia Contemporánea* (1990–92): 187–99.

Marichal, Carlos. *A Century of Debt Crises in Latin America from Independence to the Great Depression, 1820–1930.* Princeton: Princeton University Press, 1989.

Márquez, Enrique (ed.). *San Luis Potosí: Textos de su historia.* Mexico City: Instituto de Investigaciones Dr. José María Luis Mora, 1986.

Márquez, Enrique, and María Isabel Abella (eds.). *Ponciano Arriaga: Obras Completas, vol. 1: La Experiencia Potosina*. Mexico City: Pórtico de la Ciudad de México, 1992.

Mateos, Juan Antonio (ed.). *Historia parlamentaria de los congresos mexicanos de 1821 a 1857*. 25 vols. Mexico City: S. Reyes, 1877–1912.

Matteucci, Niccola. "Soberanía." In Norberto Bobbio et al. (eds.), *Diccionario de política*. Mexico City: Siglo XXI Editores, 2002. 1534–46.

Mayagoitia, Alejandro. "Apuntes sobre las Bases Orgánicas." In Patricia Galeana (ed.), *México y sus Constituciones*. Mexico City: AGN-FCE, 1999. 150–89.

Mayo, John. "Imperialismo de libre comercio e imperio informal en la costa oeste de México durante la época de Santa Anna." *Historia Mexicana* 40, no. 4 (April–June 1991): 673–96.

McGowan, Gerald L. *El Distrito Federal de dos leguas, o como el Estado de México perdío su capital*. Zinacantepec: El Colegio Mexiquense, 1991.

McGowan, Gerald L. (ed.). *El Estado del Valle de México 1824–1917*. Zinacantepec: El Colegio Mexiquense, 1991.

McKenzie Johnston, H. *Missions to Mexico: A Tale of British Diplomacy in the 1820s*. London: British Academic Press, 1992.

Medina Peña, Luis. *Invención del sistema político mexicano: Formas de gobierno y gobernabilidad en México en el siglo XIX*. Mexico City: Fondo de Cultura Económica, 2004.

Memoria en que el gobierno del Estado libre de los Zacatecas da cuenta de los ramos de su administración al congreso del mismo estado, con arreglo a lo dispuesto en el artículo 74 de su constitución. Zacatecas: Imprenta del gobierno, 1833.

Mena Brito, Bernardino. *Reestructuración histórica de Yucatán (Influencia negativa de los políticos campechanos en los destinos de México y de Yucatán de 1821 a 1855)*. 3 vols. Mexico City: Editores Mexicanos Unidos S.A., 1965.

Méndez, Don Santiago. *Representación que el gobernador de Yucatán dirige al congreso constituyente de la república mejicana en cumplimiento del acuerdo de la legislatura del estado, de 2 de junio de 1842*. Mérida de Yucatán: Imprenta de J. Dolores Espinosa, 1842.

Meyer Cosío, Rosa María. "Empresarios, crédito y especulación (1820–1850)." In Leonor Ludlow and Carlos Marichal (eds). *Banca y poder en México 1800–1925)*. Mexico City: Editorial Grijalbo, 1986. 99–117.

Meyer, Jean. "Haciendas y ranchos, peones y campesinos en el Porfiriato: Algunas falacias estadísticas." *Historia mexicana* 35, no. 3 (January–March 1986): 477–509.

———. *Problemas campesinos y revueltas agrarias, 1821–1910*. Mexico City: Sep Setentas, 1973.

Moliner, Antonio. *La guerra de la independencia en España (1808–1814)*. Barcelona: Nabla Ediciones, 2007.

Monroy Castillo, Ma. Isabel. *Sueños, tentativas y posibilidades: Extranjeros en San Luis Potosí, 1821–1845*. San Luis Potosí: El Colegio de San Luis–Archivo Histórico del Estado de San Luis Potosí, 2004.

Monroy, Ma. Isabel, and Tomás Calvillo. *Breve historia de San Luis Potosí*. Mexico City: Fondo de Cultura Económica–El Colegio de México, 1997.

Mora, José María Luis. "Catecismo político de la Federación Mexicana." In Lillian Briseño Senosiain (ed.), *Obras Completas de José María Luis Mora*. Obra Política III (series). Mexico City: Instituto Mora–CONACULTA, 1989.

———. *México y sus revoluciones*. 3 vols. Reprint, Mexico City: Fondo de Cultura Económica–Instituto Cultural Helénico, 1986.

———. *Obras sueltas*. 2nd ed. Mexico City: Editorial Porrúa, 1963.

Morange, Claude. *Una conspiración fallida y una Constitución nonata (1819)*. Madrid: CEPC, 2006.

Moreno Alonso, Manuel. *José Bonaparte: Un rey republicano en el trono de España*. Madrid: La esfera de los libros, 2008.

Moreno Toscano, Alejandra. "Cambios en los patrones de urbanización en México, 1810–1910." *Historia Mexicana* 22, no. 2 (October–December 1972): 160–87.

———. "El paisaje rural y las ciudades: Dos perspectivas de la geografía histórica." *Historia Mexicana* 21, no. 2 (October–December 1971): 242–68.

Moreno Toscano, Alejandra, and Carlos Aguirre Anaya. "Migrations to Mexico City in the Nineteenth Century: Research Approaches." *Journal of Interamerican Studies and World Affairs* 17, no. 1 (February 1975): 27–42.

Moreno Valle, Lucina (ed.). *Catálogo de la Colección Lafragua de la Biblioteca Nacional de México, 1821–1853*. Mexico City: Instituto de Investigaciones Bibliográficas, 1975.

Morton, Ohland. *Terán and Texas: A Chapter in Texas-Mexican Relations*. Austin: Texas State Historical Association, 1948.

Muría, José María. *Breve historia de Jalisco*. Guadalajara: Universidad de Guadalajara, 1988.

———. *El federalismo en Jalisco (1823)*. Mexico City: INAH, 1973.

———. *México en la conciencia nacional*. Mexico City: Instituto de Investigaciones Dr. José Luis Mora, 1987.

Muría, José María (ed.). *Historia de Jalisco*. 4 vols. Guadalajara: Gobierno de Jalisco, 1981.

Muría, José María, Cándido Galvan, and Angélica Peregrina (eds.). *Jalisco en la conciencia nacional*. 2 vols. Guadalajara: Gobierno del Estado de Jalisco–Instituto de Investigaciones Dr. José María Luis Mora, 1987.

Muro, Luis. "Relación de las fechas de las sesiones secretas de los cuerpos legislativos mexicanos (1821–1824) cuyas actos no aparecen en el libro manuscrito original." *Historia Mexicana* 32, no. 3 (January–March 1984): 459–62.

Muro, Luis (ed.). *Historia parlamentaria mexicana: Sesiones secretas 1821–1824*. Mexico City: Instituto de Investigaciones Legislativas, Cámara de Diputados, 1982.

Muro, Manuel. *Historia de San Luis Potosí*. 2 vols. San Luis Potosí: N.p., 1910.

Noriega, Alfonso. *El pensamiento conservador y el conservadurismo mexicano*. Mexico City: Instituto de Investigaciones Jurídicas, UNAM, 1972.

———. *El pensamiento conservador y el conservadurismo mexicano*. 2 vols. Serie C. Estudios históricos 3. Mexico City: Instituto de Investigaciones Jurídicas, UNAM, 1993.

Noriega Elío, Cecilia. *El Constituyente de 1842*. Mexico City: UNAM, 1996.

Noriega Elío, Cecilia (ed.). *El nacionalismo en México: VIII Coloquio de antropología e historia regionales*. Zamora: El Colegio de Michoacán, 1992.

Ocampo, Javier. *Las ideas de un día: El pueblo mexicano ante la consumación de su independencia*. Mexico City: El Colegio de México, 1969.

O'Gorman, Edmundo. *Historia de las divisiones territoriales de México*. 5th ed. Mexico City: Editorial Porrúa, 1979.

Olavarría y Ferrari, Enrique. *México independiente 1821–1855*. Vol. 4 of *México á través de los siglos*, edited by Vicente Riva Palacio. Mexico City: Ballescá y Compañía, 1888–89.

Olveda, Jaime. *Gordiano Guzmán, un cacique del siglo XIX*. Mexico City: SEP-INAH, 1980.

———. *La política de Jalisco durante la primera época federal*. Guadalajara: Poderes de Jalisco, 1976.

Olveda, Jaime (ed.). *Cartas a Gómez Farías*. Guadalajara: Gobierno del Estado de Jalisco, 1990.

Ortega Noriega, Sergio. "Hacia la regionalización de la historia de México." *Estudios de historia moderna y contemporánea de México* no. 8 (1980): 9–21.

Ortiz de Ayala, Tadeo. *México considerado como nación independiente y libre.* 2 vols. Burdeos, 1832; reprint, Guadalajara: Ediciones I.T.G., 1952.

Ortiz Escamilla, Juan. "Calleja, el gobierno de la Nueva España y la Constitución de 1812." *Revista de Investigaciones Jurídicas*, año 20, no. 20 (1996): 405–47.

———. "Defensa militar, negocios e ideología: Veracruz, 1821–1825." In S. Broseta, C. Corona, and M. Chust et al. (eds.), *Las ciudades y la guerra, 1750–1898.* Castellón: Universitat Jaume I, 2002. 155–96.

———. "Félix María Calleja: De héroe a villano." In Manuel Chust and Víctor Mínguez (eds.), *La construcción del héroe en España y México (1789–1847).* Valencia: Publicacions de la Universitat de Valencia, 2003. 337–55.

———. "Las fuerzas militares y el proyecto de estado en México, 1767–1835." In Alicia Hernández Chávez and Manuel Miño Grijalva (eds.), *Cincuenta años de historia en México.* 2 vols. Mexico City: Centro de Estudios Históricos, El Colegio de México, 1991. 2:261–82.

———. "El pronunciamiento federalista de Gordiano Guzmán, 1837–1842." *Historia Mexicana* 38, no. 2 (October–December 1988): 241–82.

Ortiz Escamilla, Juan, and José Antonio Serrano Ortega (eds.). *Ayuntamientos y liberalismo gaditano en México.* Mexico City: El Colegio de Michoacán–Universidad Veracruzana, 2007.

Otero, Mariano. *Ensayo sobre el verdadero estado de la cuestión social y política que se agita en la República Mexicana.* In Jesús Reyes Heroles (ed.), *Mariano Otero Obras*, vol 1. Mexico City: Editorial Porrua, 1995.

Pantoja Morán, David. *La idea de soberanía en el constitucionalismo latinoamericano.* Mexico City: UNAM, 1973.

Parcero, María de la Luz. *Lorenzo de Zavala: Fuente y origen de la reformal liberal en México.* Mexico City: INAH, 1969.

Payne, Stanley. *Politics and the Military in Modern Spain.* Stanford CA: Stanford University Press, 1967.

Pérez Herrero, Pedro. "'Crecimiento' colonial vs. 'crisis' nacional en México, 1765–1854: Notas a un modelo explicativo." In Virginia Guedea and Jaime E. Rodríguez O. (eds.), *Five Centuries of Mexican History.* 2 vols. Mexico City: Instituto Dr. José María Luis Mora–University of California, Irvine, 1992. 2:81–105.

————. "Regional Conformation in Mexico, 1700–1850: Models and Hypotheses." In Eric Van Young (ed.), *Mexico's Regions: Comparative History and Development*. San Diego: Center for U.S.-Mexican Studies, University of California, San Diego, 1992. 117–44.

Pérez Herrero, Pedro (ed.). *Región e historia en México (1700–1850): Métodos de análisis regional*. Mexico City: Instituto de Investigaciones Dr. José María Luis Mora–Universidad Autónoma Metropolitana, 1991.

Pérez Verdía, Luis. *Biografía del Excmo Sr. Don Prisciliano Sánchez, primer gobernador constitucional del Estado de Jalisco*. Guadalajara: Tipografía de Banda, 1881.

Pérez Verdía, Luis. *Historia particular del estado de Jalisco*. 2 vols. Originally published 1910; 2nd ed. Guadalajara: Gobierno de Jalisco, 1951.

Piñera Ramírez, David. *El nacimiento de Jalisco y la gestación del federalismo mexicano*. Guadalajara: Poderes de Jalisco, 1974.

Poinsett, Joel Roberts. *Notes on Mexico Made in the Autumn of 1822*. Reprint, New York: Frederick R. Praeger, 1969.

Poinsett, Joel Roberts. *The Present Political State of Mexico*. Edited by L. Smith Lee. Salisbury NC: Documentary Publications, 1976.

Portillo Valadés, José María. *Crisis atlántica: Autonomía e independencia en la crisis de la monarquía hispana*. Madrid: Marcial Pons–Fundación Carolina, 2006.

Potash, Robert A. *Mexican Government and Industrial Development in the Early Republic: The Banco de Avío*. Amherst: University of Massachusetts Press, 1983.

Prieto, Guillermo. *Memorias de mis tiempos (de 1840 a 1853)*. Puebla: Editorial José M. Cajica Jr., 1970.

Primer centenario de la constitución de 1824, obra conmemorativa. Mexico City: Cámara de Senadores, 1924.

Quezada, Sergio. Formas de gobierno y élites peninsulares: Federalismo y centralismo en Yucatán, 1825–1835. Manuscript.

Quijada, Mónica. "¿Qué Nación? Dinámicas y dicotomías de la nación en el imaginario hispanoamericano del siglo XIX." *Imaginar la nación: Cuadernos de Historia Latinoamericana*, no. 2 (1994): 15–51.

Quinlan, David M. "Issues and Factions in the Constituent Congress, 1823–1824." In Jaime E. Rodríguez O. (ed.), *Mexico in the Age of Democratic Revolutions, 1750–1850*. Boulder CO: Lynne Rienner Publishers, 1994. 177–207.

Quintanilla, Lourdes. *El nacionalismo de Lucas Alamán*. Guanajuato: Gobierno del Estado de Guanajuato, 1991.

Quintanilla Obregón, Lourdes. "El nacionalismo de Lucas Alamán." In Cecilia Noriega Elío (ed.), *El nacionalismo en México*. Zamora: El Colegio de Michoacán, 1992. 377–86.

Rabasa, Emilio. *El pensamiento político del constituyente de 1824 (Integración y realización)*. Mexico City: UNAM, 1986.

Rangel Silva, José Alfredo, and Flor de María Salazar Mendoza. "Élites, territorialidad y fragmentación política: La Provincia Huasteca de 1823." In Antonio Escobar Ohmstede and Luz Carregha Lamadrid (eds.), *El Siglo XIX de las Huastecas*. Mexico City: CIESAS, 2002. 59–92.

Rangel, José Alfredo, and Carlos R. Ruiz Medrano (eds.). *Discursos públicos, negociaciones y estrategias de lucha colectiva*. San Luis Potosí: El Colegio de San Luis–AHESLP, 2006.

Real Academia Española. *Diccionario de la lengua castellana compuesto por la Real Academia Española, reducido a un tomo para su más fácil uso*. Madrid: Viuda de Ibarra, 1803.

Reed, Nelson. *The Caste War of Yucatán*. Rev. ed. Stanford: Stanford University Press, 2001.

Reina, Leticia. "Una mirada a diferentes formas de reconstrucción histórica de las rebeliones. Periodo colonial y siglo XIX." In Jane-Dale Lloyd and Laura Pérez (eds.). *Paisajes rebeldes*. Mexico City: Universidad Iberoamericana, 1995. 53–76.

———. *Las rebeliones campesinas en México (1819–1906)*. 4th ed. Mexico City: Siglo Veintiuno Editores, 1988.

———. "Las rebeliones indígenas y campesinas (periodo colonial y siglo XIX)." In Carlos García Mora and Martín Villalobos (eds.), *La antropología en México: Panorama histórico*. Mexico City: INAH, 1988. 4:517–41.

Reyes Heroles, Jesús. *El liberalismo mexicano*. 3 vols. Originally published 1957. Mexico City: Fondo de Cultura Económica, 1974.

Rieu-Millan, Marie Laure. *Los diputados americanos en las Cortes de Cádiz (Igualdad o independencia)*. Madrid: Consejo Superior de Investigaciones Científicas, 1990.

Robertson, William Spence. *Iturbide of Mexico*. Durham NC: Duke University Press, 1952.

Rodríguez O., Jaime E. "Los caudillos y los historiadores: Riego, Iturbide y Santa Anna." In Manuel Chust and Víctor Mínguez (eds.). *La construcción del héroe en España y México, (1789–1847)*. Valencia: Publicacions de la Universitat, 2003. 309–35.

———. "La Constitución de 1824 y la formación del Estado mexicano." *Historia Mexicana* 40, no. 3 (January–March 1991): 507–35.

———. "The Constitution of 1824 and the Formation of the Mexican State." In Jaime E. Rodríguez O. (ed.), *The Evolution of the Mexican Political System*. Wilmington DE: SR Books, 1991. 71–90.

———. "The Constitution of 1824 and the Formation of the Mexican State," in Jaime E. Rodríguez O. (ed.). *The Origins of Mexican National Politics 1808–1847*. Wilmington DE: Scholarly Resources, 1997. 65–84.

———. "Las Cortes mexicanas y el Congreso constituyente." In V. Guedea (ed.), *La independencia de México y el proceso autonomista novohispano, 1808–1824*. Mexico City: UNAM–Instituto Mora, 2001. 285–320.

———. *Down from Colonialism: Mexico's Nineteenth Century Crisis*. Chicano Studies Research Center Publications, no. 3. Los Angeles: University of California, 1983.

———. *The Emergence of Spanish America: Vicente Rocafuerte and Spanish Americanism, 1808–1832*. Berkeley: University of California Press, 1975.

———. "The Formation of the Federal Republic." In Virginia Guedea and Jaime E. Rodríguez O. (eds.), *Five Centuries of Mexican History*. 2 vols. Mexico City: Instituto de Investigaciones Dr. José María Luis Mora–University of California, Irvine, 1992. 316–38.

———. "La independencia de la América Española: Una reinterpretación." *Historia Mexicana* 42, no. 3 (January–March 1993): 571–620.

———. *The Independence of Spanish America*. Cambridge: Cambridge University Press, 1998.

———. "Mexico's First Foreign Loans." In Jaime E. Rodríguez O. (ed.), *The Independence of Mexico and the Creation of the New Nation*. Los Angeles: UCLA Latin American Center, 1989. 215–35.

———. "Oposición a Bustamante." *Historia Mexicana* 20, no. 2 (October–December 1970): 199–234.

———. "The Origins of the 1832 Rebellion." In Jaime E. Rodríguez O. (ed.), *Patterns of Contention in Mexican History*. Wilmington DE: SR Books, 1992. 145–62.

———. "The Struggle for the Nation: The First Centralist-Federalist Conflict in Mexico, 1822–1824." *The Americas* 49, no. 1 (July 1992): 1–22.

———. "La transición de colonia a nación: Nueva España, 1820–1821." *Historia Mexicana* 43, no. 2 (1993): 265–322.

———. "The Transition from Colony to Nation: New Spain, 1820–1821." In Jaime E. Rodríguez O. (ed.), *Mexico in the Age of Democratic Revolutions, 1750–1850*. Boulder CO: Lynne Rienner Publishers, 1994. 97–132.

Rodríguez O., Jaime E. (ed.). *The Evolution of the Mexican Political System.* Wilmington DE: SR Books, 1993.

———. *The Independence of Mexico and the Creation of the New Nation.* Los Angeles: UCLA Latin American Center, 1989.

———. *Mexico in the Age of Democratic Revolutions, 1750–1850.* Boulder CO: Lynne Rienner Publishers, 1994.

———. *Mexico's Regions: Comparative History and Development.* San Diego: Center for U.S.-Mexican Studies, University of California, San Diego, 1992.

———. *Patterns of Contention in Mexican History.* Wilmington DE: SR Books, 1992.

———. *Servando Teresa de Mier, Obras Completas: La formación de un republicano.* Mexico City: UNAM, 1988.

Rojas, Beatriz (ed). *Cuerpo político y pluralidad de derechos: Los privilegios de las corporaciones novohispanas.* México City: CIDE–Instituto Mora, 2007.

———. *Mecánica política para una relectura del siglo XIX mexicano: Antología de correspondencia política.* Mexico City: Universidad de Guadalajara–Instituto Mora, 2006.

Romano, Ruggiero. "Algunas consideraciones alrededor de Nación, Estado (y Libertad) en Europa y América centro-meridional." In Antonio Annino et al. (eds.), *América Latina: Dallo stato coloniale allo stato nazione.* 2 vols. Milan: Franco Angeli, 1987. 1:1–21.

Romero, Matías. *Memoria de Hacienda y Crédito Público, correspondiente al cuadragésimo año económico presentada por el Secretario de Hacienda al Congreso de la Unión el 16 de septiembre de 1870.* Mexico City: Imprenta del gobierno, en Palacio, a cargo de José María Sandoval, 1870.

Rubin, Jeffrey W. "Decentering the Regime: Culture and Regional Politics in Mexico." *Latin American Research Review* 31, no. 3 (1996): 85–126.

Rubio Mañé, Ignacio. "Los diputados mexicanos a las Cortes españolas y el

Plan de Iguala, 1820–1821." *Boletín del Archivo General de la Nación* 2nd series, vol. 12, nos. 3–4 (July–December 1971): 347–95.

Rugeley, Terry. *Yucatán's Maya Peasantry and the Origins of the Caste War.* Austin: University of Texas Press, 1996.

Runciman, W. G. (ed.). *Weber: Selections in Translation.* Cambridge: Cambridge University Press, 1978.

Salinas Sandoval, María del Carmen. *Los municipios en la formación del Estado de México, 1824–46.* Zinacatepec, Edo. de México: El Colegio Mexiquense, 2001.

———. *Política y sociedad en los municipios del Estado de México (1825–1880).* Zinacatepec, Edo. de México: El Colegio Mexiquense, 1996.

Salvucci, Richard J. *Textiles and Capitalism in Mexico: An Economic History of the Obrajes, 1539–1840.* Princeton: Princeton University Press, 1987.

Salvucci, Richard J., Linda K. Salvucci, and Aslán Cohen. "The Politics of Protection: Interpreting Commercial Policy in Late Bourbon and Early National Mexico." In Kenneth J. Andrien and Lyman L. Johnson (eds.), *The Political Economy of Spanish America in the Age of Revolution, 1750–1850.* Albuquerque: University of New Mexico Press, 1994. 95–114.

Samponaro, Frank N. "La alianza de Santa Anna y los federalistas, 1832–1834: Su formación y desintegración." *Historia Mexicana* 30, no. 3 (January–March 1981): 358–90.

———. "Santa Anna and the Abortive Anti-Federalist Revolt of 1833 in Mexico." *The Americas* 40, no. 1 (July 1983): 95–107.

San Juan Victoria, Carlos. "Las utopías oligárquicas conocen sus límites (1821–1834)." In María del Refugio González (ed.), *La formación del estado mexicano.* Mexico City: Editorial Porrúa, 1984. 89–120.

Sánchez Lamego, Miguel A. "El Colegio Militar y el motín de la Acordada." *Historia Mexicana* 10, no. 3 (January–March 1961): 425–38.

Sánchez Luna, Gabriela. "Francisco García Salinas, gobernador de Zacatecas (1828–1834)." In Beatriz Bernal (ed.), *Memoria del IV Congreso de historia del derecho mexicano (1986).* 2 vols. Mexico City: UNAM, 1988. 2:989–1001.

Santa Anna, Antonio López de. *The Eagle: The Autobiography of Santa Anna.* Edited by Ann Fears Crawford. Austin: Pemberton Press, 1967.

———. *Mi historia militar y política (1810–1874).* Vol. 2: *Documentos ineditos o muy raros para la historia de México,* edited by Genaro García. Mexico City: Libreria de la Vda. de Ch. Bouret, 1905.

Santoni, Pedro. "A Fear of the People: The Civic Militia of Mexico in 1845." *Hispanic American Historical Review* 68, no. 2 (May 1988): 269–88.

———. *Mexicans at Arms: Puro Federalists and the Politics of War, 1845–1848.* Fort Worth: Texas Christian University Press, 1996.

Sarmiento, Domingo F. *Facundo: Civilización y barbarie.* Originally published in 1845; Madrid: Editorial Nacional, 1975.

Serrano Ortega, José Antonio. "El ascenso de un caudillo en Guanajuato: Luis de Cortázar, 1827–1832." *Historia Mexicana* 43, no. 1 (July–September 1993): 49–80.

———. *Igualdad, Uniformidad, Proporcionalidad: Contribuciones directas y reformas fiscales en México, 1810–1846.* Mexico City: Instituto Mora–El Colegio de Michoacán, 2007.

———. "Villas fuertes, ciudades débiles: Milicias y jerarquía territorial en Guanajuato, 1790–1847." In S. Broseta, C. Corona, and M. Chust et al. (eds.), *Las ciudades y la guerra, 1750–1898.* Castellón: Universitat Jaume I, 2002. 381–420.

Siemens, Alfred H. *Between the Summit and the Sea: Central Veracruz in the Nineteenth Century.* Vancouver: University of British Columbia Press, 1990.

Sierra, Catalina. *El nacimiento de México.* Mexico City: UNAM, 1960.

Sims, Harold D. *Descolonización en México: El Conflicto entre mexicanos y españoles (1821–1831).* Mexico City: Fondo de Cultura Económica, 1982.

———. "Los exiliados españoles en México en 1829." *Historia Mexicana* 31, no. 3 (January–March 1981): 390–414.

———. *La expulsión de los Españoles de México (1821–1828).* Mexico City: Fondo de Cultura Económica, 1974.

———. *The Expulsion of Mexico's Spaniards 1821–1836.* Pittsburgh: University of Pittsburgh Press, 1990.

———. *La reconquista de México: La historia de los atentados españoles, 1821–1830.* Mexico City: Fondo de Cultura Económica, 1984.

Solares Robles, Laura. *La obra política de Manuel Gómez Pedraza, 1813–1851.* Mexico City: Instituto Mora, 1999.

———. *Una revolución pacífica: Biografía política de Manuel Gómez Pedraza, 1789–1851.* Mexico City: Instituto Mora, 1996.

Sordo Cedeño, Reynaldo. "El congreso y la formación del Estado-nación en México, 1821–1855." In Josefina Zoraida Vázquez (ed.), *La fundación del estado mexicano, 1821–1855.* Mexico City: Nueva Imagen, 1994. 135–78.

———. *El congreso en la primera república centralista.* Mexico City: El Colegio de México–Instituto Tecnológico Autónomo de México, 1993.

———. "Santa Anna y la república centralista de las siete leyes." In Alicia Hernández Chávez and Manuel Miñón Grijalva (eds.), *Cincuenta años de historia en México.* 2 vols. Mexico City: Centro de Estudios Históricos, El Colegio de México, 1991. 2:283–98.

Soto, Manuel Fernando. *Noticias estadísticas de la Huasteca y de una parte de la Sierra Alta formadas en el año de 1853.* Mexico City: Imprenta del Gobierno en Palacio, 1869.

Soto, Miguel, "Mariano Paredes y Arrillaga." In Will Fowler (coord.), *Gobernantes mexicanos,* vol. 1. Mexico: Fondo de Cultura Economica, 2008. 187–201.

Staples, Anne. "Clerics as Politicians: Church, State, and Political Power in IndependentMexico." In Jaime E. Rodríguez O. (ed.), *Mexico in the Age of Democratic Revolutions, 1750–1850.* Boulder CO: Lynne Rienner Publishers, 1994. 223–41.

———. *La iglesia en la primera república federal mexicana (1824–1835).* Mexico City: Editorial Sep Setentas, 1976.

———. "Secularización: Estado e iglesia en tiempos de Gómez Farías." *Estudios de historia moderna y contemporánea de México,* 10 (1986): 109–23.

Stevens, Donald Fithian. "Autonomists, Nativists, Republicans, and Monarchists: Conspiracyand Political History in Nineteenth-Century Mexico." *Mexican Studies/Estudios Mexicanos* 10:1 (Winter 1994): 247–66.

———. "Economic Fluctuations and Political Instability in Early Republican Mexico." *Journal of Interdisciplinary History* 16, no. 4 (Spring 1986): 645–65.

———. *Origins of Instability in Early Republican Mexico.* Durham NC: Duke University Press, 1991.

———. "Riot, Rebellion and Instability in Nineteenth-Century Mexico." In Virgina Guedea and Jaime E. Rodríguez O. (eds.), *Five Centuries of Mexican History.* 2 vols. San Diego: Instituto de Investigaciones Dr. José María Luis Mora–University of California, Irvine, 1992. 1:344–54.

Suárez Molina, Víctor M. *La evolución económica de Yucatán a través del siglo XIX.* 2 vols. Mexico City: Ediciones de la Universidad de Yucatán, 1977.

Suárez y Navarro, Juan. *Historia de México y del general Antonio López de Santa Anna.* 2 vols. Mexico City: Imprenta de I. Cumplido, 1850–51; reprint, Mexico: INEHRM, 1987.

Sutro Branch, California State Library. *Catalogue of the Mexican Pamphlets in the Sutro Collection, 1632–1822.* San Francisco: California State Library, 1939.

———. *Catalogue of Mexican Pamphlets in the Sutro Collection 1823–1842.* San Francisco: California State Library, 1940.

———. *Supplement to the Catalogue of the Mexican Pamphlets in the Sutro Collection (1800–1828).* San Francisco: California State Library, 1941.

Tena Ramírez, Felipe. *Derecho constitucional mexicano.* 18th ed. Mexico City: Editorial Porrúa, 1981.

———. *Leyes fundamentales de México, 1808–1975.* 6th ed., rev. Mexico City: Editorial Porrúa, 1975.

Tenenbaum, Barbara A. "Banqueros sin bancos: El papel de los agiotistas en México (1826–1854)." In Leonor Ludlow and Carlos Marichal (eds.), *Banca y poder en México (1800–1925).* Mexico City: Editorial Grijalbo, 1986. 75–97.

———. "The Chicken and the Egg: Reflections on the Mexican Military, 1821–1846." In Virginia Guedea and Jaime E. Rodríguez O. (eds.), *Five Centuries of Mexican History.* 2 vols. Mexico City: Instituto de Investigaciones Dr. José María Luis Mora–University of California, Irvine, 1992. 1:355–70.

———. "The Making of a Fait Accompli: Mexico and the Provincias Internas, 1776–1846." In Jaime E. Rodríguez O. (ed.), *The Evolution of the Mexican Political System.* Wilmington DE: SR Books, 1993. 91–115.

———. "Merchants, Money and Mischief: The British in Mexico, 1821–1862." *The Americas* 35, no. 3 (January 1979): 317–40.

———. *The Politics of Penury, Debts and Taxes in Mexico, 1821–1856.* Albuquerque: University of New Mexico Press, 1986.

———. "Streetwise History: The Paseo de la Reforma and the Porfirian State, 1876–1910." In William H. Beezley, Cheryl English Martin, and William E. French (eds.), *Rituals of Rule, Rituals of Resistance: Public Celebrations and Popular Culture in Mexico.* Wilmington DE: SR Books, 1994. 127–50.

———. "Taxation and Tyranny: Public Finance during the Iturbide Regime, 1821–1823." In Jaime E. Rodríguez O. (ed.), *The Independence of Mexico and the Creation of the New Nation.* Los Angeles: UCLA Latin American Center, 1989. 201–13.

———. "'They Went Thataway': The Evolution of the Pronunciamiento,

1821–1856." In Jaime E. Rodriguez O. (ed.), *Patterns of Contention in Mexican History*. Wilmington DE: SR Books, 1992. 187–205.

Thomson, Guy P. C. *Puebla de los Angeles: Industry and Society in a Mexican City, 1700–1850*. Boulder CO: Westview Press, 1989.

———. "Traditional and Modern Manufacturing in Mexico, 1821–1850." In Reinhard Liehr (ed.), *América Latina en la época de Simón Bolívar: La formación de las economías nacionales y los intereses europeos 1800–1850*. Berlin: Colloquium Verlag, 1989. 55–85.

Thomson, Guy P. C., with David G. La France. *Patriotism, Politics, and Popular Liberalism in Nineteenth Century Mexico: Juan Francisco Lucas and the Puebla Sierra*. Wilmington DE: Scholarly Resources, 1999.

Tornel y Mendívil, José María. *Breve reseña histórica de los acontecimientos más notables de la nación mexicana desde el año de 1821 hasta nuestros días*. Mexico City: Imprenta de Cumplido, 1852; reprint, Mexico City: INEHRM, 1985.

Torre Villar, Ernesto de la. "El origen del estado mexicano." In Inge Buisson et al. (eds.), *Problemas de la formación del estado y de la nación en Hispanoamérica*. Cologne: Bohlau Verlag, 1984. 127–42.

Torres Bautista, Mariano. "Estado-nación y legitimidad, misma búsqueda, mismas ficciones." In Carlos Contreras Cruz (ed.), *Espacio y perfiles: Historia regional mexicana del siglo XIX*. Puebla: Universidad Autónoma de Puebla, 1989. 213–21.

Trens, Manuel B. *Historia de Chiapas: Desde los tiempos más remotos hasta la caída del segundo imperio*. 2nd ed. Mexico City: Talleres Gráficos de la Nación, 1957.

———. *Historia de Veracruz*. 6 vols. Mexico City: Editorial La Impresora, 1950.

Trueba, Alfonso. *Nicolás Bravo: El mexicano que perdonó*. Mexico City: Editorial Jus, 1976.

Tutino, John. "Cambio social agrario y rebelión campesina en el México decimonónico: El caso de Chalco." In Friedrich Katz (ed.), *Revuelta, rebelión y revolución*. 2 vols. Mexico City: Ed. ERA, 1988. 1:94–134.

———. *From Insurrection to Revolution in Mexico: Social Bases of Agrarian Violence, 1750–1940*. Princeton: Princeton University Press, 1986.

———. "Power, Class and Family: Men and Women in the Mexican Elite, 1750–1810." *The Americas* 39, no. 3 (January 1983): 359–81.

Urías Horcasitas, Beatriz. "Conciencia regional y poder central: Ensayo sobre el pensamiento separatista yucateco en la primera mitad del siglo diecinueve." *Estudios de historia moderna y contemporánea de México* 11 (1988): 59–83.

———. "El pensamiento económico moderno en el México independiente." In Jaime E. Rodríguez O. (ed.), *The Independence of Mexico and the Creation of the New Nation*. Los Angeles: UCLA Latin American Center, 1989. 265–274.

Valadés, José C. *Alamán, estadista e historiador*. Mexico City: Porrúa e Hijos, 1938.

———. *México, Santa Anna, y la guerra de Texas*. Mexico City: Editores Mexicanos Unidos, 1965.

———. *Orígenes de la república mexicana: La aurora constitucional*. Mexico City: Editores Mexicanos Unidos, 1972.

Valle, Rafael Heliodoro (ed.). *La anexión de Centroamerica a México*. 3 vols. Archivo Histórico Diplomatico Mexicano, vols. 4–6. Mexico City: Secretaría de Relaciones Exteriores, 1945, 1946, 1949.

Van Young, Eric. "Are Regions Good to Think?" In Eric Van Young (ed.), *Mexico's Regions: Comparative History and Development*. San Diego: Center for U.S.-Mexican Studies, University of California, San Diego, 1992. 1–36.

———. *La crisis del orden colonial: Estructura agraria y rebelión popular en la Nueva España, 1750–1821*. Mexico City: Alianza Editorial, 1991.

———. *Hacienda and Market in Eighteenth-Century Mexico: The Rural Economy of the Guadalajara Region, 1675–1820*. Berkeley: University of California Press, 1981.

———. "Islands in the Storm: Quiet Cities and Violent Countrysides in the Mexican Independence Era." *Past and Present*, 118 (February 1988): 130–55.

———. "Of Tempests and Teapots: Imperial Crisis and Local Conflicts in Mexico at the Beginning of the Nineteenth Century." In Elisa Servín, Leticia Reina, and John Tutino (eds.), *Cycles of Conflict, Centuries of Change: Crisis, Reform, and Revolution in Mexico*. Durham NC: Duke University Press, 2007. 23–59.

———. "The State as Vampire—Hegemonic Projects, Public Ritual, and Popular Culture in Mexico, 1600–1990." In William H. Beezley, Cheryl English Martin, and William E. French (eds.), *Rituals of Rule, Rituals of Resistance: Public Celebrations and Popular Culture in Mexico*. Wilmington DE: SR Books, 1994. 343–74.

———. "Who Was That Masked Man, Anyway? Popular Symbols and Ideology in the Mexican Wars of Independence." In *Proceedings,* Rocky Mountain Council on Latin American Studies, Annual Meeting, Las Cruces, New Mexico, 1984. 1:18–35.

Van Young, Eric (ed.). *Mexico's Regions: Comparative History and Development.* San Diego: Center for U.S.-Mexican Studies, University of California, San Diego, 1992.

Vázquez Mantecón, Carmen. *Santa Anna y la encrucijada del Estado La dictadura (1853–1855).* Mexico City: Fondo de Cultura Económica, 1986.

Vázquez, Josefina Zoraida. *Don Antonio López de Santa Anna, Mito y enigma.* Mexico City: CONDUMEX, 1987.

———. *Mexicanos y norteamericanos ante la guerra del 47.* Mexico City: Secretaría de Educación Pública, 1972.

———. "De la difícil constitución de un Estado: México, 1821–1854." In Josefina Zoraida Vázquez (ed.), *La fundación del estado mexicano, 1821–1855.* Mexico City: Nueva Imagen, 1994. 9–37.

———. "El ejercito: Un dilema del gobierno mexicano (1841–1864)." In Inge Buisson, Gunter Kahle, Hans-Joachim König, and Horst Pietschmann (eds.), *Problemas de la formación de la nación en Hispanoamérica.* Cologne: Böhlau Verlag, 1984. 319–38.

———. "El establecimiento del federalismo en México, 1812–1827." In Josefina Zoraida Vázquez (ed.), *El establecimiento del federalismo en México, 1821–1827.* Mexico City: Colegio de México, 2003. 19–38.

———. "El federalismo mexicano: 1823–1847." In Marcello Carmagnani (ed.), *Federalismos latinoamericanos: México/Brasil/Argentina.* Mexico City: El Colegio de México–Fondo de Cultura Económica, 1993. 15–50.

———. "El modelo de pronunciamiento mexicano, 1820–1823." *Ulúa* (Revista de Historia, Sociedad y Cultura) 7 (January–June 2006): 31–52.

———. "Iglesia, ejército y centralismo." *Historia Mexicana* 39, no. 1 (July–September 1989): 205–34.

———. "La crisis y los partidos políticos, 1833–1846." In Antonio Annino et al. (eds.), *América Latina: Dallo stato coloniale allo stato nazione.* 2 vols. Milan: Franco Angeli, 1987. 2:557–72.

———. "Los pronunciamientos de 1832: Aspirantismo político e ideología." In Jaime E. Rodríguez O. (ed.), *Patterns of Contention in Mexican History.* Wilmington DE: SR Books, 1992. 163–86.

———. "Political Plans and Collaboration between Civilians and the Military, 1821–1846." *Bulletin of Latin American Research* 15, no. 1 (1996): 19–38.

———. "Un viejo tema: El federalismo y el centralismo." *Historia Mexicana* 42, no. 3 (January–March 1993): 621–31.

Vázquez, Josefina Zoraida (ed.). *De la rebelión de Texas a la guerra del 47.* Mexico City: Nueva Imagen, 1994.

———. *La fundación del estado mexicano, 1821–1855.* Mexico City: Nueva Imagen, 1994.

———. *México al tiempo de su guerra con Estados Unidos (1846–1848).* Mexico City: FCE–Colegio de México–SER, 1998.

———. *Planes en la nación Mexicana. Libro dos: 1831–1834.* Mexico City: Senado de la República–El Colegio de México, 1987.

———. *Planes en la nación mexicana. Libro tres: 1835–1840.* Mexico City: Senado de la República–El Colegio de México, 1987.

———. *Planes en la nación mexicana. Libro cuatro: 1841–1854.* Mexico City: Senado de la República–El Colegio de México, 1987.

Vázquez, Josefina Zoraida, and Héctor Cuauhtémoc Hernández Silva (eds.). *Diario histórico de México 1822–1848 de Carlos María de Bustamante.* Mexico: CIESAS, El Colegio de México, 2001.

Vázquez, Josefina Zoraida, and Lorenzo Meyer. *México frente a Estados Unidos (Un ensayo histórico 1776–1988).* 2nd ed. Mexico City: Fondo de Cultura Económica, 1989.

Vega, Mercedes de. "La opción federalista en Zacatecas, 1820–1835." In Alicia Hernández Chávez and Manuel Mioño Grijalva (eds.), *Cincuenta años de historia de México.* 2 vols. Mexico City: Centro de Estudios Históricos, El Colegio de México, 1991. 2:243–59.

Velázquez, Gustavo G. *La diputación del Estado de México en el supremo congreso constituyente de 1823: Notas biográficas.* Toluca: Gobierno del Estado de México,1977.

Velázquez, Primo Feliciano. *San Luis Potosí.* San Luis Potosí: Universidad Autónoma de San Luis Potosí, 1961.

Victoria, Guadalupe. *Discursos y manifiestos.* Presentación por Salvador Reyes Nevares. Mexico City: Partido Revolucionario Institucional, 1976.

Villalpando César, José Manuel. "La evolución histórico-jurídico de la guardia nacional en México." In Beatriz Bernal (ed.), *Memoria del IV Congreso de historia del derecho mexicano (1986).* 2 vols. Mexico City: UNAM, 1988. 1:1117–62.

Villoro, Luis. "The Ideological Currents of the Epoch of Independence." In Mario de la Cueva et al. (eds.), *Major Trends in Mexican Philosophy*. Notre Dame IN: University of Notre Dame Press, 1966. 185–219.

Voss, Stuart F. *On the Periphery of Nineteenth-Century Mexico: Sonora and Sinaloa, 1810–1877*. Tucson: University of Arizona Press, 1982.

Walker, David W. *Kinship, Business and Politics: The Martínez del Río Family in Mexico, 1823–1867*. Austin: University of Texas Press, 1986.

Ward, Henry George. *Mexico in 1827*. 2nd ed. London: Colburn, 1829.

Warren, Richard A. *Vagrants and Citizens: Politics and the Masses in Mexico City from Colony to Republic*. Wilmington DE: Scholarly Resources Books, 1996; reprint, Lanham MD: Rowan and Littlefield Publishing Group, 2007.

Williams, Mary Wilhelmine. "The Secessionist Diplomacy of Yucatan." *Hispanic American Historical Review* 9, no. 2 (May 1929): 132–43.

Wortman, Miles. "Legitimidad política y regionalismo—El Imperio Mexicano y Centroamérica." *Historia Mexicana* 26, no. 2 (October–December 1976): 238–62.

Yucateco, un. *Observaciones sobre las iniciativas que han dirigido al Congreso general la H. legislatura de Querétaro y la comisión permanente de la de Jalisco, relativas a los negocios de Yucatán; y por apéndice una colección de los opúsculos que se han publicado sobre este mismo asunto en el presente año*. Mexico City: Imprenta de Galván, a cargo de Mariano Arévalo, 1831.

Yucatecos, varios. *Documentos interesantes y decretos del legítimo Congreso Constitucional del Estado de Yucatán: Los yucatecos imparciales, Impugnación a las Observaciones hechas por varios yucatecos al dictamen presentado a la Cámara de Senadores por sus comisiones reunidas en puntos constitucionales y guerra, sobre la proposición del Sr, Vargas relativa a la pacificación de Yucatán*. Mexico City: Imprenta de Galván, a cargo de Mariano Arévalo, 1831.

Zavala, Lorenzo de. *Ensayo crítico de las revoluciones de México desde 1808 hasta 1830*. 2 vols. Mexico City: Editorial Porrúa, 1969; reprint, Mexico City: Fondo de Cultura Económica, 1985.

———. *Memoria en que el gobierno del Estado Libre de México, da cuenta al honorable congreso de todos los ramos que han sido a su cargo en el ultimo año económico, presentada el día 30 de marzo de 1833*. Toluca: n.p., 1833.

Zepeda Patterson, Jorge. "La nación vs. las regiones." In Cecilia Noriega Elío (ed.), *El nacionalismo en México*. Zamora: El Colegio de Michoacán, 1992. 497–517.

Zerecero, Anastasio. *Memorias para la historia de las revoluciones de México.* Mexico City: UNAM, 1975.

Zuleta Miranda, María Cecilia. "El federalismo en Yucatán: Política y militarización (1840–1846)." *Secuencia*, Nuevo época, no. 31 (January–April 1995): 23–47.

Contributors

Shara Ali graduated from the University of St. Andrews in 2005 and completed an MA in Latin American Area Studies at the Institute for the Study of the Americas in London. She has now returned to St. Andrews, benefiting from a School of Modern Languages scholarship, and is studying the pronunciamientos of Yucatán as part of her PhD dissertation.

Timothy E. Anna is distinguished professor at the University of Manitoba. He has been in the history department since 1969. He is a fellow of the Royal Society of Canada and held a Killam Research Fellowship, 1994–96. In 2000 he received the Winnipeg Rh Institute Foundation Medal at the University of Manitoba. His books include *The Fall of the Royal Government in Mexico City* (1978); *The Fall of the Royal Government in Peru* (1979); *Spain and the Loss of America* (1983); *The Mexican Empire of Iturbide* (1990); and *Forging Mexico, 1821–1835* (1998), four of which have also appeared in Spanish. He contributed to volume 3 of *The Cambridge History of Latin America* and volume 5 of the UNESCO *Historia General de América Latina*.

Melissa Boyd is a graduate of the University of St. Andrews, where she was awarded an MA in Spanish and history in 2005. She is currently a PhD research student at the same institution. Her research interests include Mexican liberalism; nineteenth-century political thought, norms, and behavior; and political history and the history of ideas with particular reference to Mariano Otero.

Manuel Chust lectures on contemporary Latin American history at the Departamento de Historia, Geografía y Arte of the Universitat Jaume I in Castelló, Spain. He was awarded the Premio Extraordinario de Doctorado of the Universitat de Valencia (1993) and has served as secretary and director of the Departamento de Historia de la Universitat Jaume I. He is currently director of the Centro de Investigaciones de América Latina of the Universitat Jaume I. His publications add up to fourteen authored and edited books, including *Ciudadanos en armas: La Milicia nacional en el País Valenciano* (1987), *La cuestión nacional americana en las Cortes de Cádiz* (1999) *Doceañismos, constituciones e independencias* (2006); forty-five chapters in national and international volumes; and eighteen articles in academic journals.

Michael P. Costeloe is emeritus professor and senior research fellow at the University of Bristol. He has published several books and many articles on nineteenth-century Mexican history. His most recent work is *Bonds and Bondholders: British Investors and Mexico's Foreign Debt, 1824–1888* (Westport CT: Praeger, 2003), published in Spanish as *Deuda Externa de México: Bonos y tenedores de bonos, 1824–1888* (Mexico: Fondo de Cultura Económica, 2007). He is now working on Anglo-Mexican relations and has completed the biography *William Bullock, Connoisseur and Virtuoso of the Egyptian Hall: Picadilly to Mexico (1773–1849)* (Bristol: HiPLAM, 2008).

Rosie Doyle is currently completing a PhD at the University of St. Andrews under the supervision of Will Fowler as part of the Arts and Humanities Research Council–funded project on the pronunciamiento in nineteenth-century Mexico. Her area of study is the experience of the pronunciamiento in Jalisco. She has an MA in Latin American studies from the Institute of Latin American Studies, University of London, where she pursued development and gender studies and majored in human rights.

Michael T. Ducey is the author of a study of nineteenth-century rural social movements titled *A Nation of Villages: Riot and Rebellion in the Mexican Huasteca, 1750–1850,* published by the University of Arizona Press. He has also written numerous articles and book chapters in Mexican and U.S. publications on the role of indigenous villagers in the political and social life of the late colonial and early national periods. His current project traces the transformation of politics in rural municipalities as liberal models became the dominant mode of political behavior. He is currently based at the Instituto de Investigaciones Histórico-Sociales of the Universidad Veracruzana, Mexico.

Will Fowler is professor of Latin American studies at the University of St. Andrews. He is the author of *Mexico in the Age of Proposals, 1821–1853* (Westport CT, 1998), *Tornel and Santa Anna: The Writer and the Caudillo* (Westport CT, 2000), *Latin America since 1780 (London, 2002; 2nd ed., 2008)*, and *Santa Anna of Mexico* (Lincoln NE, 2007). He has published numerous articles on the early national period and edited ten volumes on Mexican and Latin American political history, including *El conservadurismo mexicano en el siglo XIX* (Puebla, 1999), and *Gobernantes mexicanos* (2 vols., Mexico City, 2008).

Ivana Frasquet is based at the Universitat de Valencia, Spain. She was awarded her PhD at the Universitat Jaume I in Castelló and was a current member of its Centro de Investigaciones de América Latina. Her publications include her monograph *Valencia en la revolución, 1834–1843: Sociabilidad, cultura y ocio* as well as several articles in academic journals concerned with the history of the Americas. She has also co-edited with Manuel Chust the recently published *La trascendencia del liberalismo doceañista en España y en América* and *Bastillas, cetros y blasones: La independencia en Iberoamérica*. Her latest work, *Las caras del águila: Del liberalismo gaditano a la república federal mexicana, 1820–1824*, has just been published.

Germán Martínez Martínez's research revolves around Latin American cultural history, literature, and film. He obtained his PhD in ideology and discourse analysis from the University of Essex in 2006, having studied previously at the Universidad Iberoamericana, Mexico City. His current research interests include Mexican national identity discourses, the imaginary construction of Latin American cities through film and literature (Buenos Aires, Havana, and Mexico City), poetics and poetry of the Americas, contemporary Mexican politics, and Latin American political culture.

Kerry McDonald graduated from the University of St. Andrews with an MA in modern languages (German and Spanish) in 2003 and obtained a postgraduate degree in translation from Herriot-Watt University in 2004, working as a translator thereafter. She is currently researching for her PhD dissertation on "The experience of the *pronunciamiento* in San Luis Potosí" benefiting from an Arts and Humanities Research Council grant.

Reynaldo Sordo Cedeño obtained his BA in history from the Universidad Nacional Autónoma de México and went on to do an MA in political science at El Colegio de México, where he was awarded his doctorate in history. He has been based at the Instituto Tecnológico Autónomo de México since 1980. In 2006 he was made distinguished professor for his contribution to academia and for his outstanding research into Mexican history. His research interests revolve around institutional political history in Mexico in the first half of the nineteenth century. He is also interested in the teaching of history to nonspecialists. His more substantial work has centered on the congresses of the early national period. Among his publications are *El Congreso en la Primera República Centralista: En defensa de la patria, 1847–1997*, co-authored with Josefina Zoraida Vázquez, and *Atlas histórico de México*, co-authored with María Julia Sierra.

Josefina Zoraida Vázquez is professor emeritus at El Colegio de México, where she has been based since 1960. She was awarded the Andrés Bello Prize of the Organization of American States in 1991 and the Mexican *Premio Nacional de Ciencias y Artes* in 1999, having been awarded grants from such eminent bodies as the Rockefeller, Guggenheim, and Fulbright foundations. Her research has centered on the history of education and the political and diplomatic history of Mexico in the nineteenth century. She has published more than 150 articles in Mexican and international academic journals and 43 book chapters in edited volumes. Her books include *Nacionalismo y educación en México; Historia de la historiografía; México frente a Estados Unidos; La fundación del estado Mexicano; Una historia de México; México y el mundo: Historia de sus relaciones exteriores (2 vols.); La enseñanza de la historia; La intervención norteamericana en México, 1846–1848; México al tiempo de su guerra con Estados Unidos; Tratados de México, 1821–1910; El establecimiento del federalismo en México, 1812–1827;* and *El nacimiento de las naciones iberoamericanas.*

Breinigsville, PA USA
26 October 2010
248033BV00001B/2/P